Genealogy 101

How to Trace Your Family's History and Heritage

Barbara Renick

Amy Johnson Crow, CG
Series Editor

Rutledge Hill Press™
Nashville, Tennessee
A Division of Thomas Nelson, Inc.
www.ThomasNelson.com

Published by Rutledge Hill Press, a Division of Thomas Nelson, Inc., P.O. Box 141000, Nashville, Tennessee 37214.

Library of Congress Cataloging-in-Publication Data

Renick, Barbara, 1950-
Genealogy 101 : how to trace your family's history and heritage / Barbara Renick.
p. cm. — (National Genealogical Society guides)
Includes index.
ISBN 1-40160-019-0 (pbk.)
1. Genealogy. 2. United States—Genealogy—Handbooks, manuals, etc.
I. Title. II. Series.
CS16 .R46 2003
929'.1—dc21
2002156110

Printed in the United States of America

03 04 05 06 07 — 5 4 3

To my family:

past, present, and future

Contents

Acknowledgments

WITHOUT THE HELP AND ENCOURAGEMENT OF CERTAIN PEOPLE, this book would never have gotten off the ground. First and foremost, recognition must go to Emily Linnell, the genealogy teacher who first taught me the principles upon which I built my own family tree. I hope this book passes on what Emily shared with me. Second, I must acknowledge my right arm and proofreader extraordinaire, Polly Bingham, who magically turned my technical phrases and German syntax into plain English. Thanks go to Beth McCarty, director of the Family History Center in Orange, California. She went above and beyond the call of duty to proofread the entire book and make sure I stated things accurately. A big thank you to Kirk Larsen whose creative ideas, brain storming, and inspiration helped make this book what it is. Last, but not least, a big hug to my husband whose patience knew no bounds during this project.

INTRODUCTION

Who Should Read This Book?

JUST AS I WAS BEGINNING TO WRITE THIS BOOK, A FRIEND CAME TO ME and asked how she could learn to do genealogy. She confessed that she didn't know the first thing about family tree tracing but really wanted to learn. With a little arm twisting, I enlisted her as one of my proofreaders.

When I delivered the first few chapters to her, I could tell she wasn't exactly thrilled at the prospect of reading what she thought was going to be a dry textbook. I made an appointment to meet her again in a week—but she didn't wait a week. Just a few days later she called me and asked to read more chapters. With excitement in her voice, she compared the manuscript to a novel that she could hardly put down. I wouldn't go that far, but I've tried to make this book entertaining by weaving in stories of my own family history adventures with my explanations of how to do genealogy.

I had three types of beginners in mind as I wrote this book. It is specifically written for those who have never done any family tree tracing. It is also for those who have already tried tracing their ancestors, but have learned quickly that, as with any puzzle, it helps to have a general idea of how to put the pieces together before you begin. The third group includes those who go on the Internet and find pieces of their family tree, but are not sure about the accuracy of what they've found (rightly so) and don't know what to do next.

This book is not just for beginners, however. The concepts discussed apply to all levels of researchers, from beginning to advanced. Even if you've been there and done that, you can use this book as a refresher course to remind you of things you have forgotten or to catch up on things you may never have learned.

At first, everyone thinks it's easy to ask questions and record your lineage. However, there are areas where experience and skill make a big difference. Recognizing what a family Bible, deed, or census record is trying to tell you seems simple until you learn how easy it is to miss vital details.

By reading this book, you'll learn a step-by-step process for getting started on your family tree quickly and easily. You'll also find tips on how to preserve your family's history and heritage. I don't know about your memory, but mine depends on names penciled on the back of family photos, and family relationships recorded in our family Bible and on my computer.

Most people are surprised at the variety of motivations for doing genealogy. Knowing the reasons why others start this hobby—one that for some becomes a passion and others a vocation—should help you clarify your own goals and decide what you want to learn first about your family tree.

I give examples of just how far back you can expect to go on your ancestral lines and how quickly you are likely to accomplish your goals. There are many roots and branches to your family tree on which to work. Remember, your family tree starts with you. I strongly encourage you to write down vignettes from your own life first. To this end, I include tips on easy ways to build your personal history one tale at a time.

Since you want to find your ancestors—and not someone else's—this book leads you through the steps to uniquely identify your ancestors. You'll learn how to gently ask living family members, neighbors, and friends important questions about your family's history. There is also a simple game plan for assembling the pieces of information you collect.

I show you how to use tools (standard genealogical charts and forms) to put your ancestors in the right positions on your family tree. I also explain the basic building blocks of pedigrees. You'll find important tips on how to avoid confusion while you look for your ancestors' names and how to work out the complex family relationships everyone encounters.

It is vital to document the drama of your search. How you get to the truth about your ancestors is often as interesting as the facts themselves. Like any treasure hunter, you'll want to record where you found each item so you can go back to it again later for more clues. I'll demonstrate the best methods for keeping track of your hunt.

Today, most genealogists use computers and genealogy programs. I offer advice on making a selection that fits your ability level and needs. You'll also learn about the methods for sharing what you find (and record in your computer) with others. Then you'll be ready to beef up your background knowledge of your ancestors: you'll learn the skills you need to track their lives, loves, and locations.

There are powerful resources to jump start your family quest, which include traditional sources, plus computerized databases and other online resources. When you are ready to go out combing for clues, you'll learn the tried-and-true places to look and how to adjust your search by location and time period as you work back in time. I'll take you through the steps for evaluating what you've found so you'll be able to go on with confidence to your next generation of ancestors.

I've learned to take pictures of family memorabilia and share them, partly because I nearly started a feud when no one in my mother's family could find the picture of her grandmother Julia. Everyone was blaming someone else in the family for having lost it. The picture was finally found when one aunt sold her house and the new owners went up in the attic. There they found a paper bag containing the missing picture. We came so close to losing this piece of our heritage forever. I'll show you how to preserve your precious family photos, stories, memorabilia, and the family tree information you've assembled.

Sooner or later, you'll need to overcome the shock of discovering the cultural differences in the older generations of your ancestry. It is always a challenge to search in other countries and centuries. This book provides a basic, but brief, overview of how to track your immigrant ancestors. Another book in the NGS series, *Online Roots* by Pamela Boyer Porter and Amy Johnson Crow, provides further help with such advanced research efforts.

Everyone occasionally needs a little help with his or her family tree. I have included sound advice on when and how to hire help, so you'll be able to decide when it makes sense to spend cents for different types of assistance.

There was no way to write a book about doing genealogy in the twenty-first century without mentioning computers and the Internet. They are wonderful, far-reaching tools. But as with any tool, the results depend upon the knowledge and skill of the person using it. In this book, I cover some of the best starting points on the Internet, clarify the principles you need to evaluate what you find (online or off), and point out the places where assumptions can leave you lost and still looking. *Online Roots* explores the world of resources available online and makes an excellent follow-up to *Genealogy 101.*

I hope this book feeds your desire to know more about your family's history by teaching you the fundamentals of how to chase dead ancestors (and living ones, too). As Tour de France winner Greg LeMond said, "Perhaps the single most important element in mastering the techniques and tactics of racing is experience. But once you have the fundamentals, acquiring the experience is a matter of time." The same is true for tracing your ancestors. Good luck with all your family tree-tracing efforts.

Chapter 1
Why Chase Dead Ancestors?

IN 1976, AS OUR NATION CELEBRATED ITS BICENTENNIAL, THE *ROOTS* phenomenon hit television audiences across America. Just by looking at his face, I could see Alex Haley had found peace and joy by coming to know his roots. As I watched this television series, I shared his sense of identity because I, too, had already begun tracing my family tree.

How Popular Is Genealogy?

Just about everyone finds genealogy enjoyable. From scrapbooking to attending family reunions to the intense thrill of the hunt for lost ancestors, people celebrate their family heritage in many different ways. Not surprisingly, surveys rank genealogy as one of the most popular hobbies in America today.

A colleague, Pamela J. Drake, wrote her psychology thesis on who is most likely to do genealogy and why ("Findings from the Fullerton Genealogy Study: A Master's Thesis Project" at *psych.fullerton.edu/genealogy/*). Her findings show that 45 percent of people in the United States were interested in genealogy in 1996. By the year 2000, that interest had grown to 60 percent. She also discovered that the average age for genealogy beginners is forty, but that genealogists range in age from grade school to retirees.

Do your own informal survey. Go to your favorite Internet search engine and compare the number of hits for *genealogy* to those for other hobbies. A search on *genealogy*

Genealogy is the art and science of tracing ancestral families and pedigrees. **Family history** has an even broader connotation as the process of coming to understand the lives of our ancestors by putting them into historical perspective. Together, they involve looking for and finding the threads of our ancestors' lives that make up the tapestry of history. Your ancestors and mine lived history. In one way or another, they all made history. Few lives are so quiet or small that they leave no ripples in the fabric of time.

at Google returns more than 16 million hits. A search on *stamp collecting* or *philatelic* doesn't even come close. The increased interest in genealogy sparked by the *Roots* TV series has not waned. Instead, it continues to grow.

Why?

Why do people spend so many four-letter words (like *time*, *work*, and *cash*) chasing dead ancestors? What motivates them to get started? The answers are as diverse as the people who pursue this popular pastime.

Human Curiosity

Quite a few people begin tracing their family trees because they really want to know if their family traditions are true or not. Is our family related to President Woodrow Wilson? Do we descend from a signer of the Declaration of Independence? Are we related to European nobility? Did Great-grandpa really jump ship and immigrate illegally, or are there records that tell how he came to America and where he came from? Are we really a mixture of Irish, Swedish, and Hungarian ancestry?

For many people, family history turns out to be even more entertaining than reality-based television shows. Judge Judy isn't seeing anything new in her court cases that genealogists haven't already encountered in old court records. Searching court records is how I learned that Edmond, my ancestor's brother, was a bigamist.

In 1860 in Tennessee, Edmond sued for a divorce from Mary, his first wife, on grounds of incompatibility (which seems a bit ironic since they already had ten children).

What he was granted was a separation of bed and board, not a full divorce. He returned his wife's dower lands to her for her support, and they lived separately.

During the Civil War, Edmond sheltered with relatives in Kentucky. Whether he was sheltering from the war or Mary is not clear. Not until 1870, after the war and his return to Tennessee, did he obtain a full divorce. Imagine my surprise when another researcher, knowing my interest in this family, sent me a copy of an 1864 marriage record for Edmond to a new wife in Kentucky.

This may seem like a slightly scandalous story, but one of the first lessons historians and genealogists learn is not to judge the past too quickly. Instead, we seek to understand the conditions under which our ancestors loved and lived. There may be unknown factors (cultural, economic, historical, religious, or social) that make your ancestor's actions logical.

The first rule of genealogy is *Keep an open mind.* The second rule of genealogy is *Always seek proof from more than one source.*

> **A genealogist** is anyone tracing his or her family tree. Genealogists range in experience from the newest beginners to experienced researchers to professionals.

Apropos to seeking proof, are you one of those people who inherited a pile of unidentified family photos? Do you wonder how all those people are related to you—especially the ones who resemble your living family members?

Goodness, Grandpa looks an awful lot like that American Indian he's standing next to in that 1940s photo! Grandpa must have been part Indian. See for yourself in Figure 1.1. Unfortunately, the U.S. Bureau of Indian Affairs won't share your certainty without a bit more proof. Yet such tales are passed down all too readily in our families. With time and frequent repetition, they take on a patina of truth. But genealogists seek truth via proof.

Genealogy readily attracts people who like mysteries, word games, and puzzles in general. Putting your family tree together is like assembling the pieces of a real-life jigsaw puzzle. Fortunately, you don't have to be Sherlock Holmes or Miss Marple to be a successful genealogist. Persistence and thoroughness count for a great deal more than occasional strokes of genius.

Honoring Your Ancestors

The idea of honoring one's ancestors has been around a long time, but people honor their ancestors in many different ways. Remembering them and preserving their life stories is just one way. Other people join a lineage or patriotic society as a way of remembering their ancestors and carrying on their goals and good works.

Figure 1.1 Grandpa Cannon *(left)* in North Carolina in the 1940s, standing next to a Native American

The number and variety of organized lineage societies are amazing. Most require you to prove a specific lineage in order to join. Membership in some societies is based on proving your ancestor was one of the first settlers in a county or state. Other societies have a religious orientation, such as the Society of Descendants of the Colonial Clergy or societies for American descendants of French Huguenot ancestors.

As the old Scottish proverb goes, "He who has in his family neither thief, knave, nor whore was begat by a stroke of lightning."

Sons, daughters, and children of Confederate soldiers have societies, as do descendants of Union soldiers. There are national societies for descendants of patriots of the American Revolution, and there is the United Empire Loyalists' Association of Canada for descendants of Loyalists. There is even an organization based in Chicago for Descendants of the Illegitimate Sons and Daughters of the Kings of Britain.

In recent times, it seems a common thing for historians to point out that our country's founding fathers were guilty of various indiscretions. Most people who join patriotic societies are quick to admit their pedigrees are not filled with perfect people; nevertheless, they find it worthwhile to trace their ancestry and join societies that honor that ancestry.

Clan Hanna-Hannah-Hannay U.S.A. participates in the Scottish Games and promotes an understanding of the history of those with the name Hanna, Hannah, or Hannay in

Finding Societies Honoring Your Ancestors on the Web

The Internet is a great resource for locating and learning more about patriotic and lineage societies.

The Lineages research firm has a page at their Web site *(www.lineages.com/usa/LinSocieties.asp?StateCode=US)* titled "United States of America: Patriotic and Lineage Societies" that provides a long and diverse list of societies.

Perhaps the best-known society is the National Society Daughters of the American Revolution. Find out more about this organization at *www.dar.org*.

Learn more about associations honoring our ancestors from other lands. For example, you can visit Clan Hanna-Hannah-Hannay U.S.A. at *homepages.rootsweb.com/~lmhannah/Clan_Hanna_Han/indexx.html*, which is devoted to ancestors from Scotland.

Scotland and elsewhere. The National Society Daughters of the American Revolution (NSDAR, commonly shortened to DAR) has specific objectives, which include historic preservation, promotion of education, and patriotic endeavors. I can tell you from personal experience as a member, the DAR awards scholarships, gives service to those less fortunate, and promotes patriotism in many ways. Along the way, we actively promote genealogy and the preservation of our legacy as Americans for future generations.

Ethnic Identity

Tracing your family tree helps build a sense of ethnic identity. This is important for young and old alike. It promotes a feeling of being part of a bigger whole.

When I was growing up, we frequently had sauerkraut and cornbread with dinner. This blending of foods was a blending of cultures in my family. My paternal grandparents were Germans from Russia. My mom's side of the family all claim to be hillbillies. My years of research have borne out the fact that there isn't a lowlander in the bunch.

Many communities sponsor ethnic festivals: Oktoberfest, Irish Days, the Italian Festival. This is a fun way to experience other times, places, and peoples. Taste the flavors, hear the sounds, and see history come alive. You risk gaining a serious amount of weight from the food, but you gain an appreciation for the culture in which your ancestors lived.

Historical Interest

History is more than just textbooks. It comes alive when you participate in historical reenactments, share your love of antiques, or travel to historic places. It is an enjoyment of biographies of famous people and a love of historical novels. Think of the stories told by James Michener and Louis L'Amour. Genealogy encompasses all the above.

Once upon a time, I was a Genealogy Merit Badge Counselor. I helped quite a few young men begin tracing their family trees. For those Boy Scouts, genealogy was a wholesome activity that sparked their interest in the past by making it personal to them. Today, with computers and the Internet, genealogy still feels like a game. (That certainly doesn't hurt when keeping half a dozen twelve-year-olds focused on the project at hand.)

Genealogy is so much fun that many public school teachers use it to make the past come alive for their students. Even some colleges and universities offer courses in family and oral history. California State University, Fullerton, where I was a graduate student, has a Center for Oral and Public History that promotes the preservation of both public and personal history.

Visit the Youth Resources Committee of the National Genealogical Society at *www.ngsgenealogy.org/youth.htm.* These Web pages contain information about genealogy and family history suitable for children ages five through eighteen and materials for teachers of grades kindergarten through high school.

I awed many of the high school teachers in my history classes with my knowledge of historical records. I particularly remember wowing my classmates by knowing how a jury panel was selected in Montana in the 1890s. Looking for ancestors in all those old court records pays off in many ways.

Genealogists develop a hunger for history as soon as they learn that it helps them find their ancestors. History is the key to knowing what types of records were created, where they are kept, and why some of them may be missing. It is also the key to correctly evaluating what we find in those records.

For instance, in the Commonwealth of Virginia before the Revolutionary War, it was illegal to belong to anything other than the official state church. It is well documented that Patrick Henry defended a Baptist minister facing a possible death sentence for practicing and preaching his religion. If your ancestors were Baptists in colonial Virginia, as mine were, don't be too surprised if they don't show up in the county marriage books for any of a number of reasons. If a nonconformist minister married your ancestors, he certainly wouldn't have wanted to report his activities to the local officials.

The more you know about the history of the times in which your ancestor lived, the better your chances of finding information about that person's life. This also means your chances of tracing your family tree back another generation are greater.

Genealogy is about real people. My family tree includes ministers, bigamists, and moonshiners. One of my friends has ancestors who accused their neighbors of witchcraft. Another friend's pedigree includes a riverboat gambler who was caught cheating and thrown overboard—even though he couldn't swim.

People are human whether they live today or lived hundreds of years ago. A study of genealogy and history teaches us not to judge others too readily while helping us avoid the mistakes of the past.

Religious Beliefs

My family tree includes Baptists, Catholics, French Huguenots, German Lutherans and Baptists, Irish Protestants, Methodists, Presbyterians, and possibly a Quaker or two. If you can't come up with religious tolerance after a lineup like that, I don't know what it would take.

Many religions around the world teach an appreciation, even a reverence, for one's ancestors. Americans with Asian ancestry often find this is a part of their cultural heritage. So do those with Native American ancestry. For members of the Church of Jesus Christ of Latter-day Saints (also known as LDS or Mormons), tracing their family trees is a matter of religious conviction. This is best explained at their Web site. Go to *www.familysearch.org* and click on Why Family History? in the information bar on the left side of your screen.

Here in Southern California, we often take visiting relatives to see the Catholic Mission at San Juan Capistrano. There, I am pleased to say, you see the physical reminders that those of the Catholic faith also care for their deceased family members. The lighted candles in that historic chapel are a beautiful reminder that the light of one's life is never gone so long as it is remembered by loved ones.

Medical Miracles

There are many reasons to search out and record your ancestors' health histories. For one thing, forewarned is forearmed. Just a few generations of a health history show family predispositions for heart problems, diabetes, or cancer. This is something we should all be recording and preserving for our descendants.

The birth of a child with a rare health problem is another reason some people begin tracing their genealogy. It helps to know that others have gone through similar trials. Docudramas, such as *Lorenzo's Oil*, graphically portray such situations and the value of positive action.

Knowing your family's past is a comfort in times of grief and loss, as I know from personal experience. I went through the trauma of infertility, only to lose my first child when I was six months pregnant. Tracing my family tree helped me realize that a number of women in my past had suffered even more devastating losses. When I did finally carry a pregnancy eight months, then gave birth to my multiply handicapped daughter, knowing the toughness of my ancestors helped me again.

The GeneWeaver software from Genes & Things, Inc., is designed to help you maintain an extensive and detailed family health history. For more information, see their Web site at *www.geneweaveronline.com*. The Family Health and Heredity Committee of the National Genealogical Society *(www.ngsgenealogy.org/comfamhealth.htm)* has even more information about family health histories.

Genealogy stretches and limbers your brain. For those of us getting on in years, it is a case of *use it or lose it.* One of the nicest things about genealogy is that you tend to get better at it the longer you do it. Staying mentally sharp adds to longevity. Genealogy keeps you mentally active and involved in life: past, present, and future.

Legal Motivation

One of my classmates from high school now traces lost heirs. She helps them prove their lineages to inherit property in Florida. Many different legal matters require proof of lineage.

Important advice for genealogy consumers can be found on the following Web pages at the National Genealogical Society site:

Consumer Protection Committee's Web page
(www.ngsgenealogy.org/comconsumer.htm)

"PSST! Wanna Buy Your Name?"
(www.ngsgenealogy.org/comconsumerpsst.htm)

A few sticky legal issues are also involved in genealogy. One classic example is the letter in the mail trying to sell you a $39.95 book claiming to contain your whole family tree, which turns out to be just a generalized background on your surname and a listing of entries from telephone books. Believe me, there are cheaper and more reliable ways to find relatives interested in your family tree. Knowing something about your family tree helps you spot the less reputable offers.

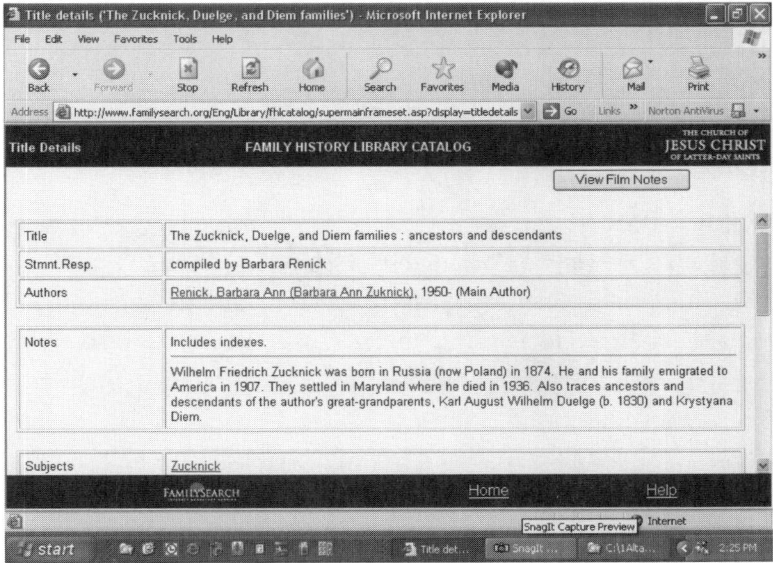

Figure 1.2 Cataloger's notes for a family history book in the Family History Library Catalog (Reproduced by permission. Copyright © 1999–2002 by Intellectual Reserve, Inc.)

Before buying any family history book, check to see how a large library catalog (like the one for the Library of Congress) describes that work. Legitimate works are easy to spot by the details included in the cataloger's notes, as shown in Figure 1.2. Such catalog checks are easy to do, thanks to the Internet.

Adoption

Another legal issue is adoption. My husband and I adopted three infants. They are all grown and out on their own now. If they ever want to trace their family trees, I am prepared to assist them.

Adoption is a challenging aspect of genealogical research. I caution adoptees to proceed with sensitivity and understanding for both birth parents and those who have spent their lives helping you grow to adulthood. But just as Alex Haley overcame many of his research challenges (with a bit of professional help along the way), so too can many orphans and adoptees.

Cyndi's List *(www.cyndislist.com)* is the best-known genealogy directory on the Internet. The directory is divided into more than 150 main categories with many subcategories leading you to lists of links about those topics. Cyndi's List includes a category called Adoption *(www.cyndislist.com/adoption.htm).*

Accepting the Baton

You may have no knowledge of or interest in genealogy, but then face an emotional quandary when an aging parent or relative pleads with you to take over and continue his genealogical research. He may even threaten to come back and haunt you in later years if you don't step forward and shoulder this responsibility. In other cases, the relative dies and you inherit cardboard boxes filled with Aunt Martha's collection of scribbles, newspaper clippings, and gravestone rubbings.

The children and relatives of genealogists face the greatest challenges when getting started in genealogy. Much of the easy work has already been done, and they are forced to start without the skills and techniques learned during those early phases of research. Later chapters in this book should be particularly helpful for those of you who make your start by reviewing what someone else has already done.

Figure 1.3 My husband's grandmother with the Eiffel Tower in the background

Consider very carefully before you throw anything out. Today's junk is tomorrow's treasure. Yes, genealogists do tend to be packrats. (See Chapter 12, "Publish . . . or Perish the Thought," for ways to find a good home for orphaned genealogical materials.)

When I was young and newly married, my husband brought home an old photo album given to him by his parents. It was moldy and full of bugs. I remember one photo well: my husband's grandmother standing on a wrought-iron balcony with the Eiffel Tower in the background (see Figure 1.3). I made my husband store this castoff family treasure in the garage. It stayed there for several years until, in a fit of cleaning, we threw it out. The saddest words a genealogist ever utters are, "If only I had . . ." (Fortunately, my husband inherited another copy of that particular picture from his uncle.)

Political Motivation

If you would rather have someone else trace your family tree, just run for office. Presidents and famous people are often handed their genealogies for free. Or you could try joining the FBI. They do in-depth background checks. (Believe it or not, through their investigations, the FBI has created some significant genealogical records over the years.)

If this doesn't work for you, consider hiring a professional genealogist to help with the rough spots on your family tree—the ones you do not want to tackle on your own. I personally know two of the professional genealogists who helped Alex Haley and his family with their research. This is a perfectly acceptable alternative when you can't go searching on location or when you need an expert to overcome a difficult problem.

The LDS Church Helps Genealogists around the World

The LDS Church is a frugal organization with no paid clergy, yet this church spends millions of dollars helping people—whether of the LDS faith or not—trace their family trees. Here are some of the ways the LDS Church helps family tree tracers:

- It has 242 microfilm cameras filming in more than forty countries around the world, preserving records of genealogical interest. Many governments, churches, and organizations have taken advantage of this free program.
- It maintains the world's largest genealogy and family history library in Salt Lake City, Utah, with
  - 2,200,000 rolls of microfilm
  - 742,000 microfiche (a good format for copying printed materials)
  - 300,000 books, serials, maps, etc.
  - For more information go to *www.familysearch.org* and click on the Library tab.
- It has more than 3,700 Family History Centers (branches of the main Family History Library in Salt Lake City) not only in the United States but also around the world, where patrons of all faiths can use the materials on hand. For more information about Family History Centers go to *www.familysearch.org,* click on the Library tab, and then click on About Family History Centers.
- One of the most helpful Web sites for genealogy beginners is the LDS Church's FamilySearch Internet Genealogy Service site *(www.familysearch.org).* Everything at this Web site is free, except for a few of the products, which you can order online.
- In the early 1980s, the LDS Church developed the Personal Ancestral File genealogy program for personal computers. The church has continued to update its features and PAF has the greatest longevity of any of the popular personal genealogy programs in the United States. The current version (PAF 5.2) is available in English as well as in several foreign languages.
- The Church's Family and Church History Department has coordinated vast volunteer record-extraction and indexing projects. Volunteers automating the Ellis Island records spent 5.6 million hours, and it took 11.5 million hours to automate the nearly 50 million names found in the 1880 U.S. census. The resulting Ellis Island records and 1880 United States Census and National Index are now searchable online. A Family History Center near you may have purchased some of the extracted records as CD sets for use by patrons.

To the Hunt

Genealogy is as addictive as treasure hunting. And like treasure hunting, with enough persistence, even the most difficult ancestry can usually be uncovered. Our motivations for doing so are varied, but as Alex Haley said, "In all of us is a hunger, marrow-deep, to know our heritage—to know who we are and where we have come from. Without this enriching knowledge, there is a hollow yearning. No matter what our attainments in life, there is still a vacuum, and an emptiness, and the most disquieting loneliness." ("What *Roots* Means to Me," *Reader's Digest,* (May 1977), 73–74)

It is my sincere hope this book helps each of you find the rich treasures buried in your past.

Chapter 2

Starting Backwards

How Far Back Can You Go?

How far back can you reasonably trace your family tree? The answer depends on the number of challenges your ancestors hand you along the way. Family trees do not necessarily grow evenly. Some branches are easier to trace than others.

One of my students traced one branch of her family tree back to 1636 in just six weeks. I recently traced a friend's paternal ancestry (her father's ancestry) back to her fifth great-grandfather, born about 1658. I did this over a period of three years in my spare moments.

My own family tree was never that easy. For example, my earliest identified ancestor was a Crook. Now, don't jump to conclusions—that was his surname, not his occupation. He was a vinedresser, and his name was Gedeon Kruk or Kruckh (or any other way a German might phonetically spell the name). He was born in 1533 near Stuttgart, Germany. It took me twenty years to trace this line because the descendant families migrated to Russia, then to Prussia, and finally to America.

After more than thirty years of searching, I'm still stuck on one paternal great-grandmother. She was from a Prussian village whose church burned to the ground in World War II. Four hundred years of christening, confirmation, and burial records went up in smoke. I haven't worked around that dead end yet, but there are still possibilities for success.

Your experience as a genealogy beginner will probably fall somewhere between these extremes.

For most areas of Europe, few records survive before the 1500s, so accurately finding European ancestors any earlier is not likely. In the United States, consider yourself lucky if you get back to the Revolutionary War. Immediately after the Revolution, our nation experienced a period of rapid westward expansion. People on the move in frontier areas generate fewer records than do settled residents. If you can accurately trace your ancestors from the United States to Europe, you may have a better chance of going back farther in time.

Another black hole for U.S. research is during the 1890s. Again, this was a period of movement within our country. Railroads stretched from coast to coast, and economic difficulties motivated many people to seek their fortunes elsewhere. To make matters worse, the 1890 U.S. census was badly charred in a warehouse fire. Only bits and pieces of that census remain.

You never run out of dead ends on your family tree. Some are just nearer to you than others. Each generation of ancestors leads back to another generation with twice as many new ancestors to chase. If you encounter difficult ancestors, tackle one who is easier to find. Then go back to the challenging ones as you gain skills. It takes time, work, and a bit of cash to trace your family tree, but you just might surprise yourself with how much you can find.

How Big Do Family Trees Get?

As you work your way back in time, most family trees end up being diamond shaped. This is due to propinquity. Propinquity means that your ancestors could only marry the people they could meet. In small communities, just about everyone ends up related to everyone else.

When your ancestry doubles back on itself, you end up with half as many ancestors from that point back. Take my husband's family tree, for example. Back in the 1790s in Lincoln County, Kentucky, two Renick brothers (Henry and Samuel) married two Hall sisters (Prudence and Ruth). Each couple had a son (Leonard Hall Renick and William Henry Renick). Those young men were double first cousins to each other, as shown in Figure 2.1. Then one son had a son (John Thomas Renick) who married the other's daughter (Ruth J. Renick). This was a case of second cousins marrying each other, and they are my husband's great-grandparents. Back

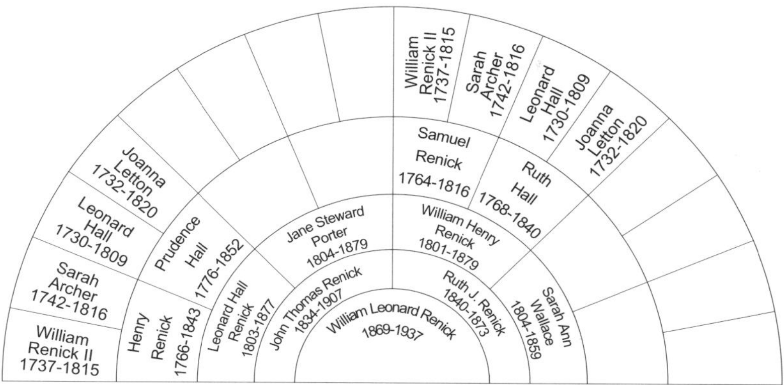

Figure 2.1 Fan chart (a type of ancestor chart) showing how Leonard Hall Renick and William Henry Renick are double first cousins.

beyond those Renick brothers and Hall sisters, two of my husband's ancestral lines are identical.

I have a Vietnamese friend who wants to find out more about her ancestors, but many of the places of her childhood no longer exist. She also knows her ancestors changed their names frequently. I advised her to ask family members to take pictures when they go back to Vietnam on visits. These pictures should be of any remaining homes they lived in, schools they attended, and religious centers significant to them as a family. I also suggested she help her parents write their life stories and urged her to start a tradition of written family records. She needs to do this while her older relatives are still alive to answer questions.

Double first cousins occur when one cousin's father and mother are the siblings of the other cousin's father and mother. This happens when two sisters from one family marry two brothers from another family, making their children double first cousins to each other. It also happens when a brother and a sister from one family marry a sister and a brother from another family. Their children then become double first cousins to each other.

Some family trees, like my Vietnamese friend's, end up short on ancestors and long on descendants. Other beginning genealogists manage to trace some branches of their family tree back into the middle ages in a matter of weeks, then spend years filling in the more challenging branches. Some of us inherit family trees that seem custom designed for puzzle lovers.

Start with the First Generation (You)

No matter how you stumble into genealogy, at some point you get bitten by the bug and want to start tracing your own family tree. Genealogists work backward in time. They start with themselves and carefully align each older generation on top of the younger—much like a toddler stacking a tower of blocks. A good place to start is with your own history. Writing your own personal history is one of the greatest legacies you can leave for the generations yet to come. It will be of value not only to your own children and grandchildren, but also to your siblings' descendants. This is especially true if you record the stories of your life growing up with your parents, siblings, and other relatives you remember.

A **personal history** is autobiographical and can take many forms: taped oral interviews or oral narrations, written stories, videotapes, scrapbooks. It can also be a part of a family history book. What is important is that a life story is recorded for posterity.

One of my most valued stories about my great-grandpa W.B. was recorded by my mother. She remembers that her youngest sister, Rena, was W.B.'s favorite grandchild. According to my mother, W.B. didn't like the rest of the grandchildren nearly as much as he liked Rena. My mother could tell because Rena used to get to sit on his lap and play with his eyeglasses. Another reason might have been that all the other grandchildren were older than Rena and liked to play with marbles. W.B. was getting on in years and was afraid of slipping on them. He told my mother to go plant her marbles in the ground and grow a marble tree. She did, but the marble tree never grew.

This story tells something about my mother and her grandfather, but it also tells something about mom's youngest sister, Rena. It is of interest not only to Mom's branch of the family, but to Rena's descendants, too. No one's life is so bland that it won't be of interest to almost everyone a hundred years from now. What I wouldn't give for a diary kept by W.B.—including his side of the marble story.

Recording Your Own Story

A personal history is autobiographical in nature, but doesn't have to be as long as a book. Start small with the basics, and as time permits, add stories. The major events in your life form the basic outline as you answer the who, what, when, where, why, and how questions:

- What was the full name you were born with?
- Was your name different at any other time in your life? How did you get that nickname?
- When were you born? What was the weather like on the day you were born? What was going on in your community and the world on the day you were born?
- Where were you born? Why were you born there?
- What are your parents' names? Are there any naming traditions in your family?
- How old were your parents when you were born?
- Do you have any siblings? Are they younger or older? What are their names and when and where were they born? Describe some of the character traits you best remember about each sibling.

Tell about each stage in your life: birth and childhood, family life and school years, courtship and marriage, your child-rearing years, your vocation and travels, middle age, and retirement as it creeps up on you. Write about your pets, your modes of transportation, and your family traditions. If you have a rich heritage of family photos, choose a photo and write about what was happening when that photo was taken.

Make a list of questions you want to answer. If you have any trouble coming up with questions to write about, consult lists compiled by oral historians and genealogists. (For some Web links to sites containing lists of questions, see the sidebar "Online Resources for Writing Oral and Personal Histories" on page 26). You don't have to reinvent the wheel. Lists of personal history (and oral interview) questions are available from many Internet sources, in adult-education classes, and in books at your public library. Your local genealogical society and any LDS Family History Centers near you are additional resources for help writing your personal history.

How to Find a Genealogical or Historical Society Near You

A **genealogical society** is usually a nonprofit organization where membership is based on an interest in genealogy. This is a place where those who share interests can network with each other and learn from more experienced members.

There are several ways to locate a genealogical or historial society in your area:

- Go to your public library and ask at the reference desk for a directory to genealogical societies in the United States. One of the best known is *Directories of Genealogical and Historical Societies, Libraries, and Periodicals in the U.S. and Canada,* edited by Dina C. Carson (Niwot, Colo.: Iron Gate Publishing, 2000).
- Call your local LDS Family History Center and ask if they have a list of local genealogical or historical societies in that area.
- Use the Society Hall search engine at *www.familyhistory.com/societyhall/* to search for a society near you. This is not a complete listing of every society in America. If you don't find an entry for a society in your area, try typing the name of your county and the words *genealogical society* in your favorite search engine. Most genealogical and historical societies have Web sites and can be found via search engines.

No matter how mundane your stories seem to you, a hundred years from now they will fascinate your descendants. They will even fascinate people not related to you. My father's life stretched from the horse and buggy days to watching a man walk on the moon. I am so glad I have his personal history.

In her personal history, my mother recorded her mother's treatment for chicken pox. When my mother caught the chicken pox, her mother laid her in the door of the log cabin and ran their chickens back and forth across her. Grandma believed this treatment lessened the severity of the pox. It is hard for my children to believe the superstitions and medical treatments of the past. What will their descendants think of our everyday lives?

Tackle writing your personal history one question at a time:

1. Select a question.
2. Think about it for anywhere from a day to a week. Carry something to jot down your thoughts about that question (a 3 x 5 card, pad of paper, day planner, or whatever you normally use to jot down a list of things to do).

3. Begin recording your thoughts, memories, and feelings about that question.
4. Set aside at least an hour each week to write what you have remembered.
5. Repeat steps 1 to 4 until you have something written about each stage of your life. You do not have to work in any special order, just be sure to cover all the stages in your life.

If you type faster than you write by hand, put technology to work for you. Computers and word processors make it easy to edit your stories as you think of things to add to your personal narrative.

My father-in-law recorded his stories with a tape recorder. It is wonderful to still be able to listen to his voice telling about his life. He told stories not only about his childhood in Montana, but also about his fraternity days in college and service in World War II. My father-in-law paid someone to transcribe his tapes and then began editing them, creating a more polished written version of many of his life stories. He died before he finished the editing, but at least he left us a rich legacy from his past.

If you record your stories on tape, be sure to make additional copies on other types of media, including one that is an optical form of storage (such as a compact disc). Cassette tapes are a magnetic form of storage. They deteriorate and demagnetize over time. Besides, in ten or twenty years, will you even have a device capable of playing those tapes?

Some people maintain elaborate scrapbooks. They document their lives with not only typed stories, but also pictures, pressed flowers, and posters of high school football games. My high school scrapbook came in handy for one of my friends when he was in charge of planning our thirtieth high school reunion. The biggest disadvantage to this method of preserving your life stories is that they are difficult to copy and share.

Once you start writing your personal narrative, you'll probably feel an urge to start photographing or videotaping the places and people you mention. Just be sure to document the Five W's of each photo or video (who, what, when, where, and why). Today's ordinary photo of a family birthday party is tomorrow's treasure, especially if fully identified.

Once you are satisfied with the completeness of your personal history, update it annually. I do this by way of my infamous Christmas newsletter. It summarizes our family's doings for the past year. Family life is fodder for family history writers. An even better method is to keep a personal diary or journal and write in it regularly.

Online Resources for Writing Oral and Personal Histories

You'll find many resources on the Web to help you record your own history and that of your family members. Cyndi's List has two useful categories:

- Oral History & Interviews *(www.cyndislist.com/oral.htm)*
- Scrapbooks *(www.cyndislist.com/scrapbooks.htm)*

Other helpful Web sites include

- PBS Ancestors *(www.pbs.org/kbyu/ancestors/records/familyhistory/)*
- Juliana Smith's article "Ten Steps to Recording Your Personal History" *(www.ancestry.com/library/print/columns/compass/928.htm)*
- Association of Personal Historians *(www.personalhistorians.org)*

The Genealogy.com Web site has a whole category of how-to articles about oral histories. You'll find lists of questions for oral history interviews that adapt well for use in personal histories.

1. Go to *www.genealogy.com.*
2. Click on the Learning Center button toward the top of your screen.
3. In the sidebar on the left side of your screen, there are several categories to choose from under Genealogy How-To. Click on Developing Your Research Skills.
4. Scroll down to the Oral Histories & Family Traditions section and click on any of the listed articles to read more.

For specific help on writing your own personal history, or the biography of a living or deceased relative,

1. Go to *www.genealogy.com.*
2. Click on the Learning Center button toward the top of your screen.
3. Click on Biography Assistant at the bottom of the Learning Center sidebar on the left side of your screen. Follow the links provided for more help.

Since your personal history will never be perfect or complete (until after you are dead), go ahead and distribute copies to family members. Make those copies on acid-free paper with a laser printer or a good photocopier. The wider the distribution, the more likely a copy will survive for your descendants to find and enjoy. Choose a date to distribute updated copies each year. Just do it.

Figure 2.2 Front entrance of the Family History Library in Salt Lake City, Utah (Reproduced by permission. Copyright © 1999–2002 by Intellectual Reserve, Inc.)

Do Your Ancestors Want to Be Found?

At times, the things that happen to people tracing their family trees are downright spooky. It seems as though your deceased relatives either are just begging to be found or are so hard to find you would gladly throttle them if they weren't already dead. After you've been at this for a while, you'll see this is true.

One of my students was a registered nurse named Pat. We decided to take a research trip to the Family History Library in Salt Lake City, Utah (the world's largest genealogy library—see Figure 2.2). This was back in the days when you could fly standby on the airlines. She was the very last person to get a seat on the plane. We joked that it must be a good omen—that she was meant to go and find lots of her ancestors.

I could tell she was excited. When we got to the library, she whipped out a long

The Seven Rules for Saving Irreplaceable Things

1. Preserve on paper, because computers are a means of losing more information faster than ever before.
2. Always make more than one copy of anything irreplaceable—even if it is just a photograph of an heirloom. And be sure to date your copies and document who had the original at the time you made the copy.
3. Be sure to copy the most recent version of computer files, personal histories, etc.
4. Always test to make sure that the copy is useable/readable/viewable.
5. Always make copies in more than one format.
   a. Word processor files should be saved in their native format (.doc or .wpd) and in a plain text format (.txt).
   b. Image files (scanned images and digital photographs) should be saved in several formats, including the popular JPEG (files ending in .jpg) for displaying and TIFF (files ending in .tif) for archiving.
   c. Information you enter in a genealogy software program should be saved in three different ways. First, make a backup on removable disks using that program's backup format. Second, copy that program's data folder directly onto a removable disk. Third, save all that database information by making a generic file called a GEDCOM file. All of today's popular genealogy programs have the capability of exchanging information via generic GEDCOM files. In most programs, you go to File on the menu bar and choose Export in the drop-down menu that appears.
   d. Save important e-mail messages in their native format and as plain text messages.
   e. Backup your Web browser's bookmarks/favorites/favorite places list both online and onto a floppy or recordable compact disc.
6. Backup on more than one type of removable media (including—but not limited to—floppy disks, recordable compact discs, removable hard disk drives, extra film negatives, etc.).
7. Store your backups in more than one location (and be sure some of those locations are off-site and out-of-state).

list of microfilmed records to search. We went to the second floor where rows and rows of microfilm cabinets are arranged in numerical order. (Figure 2.3 shows how the cabinets are arranged.) The range of numbers is posted at the end of each row and on the front of each drawer. Each box of microfilm is also clearly labeled with

Figure 2.3 Rows of microfilm cabinets at the Family History Library in Salt Lake City (Reproduced by permission. Copyright © 1999–2002 by Intellectual Reserve, Inc.)

the film number. I explained this numbering system to Pat, and she was soon happily retrieving her films.

She walked up to me a while later. She said she had gone to the film cabinets to retrieve a microfilm on her list. When she got back to the microfilm reader and looked at the film, she realized it was the wrong one. It wasn't on her list, but it was about the county where her ancestors lived. As she looked through this film, she found her ancestors mentioned throughout the record.

> Two fascinating books filled with stories of strange coincidences in genealogical research are *Psychic Roots* and *More Psychic Roots: Further Adventures in Serendipity & Intuition in Genealogy* by Henry Z. "Hank" Jones. For more information see his Web site at *www.hankjones.com/morepsyc.htm.*

When she went to put the film back in its cabinet, she was shocked to realize it wasn't in the same cabinet as the film she intended to get. It wasn't even in the same row. It was practically on the opposite side of the room. She was breathless and had the funniest look on her face. I smiled and said, "Yep. It happens that way sometimes."

Chapter 3

How to Find Your Ancestors (and Not Someone Else's)

For several years in a row, the only Christmas gifts I asked my parents for were their written life stories. I even furnished them with a list of questions to answer. Finally, one Christmas they gave me what I most wanted. They each wrote down their answers to my questions. Six months later, my father died in a boating accident. How I treasure that gift of his life story.

Get Started Now

My paternal grandparents came to America in 1907. (Figure 3.1 is a picture of their family taken in about 1913.) The last of their children died in 1997. There were twenty-five grandchildren. We cousins are now the oldest generation, and attrition is slowly reducing our numbers. Don't wait until you retire to start searching for answers about your progenitors. You just might end up with no older generation of relatives to ask about the past.

For those of you who start tracing your family trees during your early to middle years, there are probably living people who knew your grandparents. There may even be someone living who knew your great-grandparents.

Once upon a time, I was walking down the hall of a Tennessee courthouse with Cousin Jack. He was the most senior elected official in the county and knew everyone who worked there. We were talking about my great-grandpa W.B., who was Jack's grandmother's brother. I told Jack it seemed to me W.B. got along better with men

Figure 3.1 The Zuknicks, my paternal grandparents and family, about 1913

than women, seeing how he was divorced twice. Jack said he remembered W.B. as a person who liked to fish and hunt with the guys.

Suddenly, Jack grabbed my arm and turned down a different corridor. We entered an office and walked up to a man seated behind a desk. Jack asked the man if he had fished with W.B. in the old days. To our surprise, the man opened his desk drawer and pulled out an old black-and-white photograph. The picture showed him as a boy standing on the banks of a river holding a fishing pole. Next to him was another fisherman, my great-grandpa. Oh, if only there had been digital cameras back then. I could have snapped a copy of that photo and had it to show you today. The saddest words a genealogist ever utters are, "If only I had . . . ."

When I started doing genealogy, both of my father's sisters were still living, Olga and Gussie. They were the oldest surviving members of his immediate family. Each year when I visited my parents, I would take time to visit these aunts and ask them questions. After this had been going on for several years, Aunt Gussie said in exasperation, "Why don't you ask Uncle Henry?"

Uncle Henry? I didn't know a lot about my ancestors then, but I knew my father didn't have a brother named Henry. My aunt said she was talking about her

Figure 3.2 Uncle Henry *(right)* on a trip to East Germany in 1956

Uncle Henry, their mother's youngest brother, who was living in Florida. In my limited experience, I hadn't thought to ask if Grandmother had any surviving siblings.

Uncle Henry, although in his nineties, turned out to be a gold mine of information. (See his picture from his trip to East Germany in Figure 3.2.) He was present at his oldest sister's wedding in 1892 and knew all the surrounding towns there in Russia. It wasn't until a decade later that he came to the United States. Henry's letters to his oldest sister (my grandmother) were instrumental in convincing her to bring her family to America, for which I am eternally grateful.

Identity Crises

Have you ever come across someone who has the same name as you do? I was attending a genealogical conference in Richmond, Virginia, when someone at the luncheon table commented there was another Barbara Renick at the conference. Just then, a young voice chirped up, "I'm Barbara Renick!" I turned around to find a much younger Barbara Renick seated directly behind me. An online search reveals more than half a dozen Barbara Renicks living in the United States. And that's a relatively rare name.

You may think Amon Gross is a unique name, but I identified five of them—all alive in the mid-1800s from families in just one county. There were also five Isaac Lindsays in that county at that time. Genealogists encounter this sort of identity crisis all the time.

Years ago, my husband and I hired a professional genealogist to trace his Swedish ancestors. She first reviewed the records compiled by a family member in the early twentieth century. She noticed that a particular christening record was the only source used to identify one ancestor's father. A more thorough review of the records in that Swedish church proved that the supposed father died at nine years of age. Luckily, our researcher found a second christening record in the same church with an identical name but different parents. The death record for this person showed that he died at a much later date. The researcher then was able to add the correct branch of ancestors, three hundred people in all, to my husband's family tree.

Start out from the very beginning with this possibility in mind: There may be more people out there with your ancestor's name, no matter how unique you think it is. Because of this, you need to document all of the important events and relationships in each ancestor's life. One of the biggest mistakes a genealogist can make is to latch on to the wrong ancestor.

Uniquely Identify Ancestors via Events

While two people might have the same name, it is less likely they also have spouses with the same name (although in my family a father and a son, both named Isaac Agee, each married a woman named Mary Smith). Two people might even have the same name and the same birth date, but it is highly unlikely they died on the same day.

That is why genealogists use at least three significant life events (such as birth, marriage, and death) to uniquely identify each stage in an ancestor's life. That is also why you need to identify your ancestor's whole family. Identifying family relationships is central to good genealogical research. Ideally, you want to find written records for each life event and relationship. You want those written records recorded by an eyewitness. You also want them recorded soon after the event occurred. Many different types of written records about you and your ancestors are probably right there in your own home (and in the homes of your immediate family members). As you work on your personal history, consult family members about any written records they have in their homes. Make copies, and put those copies in a cardboard box for now. Having scoured your home for clues and pieces to your pedigree puzzle, go out and start interviewing your close family members.

Ask and Ye Shall Receive . . . Maybe

Just like Eve did after taking that first bite of the apple, go and get those near and dear to you involved. If you are lucky enough to have parents and grandparents still living, talk to them about your interest in tracing the family tree. They are your second and third generations of ancestors. Document their lives thoroughly. By doing so, you just might find your equivalent of my great-uncle Henry.

Relationships

The relationships that you want to document for each ancestor are

- Parents (biological, foster, guardian, and step-parents plus other persons like grandparents who played a significant parental role)
- Spouse(s)
- Children (biological, adoptive, foster, guardian, and step-children)
- Siblings (biological, adoptive, step-, and half-siblings).

Involve your siblings, aunts, uncles, and cousins in your hunt for family information. Help them get started writing their own personal histories. Practice your interviewing skills on them. This prepares you for the more intensive interviewing that comes later.

Once you have documented your living relatives' lives (through their written histories and your oral interviewing), begin collecting information about deceased family members. Your interviewing will expand to include distantly related individuals whom you may never have met. After that, interview nonrelated people who knew your deceased family members. This includes their friends, in-laws, neighbors, and associates.

A really funny, informative book on interviewing is *Make Anyone Want to Talk, No Questions Asked* by investigative reporter Don Ray (Placentia, California: Shumway Publishing, 2001).

In his later years, my father-in-law visited his hometown of Butte, Montana. As he walked into the local historical society, there on the wall was a photograph of a local social event from the early 1900s. His parents and many of their friends were in that picture. The historical society was thrilled when he was able to identify most of those people for them. The moral of this story is that success can come from interviewing an ever-widening circle of people. You never know who might pop up with the answers you need.

Preparing for an Interview

Even though you are anxious to find out about your ancestors, not everyone will share your enthusiasm at first. If your potential sources are not interested, you have to either infect them with your excitement or teach them easy ways to help you in your quest. My maternal relatives thought it a bit odd when I started chasing dead ancestors. Now they send me obituaries and articles from their local newspapers that mention our surnames. We even hold an annual family reunion that gets bigger every year.

Cyndi's List has two categories to help oral interviewers:

- Video & Audio Tapes *(www.cyndislist.com/video.htm)*
- Oral History Interviews *(www.cyndislist.com/oral.htm)*

When you set up an interview, give the person some idea of the subjects you want to discuss. This gives the brain time to percolate. Over the next few days, your interviewee will remember additional details, so your subsequent interview is likely to be more productive.

But requesting an interview also gives that person a chance to make excuses to avoid you. Be prepared. If you hear "I don't want to talk about that" or "I know nothing about that," reassure that person that you'll be happy to just hear about "the good old days." If that doesn't work, ask who else might remember the people or events you want to know more about.

Several days before you do an interview, run through your check list:

- Do you have an address and telephone number to call your interviewee if you get lost or delayed? Be sure to keep this information for future reference.
- Do you have a map, driving directions, or someone to help you find your way there? Be sure to also keep this information for future reference.
- Have you prepared a short list of questions to use if the conversation bogs down?
- Do you have a small gift to present to grease the wheels of progress? Copies of photographs of ancestors, pictures of family memorabilia, or copied pages from a family Bible all make good gifts.

- Have you assembled all the equipment you need to record the interview?
    - A tape recorder and twice as many cassettes as you think are necessary.
    - A video recorder and three times as many cassettes as you think are necessary. Video recorders that capture sounds can double as tape recorders.
    - A still camera and film or memory cards. It makes the best pictures for any family histories or scrapbooks you eventually assemble. Digital cameras make pictures that are especially easy to share.
    - Batteries and AC chargers for all of the above.
    - An extension cord and/or surge protector.
    - A pencil and pad of paper for jotting down notes and diagramming relationships.
- Have you assembled everything else you need for the interview?
    - Both blank and filled-in charts and forms showing your ancestry and the interviewee's ancestry (if you know it), plus extra copies to leave with your interviewee. (See Chapter 4 for more about charts and forms.)
    - A laptop computer or PDA (personal digital assistant, such as a Palm Pilot) for quickly consulting your notes and pedigree information. If you don't have one of these devices, you'll have to leaf through your paper charts and forms during the interview when questions arise.

The Do's and Don'ts of Interviewing

Interviews are useful because they give you clues, identify places pertinent to the events in your ancestors' lives, and identify family traditions for you to prove or disprove with further research. They reflect the good, the bad, and the ugly found in any family. Family foibles are bound to come out from time to time, especially once your interviewee becomes comfortable talking to you. Remember the first rule of genealogy: *Don't judge prematurely.*

Interviewing is like any other skill. Even if you aren't born with a talent for it, you improve with practice. One way to start an interview is to select an old photograph and make copies to give to your interviewees. Sit down with family members who remember the photo. Ask them to talk about the Five W's of that photo (who, what, where, when, and why). Ask permission to record their words for posterity.

If allowed, always tape your interviews. You can't trust your memory of an interview done thirty minutes ago, much less one done thirty years ago. More important, you are preserving the sound of the voices, accents, and phrasings—a priceless gift for future generations.

Since microphones are intimidating, do your taping as unobtrusively as possible. Don't switch the recorder off and on. It is better to use up a little tape than to distract your interviewee.

Never edit your original tapes. If you are preparing an oral history, use a copy for your editing.

I make it a priority to visit and interview older family members first. Keep your visits short so as not to wear them out. Allow their conversations to wander. You'll be amazed what you learn that way. Seemingly irrelevant material often turns out to be very important later. It is almost impossible to interview too many family members. Each person furnishes a different perspective. Each can fill in different pieces of your real-life family puzzle. Always interview someone more than once, if you can. Most people remember additional details the second time you interview them. Be sneaky. Ask the same questions again, but in different ways.

If an unfamiliar name is mentioned during an interview, ask for clarification. When my family members mention Bill, they could mean my grandfather, father, half-brother, or nephew. If in doubt, double-check.

Write down the names of all the people present at any interview. If you are taping, have each of them say their name aloud. It is a good idea to jot down their ages (no offense, but sometimes memory slips with age) and relationship to anyone mentioned during the interview. Note who did the interviewing and the date and place it was done.

Consider taking a translator with you, especially if your interviewee speaks a different language or dialect. This is necessary more often than you might think, as the following story illustrates.

The last time I went to interview Fletcher (a first cousin twice removed), I happened to take along cousins Max and Jim. We were talking about W.B. Hill (my great-grandpa who was Fletcher's dad's brother). I mentioned how W.B. was known to carry a big knife in his boot. Fletcher commented that the Hills weren't quarrelsome people. Then he grinned and said the Hills wouldn't start a feud, but they sure could end one.

He said he figured his dad "warn't a scairt a nothin'," but being scrupulously honest, added, " 'cept the painter." Max and Jim looked at me and began to smile. They could tell I didn't understand. Fletcher went on to recount how one day the painter came and screamed at the door of his parents' log cabin up on the side of the mountain. He said there was a little hole carved at the bottom of the door for the family cat to go in and out. The painter looked in that hole and screamed. Fletcher's daddy just shook with fright. A few minutes later, the painter climbed up on the roof and screamed. Fletcher's daddy was so scared he crawled under the table.

By this time, Max and Jim were nearly rolling on the floor. They could see I still didn't have a clue. Finally, Jim managed to gasp, "He's talking about the panther . . . the painter cat." I didn't know mountain lions were called "painters" in that neck of the woods. I do now.

Generally avoid asking questions that require exact answers. Your interviewee will do one of three things if you pose a pointed question:

- Answer "I don't know" and clam up, ending the conversation
- Make something up just to please you
- Surprise you by being able to give accurate, detailed information

The third category of interviewees are gold mines, once you double check the details they supply. Remember the second rule of genealogy: Seek proof from more than one source.

I had an uncle who came up with lovely, flowery details about our family's history. When asked what he remembered best about his mother, he said it was her expert tailoring. She took worn-out men's suits and cut them down to make handsome tailored clothes for her boys. I believe this much was true because I have heard it from other family members and neighbors. But my uncle went on to claim that her prowess with a sewing machine was due to her being related to the Singer sewing machine brothers. Not true. Not even close—but I didn't tell him that.

When you are told these family stories and traditions, record them for later consideration. Don't contradict the person telling the story. That is a sure way to end all help from that person. Be accepting and encouraging while doing the interview. You can investigate later. Many stories that seem wildly improbable start with a grain of truth. You want to find that grain of truth.

Tips for Interviewers

- Ask open-ended questions about the 5 W's (who, what, where, when, and why).
- Ask for only a little information at a time.
- Ask brief questions (as opposed to convoluted ones) because they are easier to understand and respond to.
- Phrase your questions simply but gently.
- Ask easily answered questions first to relax the interviewee.
- Save sensitive questions until you have established a rapport. This may take several sessions or even years.
- Give the gift of silence. Let the interviewee have time to think. When the interviewee falls silent, jot down a few notes or shuffle through your papers. If you eventually need to get the conversation going again, consult the short list of questions you prepared ahead of time.
- If you think of something else you want to ask or a point you need to clarify, jot it down on your pad of paper. Show respect and don't interrupt the interviewee's story unless you absolutely have to do so.
- Interrupt only for the purpose of steering the conversation, and then only occasionally. You risk ending the flow of memories from your interviewee.
- As Benjamin Franklin advised, hedge your bets and admit you might be wrong when stating an opinion. This allows room for the other person's point of view.
- Try to establish whether the interviewer witnessed an event, or was told or read about it later. Eyewitness accounts are usually deemed more accurate than hearsay.
- Don't wear out your interviewee. End the interview in a reasonable amount of time, as gracefully as possible. You want to leave the door open for future conversations.
- Write your interviewee a thank-you note and remember to send anything you promised to share.
- Send a progress report if your interviewee expressed interest in your efforts.
- Give your interviewee extra copies of your pedigree chart and the family group records for the families you are researching. Be sure your current contact information (name, postal address, e-mail address, and possibly your telephone number) is on those forms. Worst case scenario is that your interviewee will throw them out. Best case scenario is that your interviewee will give them to someone else who expresses an interest in the family tree.

Keep in mind that no interview ever turns out perfectly and rarely does it go exactly as planned. You will save yourself a lot of frustration—and keep your interviewees relaxed and talking—if you just let them tell their stories in their own way. You never know what you might learn.

Develop a repertoire of gently revealing questions. My seven favorite questions are these:

1. When you were a child and your family got together, who were the relatives they visited?
2. Who else did your family gossip about when you were a child?
3. Where did your family go when they went to the big city to shop?
4. What were some of the landmarks in the area where you grew up?
5. Did your family always live in the same place?
6. Who else was there when . . . ?
7. Who else might know about . . . ?

Questions one and two clarify relationships. If you have an ancestor named Mary Hill, you have a problem. Because this is a common name, you have to worry about connecting to the wrong Mary Hill. But if you know your Mary Hill had a sister Louisa who married Nathan Teaster, you have a much better chance of connecting to the correct Mary Hill.

Questions three through five are about geography. Whether you are searching in the United States or elsewhere, many places share the same name. From my research, I know there are places named Laurel in Pennsylvania, Maryland, Virginia, and Kentucky. In fact, at least eighteen states in the United States have towns named Laurel. In Germany in the 1870s, more than three hundred towns had the name Neuhof (*new town*). Geography questions help you figure out the correct place of residence for your ancestral families, which helps you know where to look for more information about them.

Questions six and seven help broaden your list of people to interview. The more people you talk to about the events, places, and people important in your ancestor's lives, the more missing pieces you are likely to find.

Standards for Sound Genealogical Research

Recommended by the National Genealogical Society

Remembering always that they are engaged in a quest for truth, family history researchers consistently

- Record the source for each item of information they collect
- Test every hypothesis or theory against credible evidence, and reject those that are not supported by the evidence
- Seek original records, or reproduced images of them when there is reasonable assurance they have not been altered, as the basis for their research conclusions
- Use compilations, communications, and published works, whether paper or electronic, primarily for their value as guides to locating the original records, or as contributions to the critical analysis of the evidence discussed in them
- State something as a fact only when it is supported by convincing evidence, and identify the evidence when communicating the fact to others
- Limit with words like "probable" or "possible" any statement that is based on less than convincing evidence, and state the reasons for concluding that it is probable or possible
- Avoid misleading other researchers by either intentionally or carelessly distributing or publishing inaccurate information
- State carefully and honestly the results of their own research, and acknowledge all use of other researchers' work
- Recognize the collegial nature of genealogical research by making their work available to others through publication, or by placing copies in appropriate libraries or repositories, and by welcoming critical comment
- Consider with open minds new evidence or the comments of others on their work and the conclusions they have reached

The Game Plan

To recap the genealogy game plan, start by working on your personal history. You don't need to put a time limit on your writing, unless you promised to present someone with a copy for Christmas or a birthday. During this time, encourage family members to record their own personal histories and share them with you.

Once your personal history is coming along, start interviewing close family members. You'll be looking for records and information about your ancestors and working on your interviewing skills.

When you begin to feel comfortable doing family interviews, move on to interviewing distant relatives plus your ancestors' neighbors, friends, and associates. The information you collect in these interviews should make it much easier for you to document the significant events and family relationships in the lives of your deceased ancestors.

CHAPTER 4

Some Assembly Required

NOW THAT YOU ARE WRITING YOUR PERSONAL HISTORY AND INTERviewing others, it is time to start assembling the pieces of your family tree. This chapter describes the get-a-box method of assembly and the standard tools used by genealogists (ancestor charts and family group sheets) to put together your family tree. Chapter 5 covers the basic building blocks (names, dates, places, and relationships) needed to fill in the details on these charts.

Ancestors Wanted: Dead or Alive

Get a box. Put it someplace obvious. Choose a place where it will remind you to look around your home for anything containing information about your relatives, dead or alive. You especially want to find anything that identifies their significant life events. When you find something, make a copy and put the copy in the box.

Don't overlook even the simplest items—for instance, a recipe titled "Aunt Annie's Banana Bread" from your mother's recipe box. Who was Aunt Annie, and how is she related to you? Other types of items you may find include

Bibles. I am sorry to tell you that the names and dates written in the family pages of a Bible are not always correct. Make sure to check them against other sources. Save a copy of the publication date of the Bible, along with the family information pages. If the family event dates (birth, marriage, and death) are two hundred years before

Exploring Home Resources at Cyndi's List

Cyndi's List *(www.cyndislist.com)* has many categories with information about the types of resources found in both yours and other people's homes. Some of these categories are a little different than the types of home resources mentioned in this chapter.

Home Resources	Categories at Cyndi's List
Bibles	Family Bibles
Biographies and family history books	Biographies
Church certificates	Births & Baptisms Marriages Religion & Churches specific denomination, such as Baptist
Civil certificates	Births & Baptisms Marriages subcategory under a locality, such as U.S.—Vital Records
Citizenship papers	Immigration & Naturalization Passports
Cross-stitch samplers and quilts	Recipes, Cookbooks & Family Traditions
Diaries, journals, and books of remembrance	Diaries & Letters Scrapbooks
Emigration/immigration records	Ellis Island Immigration & Naturalization
Family newsletters	Magazines, Journals, Columns & Newsletters Newsletters Surnames, Family Associations & Family Newsletters
Histories (published and unpublished)	Books Libraries, Archives & Museums
Hospital records	Medical & Medicine
Legal papers and documents	Land Records, Deeds, Homesteads, Etc. Wills & Probate
Letters and postcards	Postcards
Memorial cards	Cemeteries & Funeral Homes
Military records	Military Records Worldwide subcategory under a locality, such as U.S.—Military
Newspaper clippings	Newspapers
Occupational records	Occupations specific occupation, such as Mining & Miners
Photos, albums, and scrapbooks	Photographs & Memories Scrapbooks
School records	Education Schools

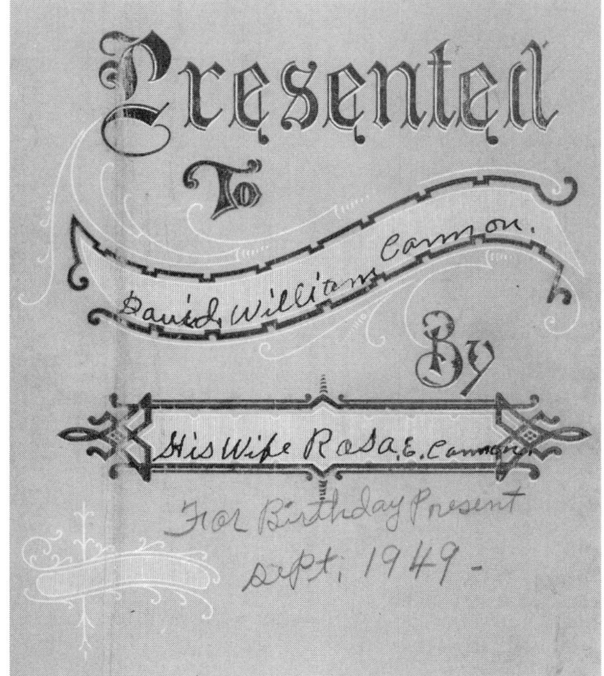

Figure 4.1 Page from my Grandfather Cannon's Bible

the Bible was published, it means the dates were not written near the time the events happened. Other relationship clues can be found on the page indicating who gave the Bible to its owner, and when. See Figure 4.1 for an example from my grandfather's Bible.

Biographies and Family History Books. If you inherited your aunt's handwritten notes about your grandmother's family, don't throw them out! You never know what little gems and pearls of wisdom are hidden in there. Compiled family history books are wonderful finds, but I have never read one that didn't contain at least a few errors. To err is human, especially when compiling a large family history book covering centuries and thousands of ancestral family members.

Church Certificates. These include christenings, baptisms, confirmations, marriages, funerals, and memorials. Church records may contain symbols representing certain events, or the condition of events, that communicate as much as the written words in

For more information on symbols used in German church records, see the following:

- German Word List found in Research Helps under the Search tab at the FamilySearch Internet site *(www.familysearch.org)*
- Genealogical Symbols and Abbreviations Web page at the German genealogy.net Web site *(www.genealogienetz.de/misc/gensig.html)*

that entry. For many centuries, births were denoted in German parish registers by a symbol that looks like an asterisk, but illegitimate births were denoted by a symbol that looks like an asterisk surrounded by parentheses.

Civil Certificates. These include official government certificates for births, marriages, divorces, and deaths. They are generally considered original sources because they are made near the time of the event by a recorder who usually can read and write competently.

One of the easiest to use sites for ordering copies of birth certificates and other vital records is VitalChek *(www.vitalchek.com)*.

Citizenship Papers. Applications for citizenship include genealogically significant information, whereas actual certificates of citizenship rarely do. Such applications in the twentieth century in the United States often include birth dates and places, your ancestor's actual signature, the port of arrival, and his or her last place of residence before coming to this country. Alien registration records also contain helpful information.

Cross-Stitch Samplers and Quilts. Occasionally, these decorative items contain the names and important dates of the immediate family or ancestry of the women who made them. Family recipes and information scribbled in cookbooks often contribute clues, too.

Diaries, Journals, and Books of Remembrance. These often provide important facts and clues genealogists need. They also reveal the personality of the people who wrote them.

Emigration/Immigration Records. This category includes such things as steamship tickets, passenger lists, ship manifests, and alien manifests. Twentieth-century alien passenger manifests often list the town of residence and the next of kin back in the old country. You may also be able to determine relatives' locations from postmarks on letters and pictures on postcards.

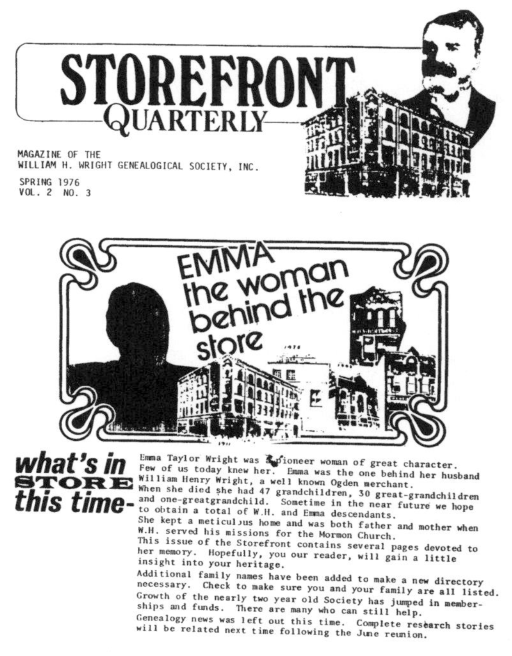

STOREFRONT QUARTERLY

MAGAZINE OF THE
WILLIAM H. WRIGHT GENEALOGICAL SOCIETY, INC.

SPRING 1976
VOL. 2 NO. 3

EMMA the woman behind the store

what's in STORE this time-

Emma Taylor Wright was a pioneer woman of great character. Few of us today knew her. Emma was the one behind her husband William Henry Wright, a well known Ogden merchant.
When she died she had 47 grandchildren, 30 great-grandchildren and one-greatgrandchild. Sometime in the near future we hope to obtain a total of W.H. and Emma descendants.
She kept a meticulous home and was both father and mother when W.H. served his missions for the Mormon Church.
This issue of the Storefront contains several pages devoted to her memory. Hopefully, you our reader, will gain a little insight into your heritage.
Additional family names have been added to make a new directory necessary. Check to make sure you and your family are all listed.
Growth of the nearly two year old Society has jumped in memberships and funds. There are many who can still help.
Genealogy news was left out this time. Complete research stories will be related next time following the June reunion.

Figure 4.2 *Storefront Quarterly*, a family newsletter

Family Newsletters. Personal computers have made it easy to publish a family newsletter. Over the years these become more and more valuable as a record of family members and to preserve the stories and memories of family members. They are often used to share the results of genealogical research. See Figure 4.2 for an example of a newsletter done by one of the branches of my husband's family.

Histories (Published and Unpublished). Just like biographies, you need to verify their facts with other sources, but histories often contain interesting information about the places people lived and the economic, social, and political events that happened during their lifetimes. The smaller the geographic area covered in a history book, the more likely you are to find your resident ancestor mentioned there.

Hospital Records. Hospital records covering births, illnesses, and deaths provide valuable information. Don't overlook work records for hospital employees.

Legal Papers and Documents. Wills, deeds, mortgages, land grants, and land surveys may contain names, dates, and places. Often they also reveal relationships.

Letters and Postcards. Personal letters frequently contain valuable information about the places people lived and the intimate details of their lives. They often reveal relationships and significant events observed in families. Postcards may mention relatives' names and the places they lived or trips they took. The postmark on a postcard may provide clues, too.

Memorial Cards. Memorial cards are sent to relatives living far away to announce a death in the family. They generally include birth and death dates, age at death, and place of burial. Many mortuaries print memorial cards as part of their services.

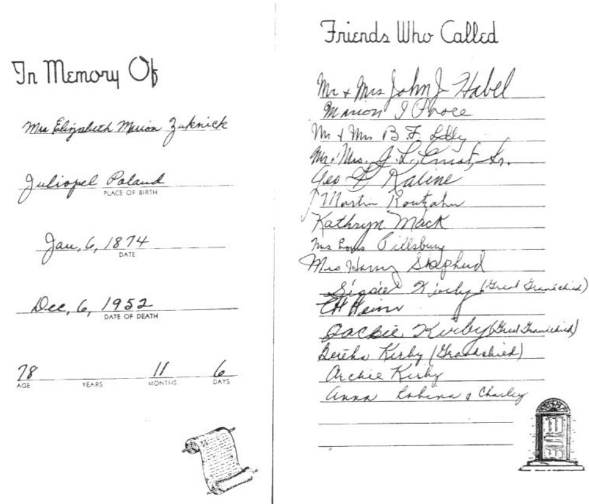

In Memory Of

Mrs Elizabeth Marion Zuknick

Juliopel Poland
PLACE OF BIRTH

Jan, 6, 1874
DATE

Dec, 6, 1952
DATE OF DEATH

78 AGE YEARS 11 MONTHS 6 DAYS

Friends Who Called

Mr + Mrs John J Habel
Kathryn Mack
Archie Kirby

Figure 4.3 Pages from the register from my paternal grandmother's funeral

Registers were often kept of the people attending a funeral. These help you identify likely people to interview (their family, friends, and associates). See Figure 4.3 for the register kept by the funeral home that handled my paternal grandmother's funeral.

Military Records. These include draft registrations, service records, medals, ribbons, pay vouchers, discharge papers, pension papers, and bounty land warrants.

Newspaper Clippings. People often save clippings of birth, marriage, and death notices, as well as articles about anniversaries, civil ceremonies, church activities, and social events. These must be verified with other sources because they are not always accurate. When you do the clipping, be sure to save the front of the section of the newspaper in which the article appears so you have the publication details needed to cite the source. Nothing is more frustrating than having an article from an unknown newspaper with no dates.

Occupational Records. These include apprenticeship and pension records, awards, citations, and pay stubs. Not only do they contain some genealogical information, but they can also teach you more about how your ancestors lived.

Photos, Albums, and Scrapbooks. Photograph albums are infamous for being full of unlabeled pictures. If that is the case, your job is to talk to living relatives and friends to identify the people in those pictures. Some types of albums are notorious for destroying photos. If your photos are stuck, do not force them out. Scan them through the plastic pockets of the plastic pages.

School Records. These generally contain such information as birth dates and family relationships, achievements and awards, and graduation dates. You can approximate an ancestor's age from the date and grade on a report card.

Not until my fifth interview with Aunt Olga did she finally dig out her mother's 1907 steamship ticket, which Aunt Olga had kept for seventy years (see Figure 4.4). The card was punched each day its holder was on the ship. It contains some interesting information, including the fact that Grandmother claimed to be six months pregnant when they left Bremen, Germany. Steamship passengers were not allowed to travel if

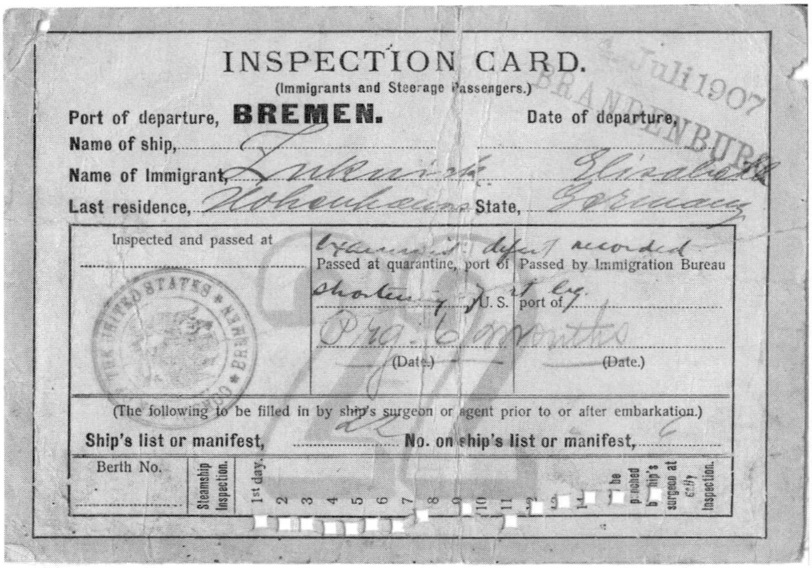

INSPECTION CARD.

(Immigrants and Steerage Passengers.)

Port of departure, **BREMEN.** Date of departure,

Name of ship,

Name of Immigrant,

Last residence, State,

Inspected and passed at | Passed at quarantine, port of U.S. | Passed by Immigration Bureau port of

(Date.) (Date.)

(The following to be filled in by ship's surgeon or agent prior to or after embarkation.)

Ship's list or manifest, No. on ship's list or manifest,

Berth No. Steamship Inspection. 1st day. 2 3 4 5 6 7 8 9 10 11 12 13 14 To be punched by ship's surgeon at daily inspection.

Figure 4.4 My paternal grandmother's 1907 steamship ticket

they were more than six months pregnant. Apparently, steamship companies didn't want to deliver babies aboard ship. Because my father was born just two months after their departure date (and was full term, according to his sisters), I know Grandmother was seven months pregnant when they boarded the steamship. Was she simply unaware of how far along she was, or did she tell a little white lie in order to travel with her family to America? Would you be tempted to do the same thing?

Finding Your Way with Charts

Oh, what a tangled web we weave when a family tree we try to perceive. Keeping track of all those pieces of information would be a nightmare if genealogists didn't use charts, forms, and computer programs. Just imagine all those names, dates, places, and relationships whirling around in your head. With our modern tools, it is easy to tell where you have been and where you are going with your family tree tracing.

The genealogist's basic tools include ancestor charts and family group sheets. They help you map the tangled branches of your family tree. Once filled out, you study them to see what you know and don't know about the members of your ancestral families.

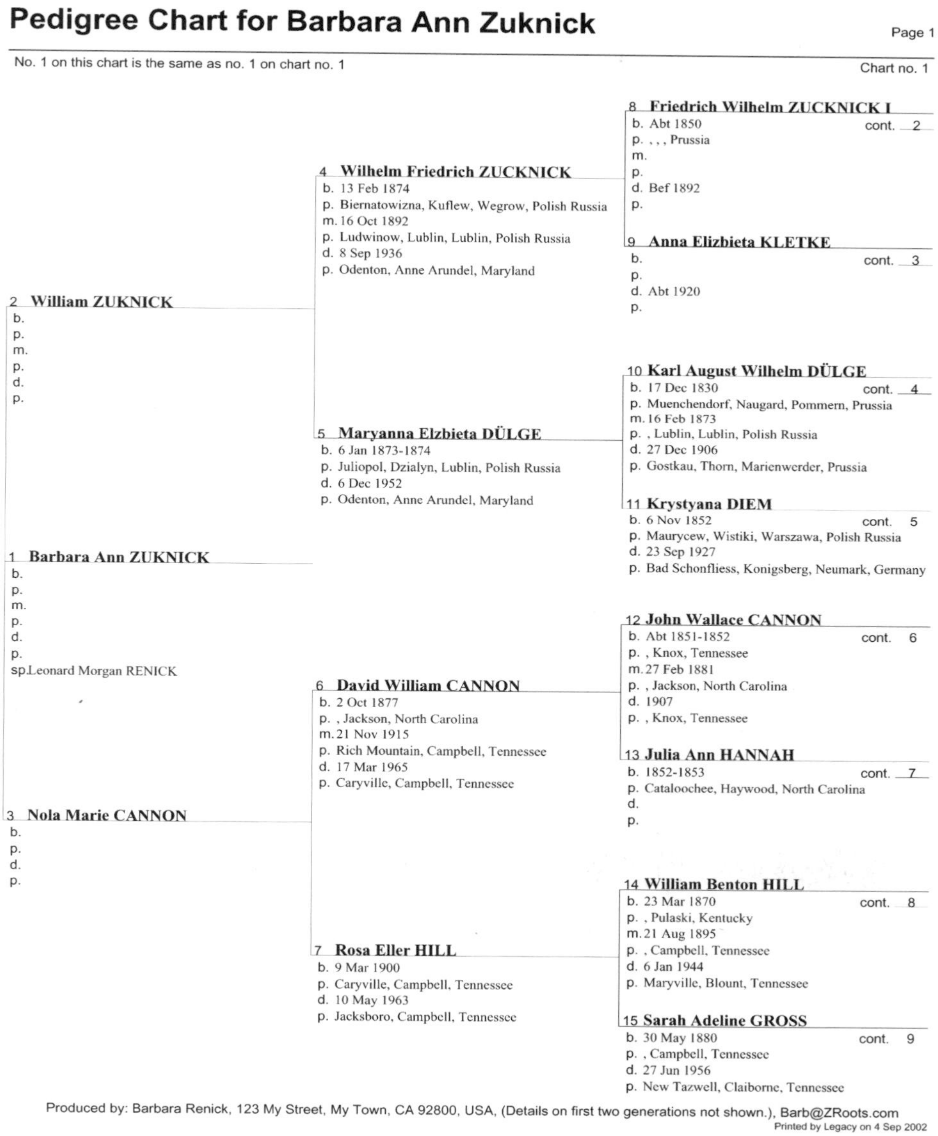

Pedigree Chart for Barbara Ann Zuknick

Page 1

No. 1 on this chart is the same as no. 1 on chart no. 1

Chart no. 1

8 Friedrich Wilhelm ZUCKNICK I
b. Abt 1850 cont. 2
p. , , , Prussia
m.
p.
d. Bef 1892
p.

4 Wilhelm Friedrich ZUCKNICK
b. 13 Feb 1874
p. Biernatowizna, Kuflew, Wegrow, Polish Russia
m. 16 Oct 1892
p. Ludwinow, Lublin, Lublin, Polish Russia
d. 8 Sep 1936
p. Odenton, Anne Arundel, Maryland

9 Anna Elizbieta KLETKE
b. cont. 3
p.
d. Abt 1920
p.

2 William ZUKNICK
b.
p.
m.
p.
d.
p.

10 Karl August Wilhelm DÜLGE
b. 17 Dec 1830 cont. 4
p. Muenchendorf, Naugard, Pommern, Prussia
m. 16 Feb 1873
p. , Lublin, Lublin, Polish Russia
d. 27 Dec 1906
p. Gostkau, Thorn, Marienwerder, Prussia

5 Maryanna Elzbieta DÜLGE
b. 6 Jan 1873-1874
p. Juliopol, Dzialyn, Lublin, Polish Russia
d. 6 Dec 1952
p. Odenton, Anne Arundel, Maryland

11 Krystyana DIEM
b. 6 Nov 1852 cont. 5
p. Maurycew, Wistiki, Warszawa, Polish Russia
d. 23 Sep 1927
p. Bad Schonfliess, Konigsberg, Neumark, Germany

1 Barbara Ann ZUKNICK
b.
p.
m.
p.
d.
p.
sp. Leonard Morgan RENICK

12 John Wallace CANNON
b. Abt 1851-1852 cont. 6
p. , Knox, Tennessee
m. 27 Feb 1881
p. , Jackson, North Carolina
d. 1907
p. , Knox, Tennessee

6 David William CANNON
b. 2 Oct 1877
p. , Jackson, North Carolina
m. 21 Nov 1915
p. Rich Mountain, Campbell, Tennessee
d. 17 Mar 1965
p. Caryville, Campbell, Tennessee

13 Julia Ann HANNAH
b. 1852-1853 cont. 7
p. Cataloochee, Haywood, North Carolina
d.
p.

3 Nola Marie CANNON
b.
p.
d.
p.

14 William Benton HILL
b. 23 Mar 1870 cont. 8
p. , Pulaski, Kentucky
m. 21 Aug 1895
p. , Campbell, Tennessee
d. 6 Jan 1944
p. Maryville, Blount, Tennessee

7 Rosa Eller HILL
b. 9 Mar 1900
p. Caryville, Campbell, Tennessee
d. 10 May 1963
p. Jacksboro, Campbell, Tennessee

15 Sarah Adeline GROSS
b. 30 May 1880 cont. 9
p. , Campbell, Tennessee
d. 27 Jun 1956
p. New Tazwell, Claiborne, Tennessee

Produced by: Barbara Renick, 123 My Street, My Town, CA 92800, USA, (Details on first two generations not shown.), Barb@ZRoots.com

Printed by Legacy on 4 Sep 2002

Figure 4.5 Ancestor chart in the classic pedigree tree shape

An ancestor chart (also called a pedigree chart) shows your progenitors—your parents, grandparents, great-grandparents—with your ancestral lines arranged in different shapes. The most common shape for an ancestor chart is shown in Figure 4.5. This standard ancestor chart is especially useful to family tree tracers because it shows at a glance which lines of ancestry you have identified and which are still missing from your family tree.

Ancestor charts come in many different shapes, sizes, and styles. The most common is a four-generation chart (in pedigree tree shape) on standard 8½ x 11-inch paper. Five- and six-generation charts are also available in this shape, but the width of each column is necessarily narrower. They allow you to fit more generations onto a page, but with less information about each ancestor on the chart.

Large, wall-sized ancestor or descendants charts (ones you fill in by hand) are available for purchase. Many genealogy programs print wall-sized charts in pieces that you cut and paste together. Several companies take a special file you give them (created in your genealogy program—including pictures) and print out truly gargantuan charts on photographic-quality paper. These are wonderful for big family reunions.

Parts of an Ancestor Chart

Allowing for styling differences, the parts of an ancestor chart (see figure 4.5) include the following elements:

Title. The title can be anything you want to use to identify whose ancestry is on that chart.

Column	Generation	Position	Whose Name Goes There	Relationship to You
1	1st	1	Yours	You
2	2nd	2	Your father's	Father
		3	Your mother's	Mother
3	3rd	4	Your father's father's	Paternal grandfather
		5	Your father's mother's	Paternal grandmother
		6	Your mother's father's	Maternal grandfather
		7	Your mother's mother's	Maternal grandmother
4	4th	8	Your father's father's father's	Great-grandfather
		9	Your father's father's mother's	Great-grandmother
		10	Your father's mother's father's	Great-grandfather
		11	Your father's mother's mother's	Great-grandmother
		12	Your mother's father's father's	Great-grandfather
		13	Your mother's father's mother's	Great-grandmother
		14	Your mother's mother's father's	Great-grandfather
		15	Your mother's mother's mother's	Great-grandmother

Figure 4.6 Numbered positions on your ancestor chart (see the example in Figure 4.5)

> To find your mother's parents on a typical ancestor chart (like the one in Figure 4.5), simply locate the couple to her right on the chart. Notice that you take your mother's number (3) and double it to locate her father (6), or double it and add 1 to find her mother (7). The same rule applies to find your father's parents.

Numbered Positions. Figure 4.6 shows the assignment of numbered positions on your ancestor chart. A four-generation ancestor chart has your ancestors arranged in generations in columns left to right, as you go back in time. Write your name in position number 1 in the far left column. Except for position number 1, males are always even numbers on the upper lines, and females are always odd numbers on the lower lines. So if your name is on line 1, your father's name goes on line 2 and your mother's name on line 3. Under line 1 is a place to include your spouse's name.

Life Events. Under each numbered line on an ancestor chart (see Figure 4.5) are the following words (or abbreviations standing for those words):

- **Born:** (the date that person was born)
- **Place:** (the place that person was born)
- **Married:** (the date that person was married, not duplicated on the wife's list)
- **Place:** (the place of the marriage)
- **Died:** (the date that person died, if applicable)
- **Place:** (the place that person died)

Chart Number. The chart number is usually located in the upper right corner of the chart. The chart on which you appear in position number 1 is labeled chart number 1.

Continuation Chart Numbers. Continuation numbers are located on the far right edge of some charts. On the four-generation chart shown in Figure 4.5, the first continuation chart number is 2 (at the top) through 9 (at the bottom). On my ancestor chart number 1, Great-grandpa W.B. Hill's name appears in position number 14 because he is my (1) mother's (3) mother's (7) father (14). His continuation chart number is 8. There are other chart numbering systems, but this is the most common for at least the first nine charts on which you display the first seven generations of your ancestry.

Chart Number Statement. This statement is located under the title in the upper left corner of most ancestor charts. For chart number 1 (where your name is in position number 1), the statement reads "No. 1 on this chart is the same person as No. 1 on chart No. 1." For Great-grandpa W.B. Hill's continuation chart (ancestor chart number 8 where his name appears in position number 1), this statement reads "No. 1 on this chart is the same person as No. 14 on chart No. 1."

My Kathy Story

Many years ago, I was sitting in the lobby of the Family History Library in Salt Lake City. The library was closing and I couldn't spend the night. While I was waiting for my roommate who had not yet exited the library, a little old lady came out and sat down by me. I was startled when she called out her good-byes to other people leaving the library. Her German accent sounded so much like my grandmother's accent.

I introduced myself and asked where in Germany she came from. She said her name was Kathy and she came from Stettin. This was very near where my grandmother's ancestors lived. I gave Kathy an extra copy of my ancestor chart (I always come prepared) and asked her to contact me if she ever found any of my ancestors in that area. She kindly promised to do so.

The next year, my husband and I moved. Eight years later, Kathy sent a handwritten letter to my old address, which was on my ancestor chart. She had found my grandmother's ancestors and added three new generations to that branch of my family tree.

The letter went to my old address. The people who had purchased our house crossed out their address and wrote in the address I had given them eight years before. By some miracle, the post office forwarded the letter to me. Kathy and I reestablished contact and worked together on my family tree. All thanks to an extra ancestor chart, Kathy's kindness, and a post office miracle.

Preparer's Statement. A preparer's statement gives the preparer's name and contact information (postal address, e-mail address, telephone number) so others who see the chart can contact the preparer. The contact information usually appears in a box in the lower left corner of the page or in very small print across the bottom.

Date Prepared. The date the chart was prepared should appear somewhere on the chart.

Filling in Family Group Sheets

The purpose of a family group sheet is to display the basic information you have about one family. This includes their major life events and relationships. It should also include a list of your sources (what you used to identify all the members of that family) plus any notes or comments you want to add. It works like a score sheet—showing you at a

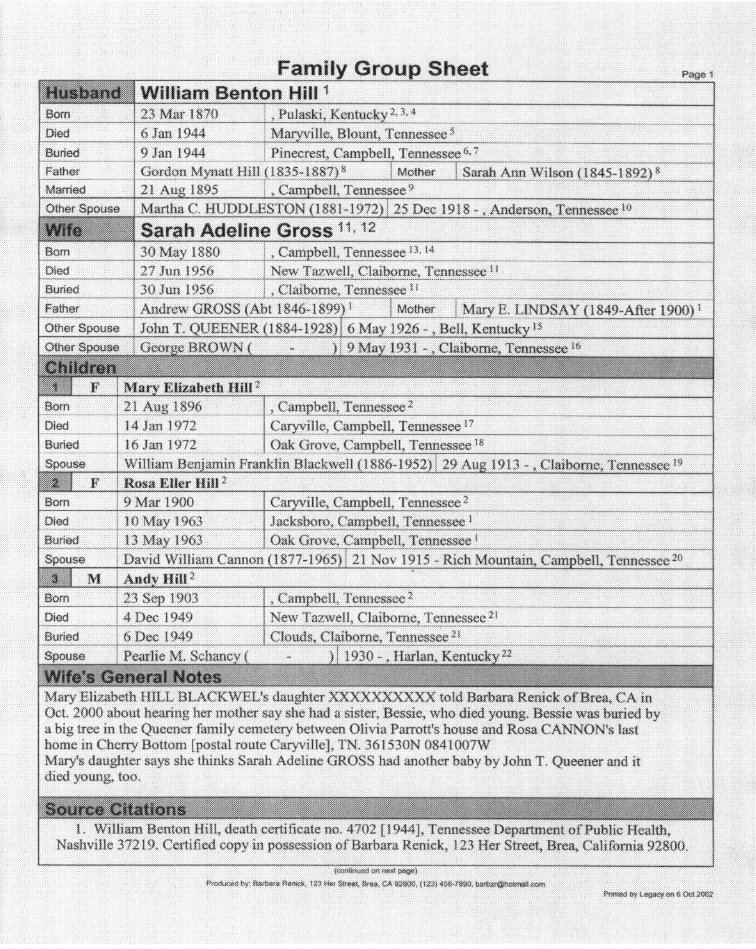

Family Group Sheet Page 1

Husband	William Benton Hill [1]		
Born	23 Mar 1870	, Pulaski, Kentucky [2, 3, 4]	
Died	6 Jan 1944	Maryville, Blount, Tennessee [5]	
Buried	9 Jan 1944	Pinecrest, Campbell, Tennessee [6, 7]	
Father	Gordon Mynatt Hill (1835-1887) [8]	Mother	Sarah Ann Wilson (1845-1892) [8]
Married	21 Aug 1895	, Campbell, Tennessee [9]	
Other Spouse	Martha C. HUDDLESTON (1881-1972)	25 Dec 1918 - , Anderson, Tennessee [10]	
Wife	**Sarah Adeline Gross [11, 12]**		
Born	30 May 1880	, Campbell, Tennessee [13, 14]	
Died	27 Jun 1956	New Tazwell, Claiborne, Tennessee [11]	
Buried	30 Jun 1956	, Claiborne, Tennessee [11]	
Father	Andrew GROSS (Abt 1846-1899) [1]	Mother	Mary E. LINDSAY (1849-After 1900) [1]
Other Spouse	John T. QUEENER (1884-1928)	6 May 1926 - , Bell, Kentucky [15]	
Other Spouse	George BROWN (-)	9 May 1931 - , Claiborne, Tennessee [16]	
Children			
1 F	**Mary Elizabeth Hill [2]**		
Born	21 Aug 1896	, Campbell, Tennessee [2]	
Died	14 Jan 1972	Caryville, Campbell, Tennessee [17]	
Buried	16 Jan 1972	Oak Grove, Campbell, Tennessee [18]	
Spouse	William Benjamin Franklin Blackwell (1886-1952)	29 Aug 1913 - , Claiborne, Tennessee [19]	
2 F	**Rosa Eller Hill [2]**		
Born	9 Mar 1900	Caryville, Campbell, Tennessee [2]	
Died	10 May 1963	Jacksboro, Campbell, Tennessee [1]	
Buried	13 May 1963	Oak Grove, Campbell, Tennessee [1]	
Spouse	David William Cannon (1877-1965)	21 Nov 1915 - Rich Mountain, Campbell, Tennessee [20]	
3 M	**Andy Hill [2]**		
Born	23 Sep 1903	, Campbell, Tennessee [2]	
Died	4 Dec 1949	New Tazwell, Claiborne, Tennessee [21]	
Buried	6 Dec 1949	Clouds, Claiborne, Tennessee [21]	
Spouse	Pearlie M. Schancy (-)	1930 - , Harlan, Kentucky [22]	

Wife's General Notes

Mary Elizabeth HILL BLACKWEL's daughter XXXXXXXXXX told Barbara Renick of Brea, CA in Oct. 2000 about hearing her mother say she had a sister, Bessie, who died young. Bessie was buried by a big tree in the Queener family cemetery between Olivia Parrott's house and Rosa CANNON's last home in Cherry Bottom [postal route Caryville], TN. 361530N 0841007W

Mary's daughter says she thinks Sarah Adeline GROSS had another baby by John T. Queener and it died young, too.

Source Citations

1. William Benton Hill, death certificate no. 4702 [1944], Tennessee Department of Public Health, Nashville 37219. Certified copy in possession of Barbara Renick, 123 Her Street, Brea, California 92800.

(continued on next page)

Produced by: Barbara Renick, 123 Her Street, Brea, CA 92800, (123) 456-7890, barbzr@hotmail.com

Printed by Legacy on 6 Oct 2002

Figure 4.7 Family group sheet for W.B. Hill printed out by my genealogy program

glance what key information you have and what is missing. See Figure 4.7 for an example of what a family group sheet for my great-grandpa William Benton (W.B.) Hill looks like when printed out by my genealogy program.

Your notes include anything pertinent about anyone in that family. A good example is the location of each family member's grave. This is especially important if the cemetery is large or you fear the stone may not be there the next time you visit.

Along with your ancestor chart, make a family group sheet for each couple represented on that chart. When your four-generation ancestor chart is finally filled, this will be eight family group sheets (see Figure 4.8). If you or one of your ancestors had more than one marriage, make additional family group sheets for each additional marriage or association.

1 family group sheet	For yourself as a parent with your spouse and children
1 family group sheet	For your parents with their children
2 family group sheets	For your grandparents with their children
4 family group sheets	For your great-grandparents with their children
More family group sheets	For any additional marriages and the children from those marriages

Figure 4.8 The family groups represented on one four-generation ancestor chart

Family group sheets are divided into sections. The husband's event information is listed in the first section, the wife's in the second section, and the children's information in the sections following their parents'. Your notes and sources for each of these individuals follow in this same order at the end of the youngest child's event section.

On most styles of family group sheets,

- The husband's and wife's sections include at least their
  - Name
  - Birth date and place (or christening date and place, or both)
  - Death date and place (or burial date and place, or both)
  - Father's name
  - Mother's name
  - Marriage date and place (not duplicated in the wife's section)
  - Other spouses' names, if any

- Each child's section includes at least that child's
  - Number in birth order (oldest is number 1, next oldest is number 2, etc.)
  - Sex (M (male), F (female), U (unknown))
  - Name
  - Birth date and place (or christening date and place, or both)
  - Death date and place (or burial date and place, or both)
  - Marriage date(s) and place(s) and spouse(s)'s name(s)

Finding Genealogical Charts and Forms on the Internet

Cyndi's List has six categories of links to Web sites that have charts and forms:

- Supplies, Charts, Forms, etc. *(www.cyndislist.com/supplies.htm)*
- Software and Computers *(www.cyndislist.com/software.htm)*
- Organizing Your Research *(www.cyndislist.com/organize.htm)*
- Novelties *(www.cyndislist.com/novelty.htm)*
- Beginners *(www.cyndislist.com/beginner.htm)*
- Timelines *(www.cyndislist.com/timeline.htm)*

The Research Helps section at FamilySearch Internet includes many free charts and forms:

1. Go to *www.familysearch.org.*
2. Click on the Search tab.
3. Click on the Research Helps subtab.
4. Click on Sort by Document Type in the options bar on the left side of your screen.
5. Under Document Types click on Forms.

If it says [PDF] after the name of a form, you can print it with the free Adobe Acrobat Reader program that comes pre-installed on many computers. If you don't have a copy on your computer, download it from *www.adobe.com/products/acrobat/alternate.html*.

Each family group sheet also includes the preparer's name and contact information, and the date the family group sheet was prepared.

Where to Obtain Charts and Forms

If you don't have a computer, check with your local genealogical society or LDS Family History Center for preprinted charts and forms. The Family History Center where I work sells ancestor charts and family group sheets for ten cents a sheet.

If you own a computer and have an Internet connection, you have two ways to produce both ancestor charts and family group sheets. The first way is to go to Web sites that provide a variety of blank charts, usually in a format that uses the free version of Adobe Acrobat Reader to print them on your printer.

Another way to obtain blank charts and forms is to print them using a genealogy program installed on your personal computer. Several free genealogy programs (such as PAF or Legacy) can be downloaded from the Internet. See the Software and Computers category at Cyndi's List online for links to download these free programs or to try out one of the commercial programs. For more about genealogy computer programs, see Chapter 7.

Once you enter information about your family and your ancestors in any genealogy program, you'll be able to create a variety of printouts. Legacy, for example, does one hundred three different varieties of charts, forms, lists, and reports. Most up-to-date genealogy programs print out a book with a title page, table of contents, chapters, and rough index from the information you enter. Even the free PAF and Legacy programs do so. One of the joys of using genealogy software is that you type the information only once, but use it in a number of different ways.

Chapter 5

The Building Blocks of Family Trees

REMEMBER IN CHEMISTRY CLASS WHEN YOU FIRST LEARNED ABOUT molecules (like H_20 for water)? Next, you had to grasp the concept of something even smaller—atoms. Well, documenting the major events in your ancestors' lives follows the same pattern.

Getting to the Root of the Matter

In your box filled with family information, you'll find some items (like Aunt Annie's Banana Bread recipe) that mention just a name. Other items probably contain details about the events in your ancestors' lives—especially births, marriages, and deaths. Those events are like molecules. They define your ancestors' lives, but they also can be broken down into their component parts: names, dates, places, and relationships.

In chemistry, you need to know the difference between H_20_2 (hydrogen peroxide) and H_20 (water). In genealogy, you need to know standard ways to tell the difference between first names and last names, the date on a marriage license versus the actual date the marriage was performed, and the town of Clinton from the county of Clinton in Missouri.

Few things are more frustrating than searching and searching in Clinton County, Missouri, for records of your ancestors—only to find that Grandma's diary meant the town of Clinton in Henry County, Missouri. Another frustration results when you learn your Tennessee ancestors came from Washington County—and you assume that means

Washington County, Tennessee. This is dangerous since there is also a Washington County, Virginia, nearby.

Genealogists, like chemists, have standard methods of notation—ways of writing down names, dates, places, and relationships—to avoid confusion. Any failure to follow these rules leads to chaos.

Decades ago, I heard a story in a beginning genealogy class that illustrates this point. One day, a patron came into a Family History Center and asked a volunteer staff member for help. The patron explained he was having a great deal of trouble tracing an ancestor with the last name of Unk. The volunteer had never heard of anyone with the last name of Unk, so she asked, "Where did you first find that name?" The patron pulled out an old family group sheet prepared by someone years before. On it was his ancestor's name: Mary Unk. The volunteer had to tell him that *Unk* probably meant *unknown*, rather than the last name of his ancestor.

Family group sheets are compiled records. They are not original resources. This patron spent countless hours researching the wrong name because someone didn't follow the genealogical standards for writing names.

What's in a Name?

Genealogists almost universally write surnames in capital letters. If you find an ancestor's name written as James Thomas, you don't know if Thomas is that ancestor's middle name or last name (surname). If someone was a sloppy writer and left out a comma, Thomas might even be his first name. But if you see that ancestor's name written as James THOMAS, you know that someone is indicating Thomas was his surname.

An exception applies when you transcribe an original record (like a will or a page from a family Bible). Then you want to create as accurate a typed copy as you can—as true to the original as a typed copy can be.

If you do not know someone's last name, leave it blank. Most computer programs give you an option to indicate the name was not known or the individual has not been identified.

If you are writing down a name by hand, list it as first, middle, then just the last name in all capitals. But if you are typing the name in a genealogy software program, follow that program's recommendations for entry. Once set (configured) to capitalize surnames, genealogy programs display and print all last names in capitals.

Some programs have a box (field) labeled Surname or Last Name. Others have just one big field for people's names. These programs have you indicate the surname by surrounding it with slashes (*James /thomas/*). The program then displays and prints the name as James THOMAS.

Do not assume an ancestor's gender based upon the name. Was Ury a girl or a boy? I have friends with husbands named Lyn and Gay (short for Gaylord). If some other record doesn't indicate the person's gender, don't guess. Genealogists and genealogy programs recognize three sexes: male (M), female (F), and unknown (U).

Spelling Variations

The idea of spelling names one correct way is largely a twentieth-century concept. Genealogists quickly learn that names are spelled any way the record taker heard them. The surname Renick has been spelled thirty-one different ways in American records since the family arrived here in the early 1700s. These spelling variations range from two N's in Rennick, to Wrennix, to the historical character Chief Joshua Rye Neck.

One of my surnames is pronounced like the word *team* but spelled Diem (the German spelling) here in America. In Polish records, it is spelled Duem. In Russian records, it is spelled Dym and Tym. Way back in Switzerland, where the name probably originated, it was spelled Thieme.

Most genealogists choose to standardize the spellings of names entered in the name

Finding Spelling Variations for Names

Use the following steps to find spelling variations for names in the International Genealogical Index (IGI) at FamilySearch Internet:

1. Go to the FamilySearch Internet Site *www.familysearch.org.*
2. Click on the Search tab.
3. By default you should be in the Search for Ancestors section.
4. Click on International Genealogical Index in the options bar on the left side of your screen.
5. Type your ancestor's name in the boxes and choose a region.

Notice the spelling variations for both the first and last names that come up in the first 200 matches displayed on the search results list.

field of a genealogy program because of the way computers sort and search records alphabetically. Figure 5.1 shows you how the computer sorts if you don't standardize names, and Figure 5.2 shows you the same file with the names standardized.

RIN	Name	Sex
341	Cook, Josephine	F
225	Cotrell, David Chadwell	M
224	Cotrell, Moses	M
244	Cotrell, Samuel Ewing	M
246	Cotrell, Virginia A.	F
256	Cottrel, Albert W.	M
345	Cottrel, Chadwell Briton	M
337	Cottrel, J. D.	M
339	Cottrel, Roxie	F
343	Cottrel, Travis Josephine	F
258	Cottrell, Barthena	F
255	Cottrell, Chadwell B.	M
344	Cottrell, Chadwill Britton	M
250	Cottrell, China W.	F
342	Cottrell, Dudley Dewitt	M
346	Cottrell, Elisabeth Ann	F
226	Cottrell, Elizabeth A.	F
348	Cottrell, Elliott	M
347	Cottrell, Elsbeth Ann	F
249	Cottrell, Fountain	M

Figure 5.1 Genealogy database with names not standardized

RIN	Name	Sex
341	Cook, Josephine	F
256	Cottrell, Albert W.	M
258	Cottrell, Barthena	F
255	Cottrell, Chadwell B.	M
344	Cottrell, Chadwell Britton	M
345	Cottrell, Chadwell Britton	M
250	Cottrell, China W.	F
225	Cottrell, David Chadwell	M
342	Cottrell, Dudley Dewitt	M
226	Cottrell, Elizabeth A.	F
346	Cottrell, Elizabeth Ann	F
348	Cottrell, Elliott	M
347	Cottrell, Elsbeth Ann	F
249	Cottrell, Fountain	M
248	Cottrell, Gray Garrett	M
337	Cottrell, J. D.	M
253	Cottrell, Louisa D.	F
254	Cottrell, Marshall	M
245	Cottrell, Mary Harriett	F
252	Cottrell, Morgan Vandemon	M

Figure 5.2 Genealogy database with names standardized

If your ancestors are like mine, their names were spelled differently in every record you find. You might as well standardize the spelling in your genealogy program, then record the exact spelling when you enter the information about that specific source. Add any of their nicknames or aliases in the fields specifically labeled for that information (fields such as Also Known As, Alternate Names, Married Name, Naming, and Nicknames—each computer program calls it something a little different).

When Names Changed

Confusion often results when an ancestor changed his or her name. This happened for a variety of reasons and may or may not have included a legal registration of the change. One example of a legal name change is when a woman marries and takes her husband's surname. In genealogy, we solve this confusion by always referring to women by their maiden names.

Many emigrants to the United States changed their foreign-sounding names (both given names and surnames) to versions that sounded more "American." This was done in different ways:

- Shortening the name (Kowalczorski to Koval)
- Translating the name (the German name Bauer to the English equivalent Farmer)
- Phonetically spelling the name (the German names Viegel spelled as Faigal, and Kreter spelled as Greater)
- Taking a totally unrelated name (Kowalczorski becoming Ford).

Caution: In some cultures women don't take their husband's surname when they marry. In other cultures a person's family name (surname) is listed first with their given name listed second. This is common in many Asian cultures.

Adding Confusion to Names

Prefixes and suffixes add confusion to names—while giving you clues for further research. It would be nice if John Dick Jr. were always the son of John Dick Sr. Unfortunately, this isn't true. Junior could be his nephew, his grandson, or just a younger man in the same area with the same name.

In 1800 in Pulaski County, Kentucky, a John Dick Sr. arrived from South Carolina with his children and their families. John Dick Sr.'s oldest son was Samuel Dick. In Pulaski County records, it was Samuel's son John who was called John Dick Jr.—not John Dick Sr.'s son John. By the way, at least seven of John Dick Sr.'s nine children had sons named John, all in the same county.

To confuse things even more, when John Dick Sr. died, who then became John Dick Sr.? Was it the original John Dick Sr.'s son or grandson? A man's postnomial can change during his lifetime.

I found my German grandmother's name confusing. Everyone in America knew her as Elizabeth Marion. It wasn't until her marriage record was located in Poland that I realized her full name was Maryanna Elzbieta Dülge and that grandfather Wilhelm's name was really Friedrich Wilhelm Zucknick. It was not uncommon for German children to be given several names. The first name(s) listed on records were often their christening names, followed by their given name(s). This given name was usually the one they were known by in the family.

Naming Patterns

In Scandinavia, a naming system called patronymics was used until the 1800s. The child's surname was derived from the father's first name. For example, Lars, the son of Peder Jensen, would be called Lars Pedersen. When Lars Pedersen had a son Nels, his name would be Nels Larsen. When Lars Pedersen had a daughter Anna, her name would be Anna Larsdotter (the feminine ending). A friend, who is a professional genealogist from Finland, says she standardizes all the female entries in her computer files with the male form of the name. In the case above, Anna Larsdotter would be listed as Anna Larsen, but the exact spelling of her name would be included with the source for her information.

Hispanic naming practices can be even more confusing. Sometimes the child carried both the father's and the mother's names, as in Maria Rodriguez Martinez or Juan Carlos Fernando Yorba y Bernardo. Once you understand this naming system, the pattern gives you clues about the next generation of ancestors.

I have never proven who John Dick Sr.'s parents were to my satisfaction. I suspect, based upon the naming pattern of his sons, that his father's name was Samuel. I deduced this because his oldest son was named Samuel, his second son was James, and his third son was John. Knowing that John Sr.'s wife, Margaret, was the daughter of James Wylie, I suspect this family followed the pattern of naming the first son after the husband's father, the second son after the wife's father, and the third son after the husband.

This is not solid proof, but there are other clues. John Dick (Sr.), as an Irish Protestant emigrant, obtained a land grant in South Carolina on the same day and in the same area as a Samuel, Charles, and Agnes Dick. Both Charles and Agnes also had sons named Samuel. I need to further investigate this Samuel Dick as a possible father for my John.

And just when you think you have the naming pattern figured out, a family will use just the opposite pattern: first son named for wife's father, second son for husband's father, and third son for father. The key is if the third son is named for his father; watch the names of the first two sons. They may have been named after their grandfathers. There are identical patterns for naming the first two daughters after their grandmothers and then the third daughter after the mother.

Some families in southern Germany gave all their sons the same first name as the father. If the father's name was Wilhelm, the sons would be Wilhelm Adolph, Wilhelm Bernhard, and Wilhelm Carl—all with the same first name. This pattern was also followed with daughters carrying their mother's name.

Date Dilemmas

Figure 5.3 Gravestone with death date and exact age

Dates can be just as tricky to interpret as names. Dates recorded as numbers are not clear. What date is 1/2/02? Is it January 2 or February 1? Is the year 2002, 1902, or 1802? To avoid confusion, genealogists write dates in a DD MMM YYYY pattern, like 7 Jun 1947 (day month year). If I were handwriting this date, I might even write 7 June 1947 because a sloppily written Jun can look like Jan, and vice versa. Genealogists write out the full four-digit year because we cover so many centuries with our family trees.

Sometimes you won't find an exact birth date, but you might find a death date and an exact age at death, like the gravestone shown in Figure 5.3. (Figure 5.3 is a classic example of why digital cameras are so popular among genealogists. They allow you to immediately check to see if you got the whole picture.) This gravestone says: "WILLIAM WHITMAN DIED Sep. 19, 1838 Aged 49 Yrs 3 Ms 12 Ds." You could do the math, but it is easier to use your genealogy software, which should include a date calculator. Figure 5.4 shows the date calculator tool in the genealogy program I use. There are also Web sites that easily calculate the birth date for you.

See the Calendars & Dates category at Cyndi's List *(www.cyndislist.com/calendar.htm)* for links to Web sites with Date Calculators.

At other times, the best you can find is an ancestor's stated age on a certain date, perhaps from a census record. You know that on 1 June 1880 (the official date for the census information), W.B. Hill was listed as ten years old. You might quickly do the math and say he was born in 1870, but if he had not yet had his birthday by 1 June, his year of birth was 1869. In other words, he was ten when the census was taken, but his eleventh birthday came later that year. Genealogists often record this "calculated date" with a slash (1869/70), but there are several other ways to record calculated dates.

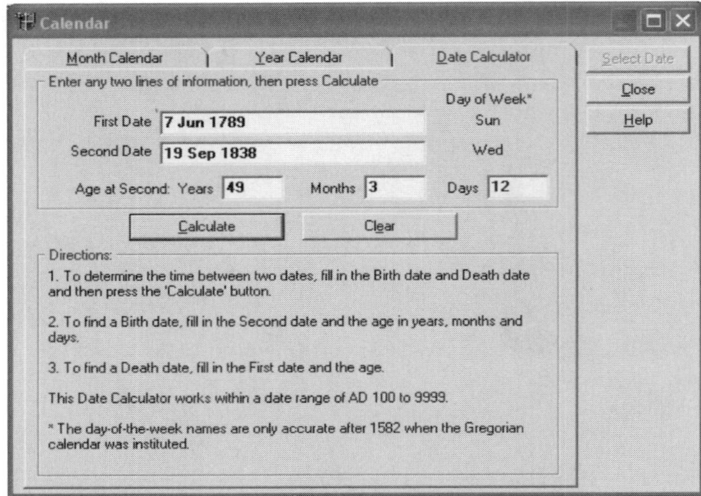

Figure 5.4 Legacy's date calculator tool

See Figure 5.5 for a list of standard ways to indicate calculated and approximated dates with prefixes. Consult your genealogy program's help files to determine the options it gives you for entering dates.

A **calculated date** is determined by a person's known or stated age at another event.

An **approximated date** is an educated guess based upon known facts.

If you can't find either a birthday or that person's age on a specified date, then approximate her age from what you know. If your ancestor lived in Tennessee, got married in 1806, had her first child in 1808, had her last child in 1838, and died in 1875, you can guess

- That she was probably 16 to 21 years old when she married, so was born between 1785 and 1790
- Which would make her 18 to 23 years old when her first child was born

- And 48 to 53 years old when her last child was born
- And, therefore, 85 to 90 years old when she died

For this ancestor, I would write her birth date as "about 1790." Again, check to see what words your genealogy software allows in its date fields.

It is much better to calculate or approximate a date to enter on your charts (or in your genealogy program) than it is to leave the date blank. A genealogy database containing fifteen William Whitmans with no event dates gets confusing. An approximated or calculated date is definitely better than no date at all—as long as you include a prefix to indicate it is not an exact date.

You Type	Your Program Displays or Prints
About 1869	ABT 1869
After 1869	AFT 1869
Age 10 (1870)	1869/70
Before 1869	BEF 1869
Between 1869 and 1875	BETWEEN 1869/1875 or 1869-1875
Calculated 1869	CAL 1869
Circa 1869	c1869
Estimated 1869	EST 1869
Human- or computer-generated estimate	<1870>

Figure 5.5 Ways to indicate calculated and approximated dates

If you have ancestors who were Asian, Quakers, or Orthodox Jews, you may encounter different calendar systems and different ways of calculating dates. To learn more about calendar systems around the world and throughout time, visit the Calendar Zone *(www.calendarzone.com).*

Place Perplexities

Genealogists write the names of places (left to right) from smallest geopolitical division to largest. Write United States locations as city, county, state, country. Write European locations as village, parish, county or shire, province or state, country.

Genealogists are adamant about their comma rules for listing places. This is because we get so frustrated when we run across an entry like "Orange, CA." If I find this place information on an address label with a zip code after it, I am confident it means the city of Orange in California. But if I find "Orange, CA" on a family group sheet, I cannot assume it means the city of Orange because there is also a county of Orange in California.

Years ago, my father-in-law hired a professional genealogist to find out more about his grandfather, George W. Roberts, who lived in Clinton, Missouri. The researcher looked and looked in Clinton County, but couldn't find any record of a George W. Roberts. She soon realized there were plenty of records in Clinton, Henry County, Missouri for Sheriff George W. Roberts.

Because I communicate with so many relatives who are not trained genealogists, I tend to use the abbreviation "Co." after the name of a county whenever I am handwriting a place name in my research notes or typing it in a letter or e-mail message.

Abbreviations for place names are dangerous. Over the years, genealogists have come up with a number of different abbreviation systems, but no one has ever come up with a system that didn't confuse someone. Even the official U.S. Postal Service two-letter state codes can be confusing. Can you correctly name the 2-letter postal codes for Alabama, Alaska, Arizona, and Arkansas? Is Indiana abbreviated IA, or is that Iowa?

While CA on an address label may mean California, at the end of a URL for a Web site it means Canada. Does MA stand for Massachusetts or Madagascar? It all depends. A wise genealogist avoids abbreviations.

There may be more than one place in a state with the same name. This is especially important to genealogists if these places are in different counties. Many records of genealogical significance are created at the county level. If you are not certain what county a particular town belongs in, do not guess. Look it up in an atlas or gazetteer.

Comma Rules for Place Names

Genealogists use commas to differentiate between place levels in place names:

- ,Orange, California, USA = the county of Orange in California (the comma before the name of the county indicates the name of the town is missing).
- Orange, , California, USA = the city of Orange in California (the two commas between the name of the town and the name of the state indicate the county name is missing).

By following these rules, you are less likely to confuse yourself and others.

Back before the Internet, I remember finding a source that said my ancestor lived in Coal Creek, Tennessee. I looked in my atlas, but there wasn't a town in that area called Coal Creek. There wasn't even a Cole Creek or anything like it. Weeks later, I finally found a historical gazetteer for Tennessee which explained that after the Tennessee Valley Authority built Norris Dam, the town of Coal Creek changed its name to Lake City. I knew where that was. I had walked there along the railroad tracks to go grocery shopping with Grandma and my cousins.

When I called my mother the next day, I told her about my search for Coal Creek and how it had turned out to be Lake City in disguise. She laughed and said, "Why honey, I could have told you that."

A gazetteer is a dictionary of place names.

One of my students claimed that her ancestors, over a period of two hundred years in the United States, lived in four states and seven counties—and never moved. My paternal grandmother was born in Russia. Today, that town is in Poland. Geopolitical boundaries change, so they affect where you look for records about your ancestors.

Using the GNIS Search Form

The Geographic Names Information System (GNIS), developed by the U.S. Geological Survey, lists two million places and geographic features in the United States. It is a valuable, free tool. See it at *geonames.usgs.gov*. The GNIS search form includes an option to search variant spellings (Query Variant Name?). Unfortunately, the default is set to not search for variants, and you have to manually change it when filling in the form for a search. See the accompanying two figures showing my GNIS search and the results for Coal Creek.

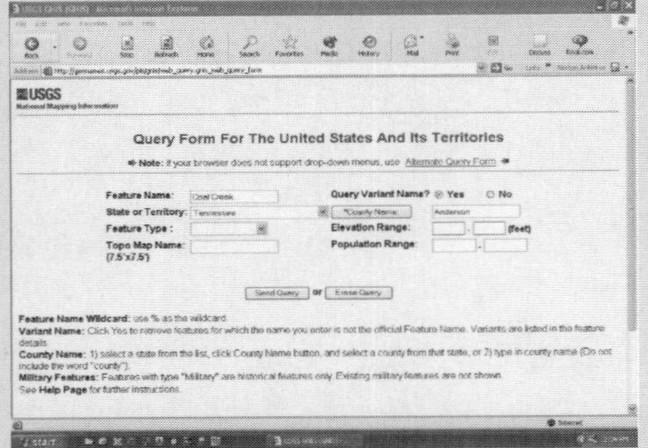

GNIS search form

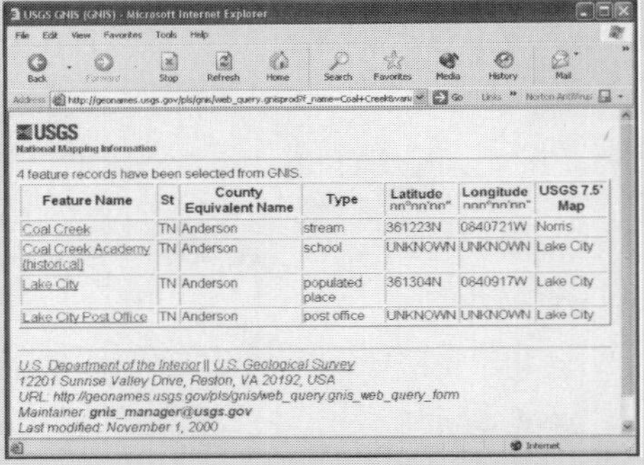

Results of GNIS search for Coal Creek

List place names as they were when that event occurred in your ancestor's life. Listing an ancestor's birthplace as Manakin, Goochland, Virginia, USA is incorrect if she was born there in 1751—before there was a United States of America.

The death certificate for my husband's great-grandmother Maggie (the one who married George W. Roberts in Clinton, Henry County, Missouri), gives her birth place as Virginia in the year 1842. But the 1870 U.S. census for Henry County lists her birth place as West Virginia. Both may be right. When she was born in 1842, there was no state of West Virginia, so technically she was born in Virginia. Then in 1870, after the Civil War, the census taker received an answer based upon the changed geopolitical boundaries for the place where Maggie was born. This information helps narrow down our search for Maggie's parents.

Because library catalogs list places as they are now and from the biggest to smallest geopolitical unit, it is good to write down what you know about place name changes in your research notes. For example, my grandparents left their farm near Bromberg, Posen, Prussia, in 1907 to come to America. Today, that city is Bydgoszcz, Bydgoszcz, Poland. I always search under both designations in library catalogs.

For more about geography and geographic tools (such as maps, atlases, and gazetteers), go to Cyndi's List *(www.cyndislist.com)* and find the name of the country or region you are researching. Browse your way down to smaller geopolitical units and Cyndi's lists of links for those subcategories.

Family Relationships

Genealogy is all about relationships. In this book, I use the word *ancestor* to mean a person whose name appears on your ancestor chart and from whom you *directly* descend, but genealogists think in terms of ancestral family relationships. As previously explained, researching the entire family of your direct ancestor helps you avoid connecting your family tree to the wrong person.

The Scoop on Cousins

Here are some resources to help you unravel cousin issues:

- One of the clearest explanations of the degrees of cousinship is found at Genealogy.com's Learning Center in an article titled "What Is a First Cousin, Twice Removed?" *(www.genealogy.com/genealogy/16_cousn.html)*.
- For more help online, see the Cousins & Kinship category at Cyndi's List (*www.cyndislist.com/cousins.htm*).

There are two useful relationship calculators you can download:

- The Cousin Calculator at iRoots.net *(www.iroots.net/tools/cusncalc/)*
- The Relationship Chart at David Sylvester's Web site *(www.mdwsweb.com/genealogy/relationship.html)*

I must confess that beyond the level of first cousin (the child of an aunt or uncle), I think of relatives as "distant cousins" and consult a relationship chart when I need to be more specific. Do you know the difference between a first cousin once removed and a second cousin? The way I remember the difference is that a remove means a difference in generation (or vertical level) whereas the degree of cousinship (first, second, third cousin, etc.) is a move laterally (or to the side that drops down an equal number of generations on both sides). And that's probably as plain as mud.

The easiest way to calculate the relationship between two people is to have your

Relationship Definitions

Siblings: Your brothers and sisters are your siblings.

Half-siblings: Person with whom you share just one parent. Includes half-brothers and half-sisters.

Step-siblings: The children of someone your parent marries; you share no biological ancestors. Includes step-brothers and step-sisters.

Step-parent: A person who marries one of your parents. Includes step-mother and step-father.

Grand-aunt or **grand-uncle:** Your grandparent's sibling. Many people (myself included) use the less precise designation of great-aunt or great-uncle for a grandparent's sibling.

Great-grand-aunt or **great-grand-uncle:** Your great-grandparent's sibling.

Great-grandparents: The parents of your grandmother or grandfather.

Paternal: Pertaining to your father's side of the family tree.

Maternal: Pertaining to your mother's side of the family tree.

Ancestor: A person who appears on your ancestor chart from whom you directly descend, and from whom you inherited part of your genetic makeup.

Descendant: A person who has you on their ancestor chart (like a daughter or a grandson), and who inherited part of your genes as their genetic makeup.

Collateral relations: Relatives with whom you share an ancestor but who do not appear on your ancestor chart. Examples: your cousin or your grand-aunt.

Collateral lines: People with whom you share no immediate genetic connection, but who are of interest genealogically because they married your ancestors or collateral relatives.

genealogy program do it for you. This works if you have entered all the generations of connecting individuals in your program. Otherwise, consult a chart to figure out how you are related to someone else—if you both can trace your ancestry back to an ancestor you share. I often use that shared ancestor's surname to define which branch of my family tree we share. Thus, my Lindsay cousins are related to Mary E. Lindsay (my great-great-grandmother), while my Gross cousins (nothing personal there) are related to her daughter Sarah Adaline Gross (my great-grandmother).

While you are working with just your first few generations of relatives (your parents, aunts, uncles, and close cousins), you may be able to get away with merely recording names on your ancestor charts and family group sheets. (However, to do so would be a disservice to future generations who will want to know where you found your information.) If that is as far as you hope to go with your family tree, you may not need to document where you found each name, date, and place.

As they grow, every family tree gets tangled (see Figure 5.6). Sooner or later, conflicting names, dates, and places arise for the events in your ancestors' lives.

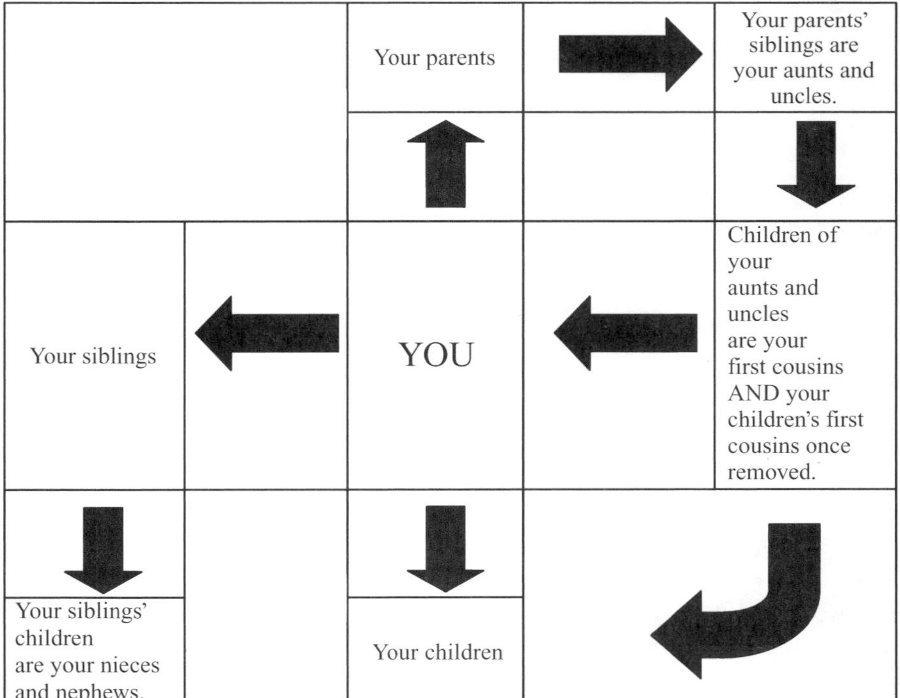

Figure 5.6 The directions of relationships

People who start out just writing down names usually end up wanting to kick themselves later for not recording where they got their information.

Make all your efforts to compile your family tree count. Start from the very beginning—from the very first source of information you find—to record everything you use to put together your family tree. You'll be documenting the drama of your ancestors' lives.

CHAPTER 6
Document the Drama

COULD YOU PUT TOGETHER A FIVE-HUNDRED-PIECE JIGSAW PUZZLE IF you were allowed to pick up each piece only once? Putting together your family tree is a lot like putting together a puzzle. You sort through the pieces until you find where they fit. This process goes more smoothly if you have a system of organization in place before you get started.

In the first four generations on your family tree, there are at least eight families. Each family is composed of individuals, each of whom needs to be uniquely identified. Each individual has life events that uniquely identify that person. Each life event has identifying pieces (names, dates, places, and relationships). So there are many pieces to even the smallest family trees. As Figure 6.1 illustrates, there are many parallels between putting together a puzzle and putting together a family tree.

Puzzle	Family Tree
1. Dump the pieces out of the box.	1. Collect copies of the pieces in a box.
2. Sort the pieces by shape (corner piece, flat edge, or other shape).	2. Sort your copies by the surname documented.
3. Sort the other shapes by color.	3. Further sort your copies according to the generation they document.
4. Begin assembly.	4. Begin assembly by recording what you have already found and where you found it.

Figure 6.1 The stages of assembly

Archaeologists take along tools not just to dig, but also to organize what they find. Genealogists need to be similarly prepared. Unfortunately, many genealogists do not start out with a system of organization, so they end up with unidentified photocopies and handwritten notes from who knows where—like pieces of a puzzle with the picture side torn off.

The further back you go, the more pieces there are in each earlier generation, the harder you have to search to find those pieces, and the more difficult it is to put them together. Therefore, the further back you go, the more organized you need to be.

Despite all the personal computers I've owned over the years, I still have fifteen feet of hanging paper files from the fifteen years of research I did during the typewriter era. These files contain my research logs, copies of all the genealogical correspondence I ever sent or received, and copies of what I found. I'm still struggling to scan and type all my past research into my personal computer.

If at all possible, record your research in a personal computer as you evaluate it (and make plenty of backups). You'll still have to keep paper files—but it will be much easier to search and sort through your family tree on the computer. In this book, I describe just the basics of organization to get you started. See the Organizing Your Research category at Cyndi's List *(www.cyndislist.com/organize.htm)* for more information.

Putting Together a Family Tree

Now that you have a box filled with copies of bits and pieces from around your home, you need to organize. The box is only a temporary storage location to get you started. It is time for you to record what you have found onto research logs. Research logs document the drama of your search. A research log (also known as a research calendar) is a form used to record both past and planned searches.

The research log is where you record what you are planning to look for and where you plan to look for it. When you make the search, write the letter, send the e-mail message, or actually do the interview, record the details of when, where, who, and what you did. I also write down comments about problems I had with that source (it was hard to read, the author is prone to err, the dirt road to the cemetery is graded only once a year, etc). Be especially careful to write down all the details about that source (author, title, publication information, the volume and page that mentions your ancestor, etc.).

This information is needed so you can analyze and evaluate what you used. How thoroughly you record this information determines, to a great extent, whether you will be able to find that source when you need it again. When you get home, don't forget to write in your research log where you filed your finds (paper copies, digital images, audio- or videotapes).

A research log functions much like a table of contents. It helps you remember why you wrote a letter to Jane Doe eight months ago. It provides a means of noting difficulties you encountered with a source. It jogs your memory about searching a particular source so that you won't search that source again unless you mean to do so.

Some genealogists like to keep separate "before" and "after" logs. They record only the research they have completed (what they found or didn't find) on their research calendars. Many genealogists keep separate correspondence logs, too. I like to keep things all together in one log.

As you see in Figure 6.2, my earliest research logs included a column for the date I did each search, interview, or letter. My research ideas were recorded right on my

SURNAME CANNON

RECORD JURISDICTION Civil

PAGE 1

RESEARCH INDEX
(INCLUDING CORRESPONDENCE)

SEARCH #	DATE OF SEARCH	BRIEF ACCOUNT OF EACH SEARCH: (SUBJECT AND PURPOSE OF SEARCH, ADDRESSES & CALL NUMBERS	NOTES ON WS NIL OR DATE OF REPLY	EXTR. # IF ANY
1	5 Oct 1975	Death Certificate Roas Ella CANNON	WS	1
2	5 Oct 1975	Death Certificate David William CANNON	WS	2
3	5 Oct 1975	Death Certificate Lora Irene ZUKNICK (daughter of D.W. & Rosa E. CANNON)	WS	3
4	23 Sep 1975	Soundex 1880 Census NC all counties searched for David William CANNON	NIL	----
5	23 Sep 1975	1850 Census Haywood Co., NC F572 (LNA) searched for any CANNON	NIL	----
6		Tax Lists Haywood and Jackson Co.'s, NC for John W. & Owen R. CANNON		
7		Voting Records (Pole Rec.) Haywood & Jackson Co.'s, NC for any CANNON		
8	15 Oct 1975	Soundex 1900 Census Tennessee for John W. CANNON or David Wm. CANNON (C-550)	NIL	----
9	15 Oct 1975	Soundex 1900 Census Missouri for John W. CANNON or David Wm. CANNON (C-550)	NIL	----
10	10 Dec 1975	Write Norton, VA for Minnie CANNON's death certificate in fall 1957	WS	25
11	3 Feb 1976	Soundex 1880 Census NC for John W. CANNON and Julia A. CANNON	NIL	----
12	3 Mar 1976	Deeds--Grantors Haywood Co., NC (GS 463,111) John W. CANNON	NIL	----

Figure 6.2 My early Cannon research log

research log. Pending items are easy to spot because they don't have anything in the Date of Search column. My only regret is that I didn't include more details about my finds on my early research logs.

Finding a Research Log That Fits

Every research-log designer has a different idea about what should be included. Only you can decide which design best fits your needs. Custom design your own form using a word processor, or use the research-log feature found in some genealogy programs. (Programs may use various names for this feature, such as Research Log, Research Journal, or To Do List.)

Base your decision on what to include in your research log upon the following ten questions. When you look at that research log twenty years from now, you will want to be able to answer them!

1. Who were you looking for?
2. Where were you looking for them?
3. What was your objective or goal?
4. What did you look at?
5. When did you look at it?
6. Where did you find it?
7. Who had it?
8. Who originally created it?
9. What was in it?
10. Where can you find it again?

Research logs are available in a surprisingly large number of places. If you do not use a computer, purchase preprinted forms at your local genealogical society or LDS Family History Center. You can also telephone the LDS Salt Lake Distribution Center at 800-537-5950 to order their research log.

If you own a computer with an Internet connection, you have three options. You can find different styles of research logs online by going to the Organizing Your Research category at Cyndi's List and scrolling down to Online Charts & Forms to Print or

Download. You can print the blank forms provided by your genealogy program. Or if necessary, use your word processor to custom design a research log to fit your exact needs.

As Valuable as a Treasure Map

At first, it may seem like needless work to keep a research log. Sure, treasure hunters and archaeologists keep detailed logs, but why should genealogists?

I always depended on Mark Hannah, retired park ranger and distant cousin, to show me the way to the log cabin our ancestor built in the Great Smokies—but now he's dead. How am I going to find the cabin again? MapBlast and MapQuest (Internet sites that provide maps and driving directions) don't show the dirt road that leads to the cabin. How will I find our Hannah Family Cemetery? I remember the path branched off where the road takes a bend at the bottom of the hill, but which hill?

These are the types of questions that are easily answered if your research log is full of the details about what you have done and where you have been, as well as what you found. One of the best pieces of advice my first genealogy teacher gave me was to keep research logs. Her second best piece of advice was to use as many lines on those logs as it took to record all the information about each search I made, every interview I conducted, and each letter (or e-mail message) I sent or received. I wish I had done a better job of recording the details of my searches. You should be sure to follow her advice.

How to Organize Your Research Logs

Some genealogists keep a different research log for each person they study. Others keep a different log for each family. Still other genealogists keep logs for each geographic area searched, recording searches for all their surnames in that area.

I keep research logs for each of my surnames, but I divide my logs into four sections: civil (government), church, family, and miscellaneous sources. Frankly, after thirty-two years of searching, my surname logs are getting a bit long. For example, I have ten pages of civil-record searches recorded for my Cannons. (See Figure 6.2 for page 1 from my earliest Cannon research log.) There is no way I could remember all those searches over all those years. I finally had to further divide my research logs geographically (Tennessee Cannons and North Carolina Cannons).

I label each page with the state, surname, source type, and log page number (Tennessee Cannon Civil Sources page 11). On research trips, I take blank research logs to write on, plus a copy of my up-to-date printed research logs. Another copy stays home in my hanging file arranged by surname (if small) or state plus surname (if large).

Research Logs and Computers

When I get home from a research trip, I sit down and analyze what I did. As I organize my finds, I frequently realize I should have looked for Grandpa not only as David Cannon, but also as D.W. Cannon, or even William Cannon (his middle name). Did I look for Cannon spelled different ways? Since his parents were divorced, I should also have looked for him under his mother's maiden name. I write down all these ideas for the next time I search.

If you take a laptop computer with you on research trips, don't enter anything into your genealogy program while in the middle of doing research. When in hot pursuit of ancestors, it is too easy to make a mistake and add something to the wrong record or to change the wrong person's death date. Wait until you can calmly evaluate what you have found before entering anything new or making any changes.

Make certain you enter all your searches on your research logs (whether you use paper forms or your genealogy program), even if you find nothing. In my research log, I write "NIL" (for "no information located") when I find nothing that seems to apply to my search. Your computer program will then be able to sort, search, or print a master list of the sources you have consulted.

If you cannot use a computer for one reason or another, be sure to keep a paper research log. When you get home, use your log to cite the sources you searched on the appropriate family group sheets and ancestor charts. If there isn't room on those paper forms to list all your source citations (and there usually isn't), attach additional sheets of paper to those forms to list all your sources and comments. Use superscripted numbers to indicate which sources and comments apply to which names, dates, places, or relationships.

So take blank log pages with you and fill them in while you are interviewing or searching. Later, after your evaluation and analysis, enter all your new information and changes either to your computer or on your paper forms. This evaluation and analysis step is a pivotal part of genealogical research.

Make Lots of Copies

While you are out searching, make copies of anything and everything you find. The details contained within a source may not seem important until you compare them to other pieces of your family puzzle.

In a book, don't copy just the one page that mentions your ancestor. From the very beginning, I knew I needed to copy both sides of the title page of any book because they contain the details I need for my source citation. I soon learned it is also important to copy

- Index pages (I highlight the names I searched for)
- Table of contents (so I have some idea of what was in that book)
- Foreword section of the book (if it contains explanations)
- Explanatory pages anywhere in the book pertinent to my search
- First page of any chapter mentioning my ancestor(s)
- Lists of abbreviations used and their meanings

Basically, you want to copy anything that helps you interpret what is on your ancestor's page in that book.

This was difficult to do before copiers, computers, and digital cameras. Today, copiers are a standard feature in most libraries, archives, and government buildings. Some digital cameras and camcorders have low-light settings that work well in dimly lit courthouses and archives. My camcorder copies images displayed on a microfilm reader and is gentle to fragile and irreplaceable resources (where strong light and even the gentlest handling deteriorate the original). There are fewer excuses than ever before for failing to make copies of what you find.

Write down the details about each source you use—not only in your research log, but also on the front of each copy you make. (But *never* deface any original by writing on it.) You'll thank yourself the next time you drop a stack of copies at the airport or in your driveway. Taking a little extra time to mark your copies when you make them saves countless hours of frustration later.

Log the Path to Success

For nine years, I searched for a marriage record of my great-great-grandparents Gordon Mynatt Hill and Sarah Ann Wilson. I suspected their marriage took place in Pulaski County, Kentucky, during the Civil War. While reading a microfilmed copy of the county marriage book, I noticed there was a six-month period in 1864 when no marriages were recorded by the county clerk. This was during a time when there was much fighting in that area. In my research log, I noted the existence of this gap in the microfilmed marriage records so that I would remember to make it part of my analysis later.

When I finally visited the courthouse, I viewed the actual book to make sure the pages weren't stuck together or torn out, but the book appeared intact. I asked if a separate marriage license or minister's return for my ancestors' marriage might have survived. The clerks denied having any other marriage records. This, too, was recorded in my research log.

I proceeded to search in the surrounding counties for my ancestors' marriage. I searched at the state library and archives. I searched at the state historical society. I searched for any other type of record that might give me that information (church records, family Bibles, newspapers, census records, land deeds, pension applications, and even their siblings' probate records).

I kept track of every record I looked at and every place I searched in my research log so that I would not waste time repeating any part of this hunt. After exhausting every possibility I could think of, I finally had to resign myself to the reality that I might never find their marriage information.

Years later, I included a six-generation ancestor chart in a letter to a retired teacher in Pulaski County. The fact that I didn't have a marriage date or place for Sarah Ann Wilson caught this teacher's attention. She wrote back to me with exciting news.

She was on the local historical society's committee, which had just completed its third volume of extracted marriage records, including the year 1864. She, too, had noticed the gap in the clerk's marriage record book. As the current clerk's ex-teacher, her enquiries turned up a box on a top shelf in the coat closet. It was filled with marriage licenses from that missing six-month period. Gordon and Sarah's marriage information had been uncovered at last.

Because I had searched so many other records about Sarah and her family, I recognized the significance of details I might have ignored had I found the license years earlier. She was married at the home of William Wilson (her oldest brother) by Rev. Bird S. Wilson (another brother who was a Baptist minister) with John H. Wilson (yet another brother) as a witness. While it identified both her husband's parents, it identified only her father. Because of my previous research, I knew her mother had died in 1857—seven years before Sarah's marriage. The whole picture doesn't come clear until you put together all the pieces of the puzzle.

With your research log and copies in hand, sit down and carefully evaluate what you do and don't know before adding anything to your paper ancestor charts and family group sheets or to your genealogy program. Then file your copies so you can find them again.

Once you have analyzed all the pieces, adding new information to your paper forms or computer files is a two-step process. First, record any new event data (the names, dates, places, and relationships), then record the details about the sources you used to put together that event data. If you don't do the second step, all you end up with is a fairy tale. Your research logs and copies are the foundation for your family tree. Citing your sources is what gives your work credibility.

It's Vital to Cite

I have never been disgusted with myself for putting too much information into a research log or source citation. But on more than one occasion, I have been distraught when I failed to fully record my source. What is most important is that you take the time to do it.

One reason to always cite your sources for any family information is to give yourself, or someone else, the best possible chance of locating that source again at a later time. You may need to look for more names you identified later, or you may need to recheck conflicting information that crops up.

Another reason to keep research logs and to cite your sources is that life gives you only a few windows of opportunity to trace your family tree. You may have to put away your genealogy for months, or even years, at a time. When you come back to this puzzle, it is nice not to have to start all over again. With completed research logs and your sources fully cited on your paper forms or in your computer files, you can pick up where you left off.

Adding Source Citations

Always cite your sources, whether you use paper forms (ancestor charts and family group sheets) or a computer and a genealogy program. Your source citations tell where you found each piece of information about each person.

In genealogy programs, you have the option to attach one or more images to each source citation. They also provide a field to type in (transcribe) all or part of the original source. As mentioned in Chapter 5, this is where you type the person's name exactly as it was spelled in that source. Most programs give you an additional field for your comments. Include such details as that source's condition when you looked at it or whether the author is prone to err (like my uncle's story about being related to the Singer sewing machine brothers).

When it comes to analyzing what you have found and then citing your sources, there is one small book that every genealogist should own: *Evidence! Citation and Analysis for the Family Historian* by Elizabeth Shown Mills (Baltimore, Maryland: Genealogical Publishing Company, 1997). The first part of her book explains the fundamentals of analyzing genealogical evidence and then citing your sources. The second part, which I consult repeatedly, is filled with examples of citation formats from a wide variety of sources including electronic ones, such as e-mail messages and online databases at Web sites.

Another helpful book about citing your sources is *Family History Documentation Guidelines* by the Silicon Valley PAF Users Group (San Jose, California: SV-PAF-UG, July 2000). Visit their Web site at *www.svpafug.org* to obtain a copy. I take both books along with me on research trips. Fortunately, they are small and easy to pack.

They don't sound like exciting travel companions until you are standing in the family cemetery plot in Great Smoky Mountains National Park—worrying about bears, ticks, and chiggers and trying to remember what pieces of information to record. If you have one or both of these books with you, all you have to do is turn to the examples for grave markers or cemetery records. Use them as a checklist to determine what source details to record on your research log and copies. Elizabeth's book has three different types of cemetery citations: published book, rural, and large urban. The SVPAFUG has two types: published book and headstone.

Not only do I record all the source details, but I also take pictures of the gravestones and write down what they say (my pictures don't always turn out readable). I record how the markers are arranged in relationship to each other (who is buried next

Safeguard Your Work

Why write down what is written on a gravestone if you've taken a picture of it? Because you don't know if your developed picture will be readable, or if the film will make it through the x-ray machines at the airport, be erased accidentally in your digital camera, or be destroyed at the developers (all of which have happened to me). For more information, see the sidebar in Chapter 2 titled "The Seven Rules of Saving Irreplaceable Things."

How to Cite Your Sources

Here are examples of citations in footnote or endnote style for some commonly encountered sources.

Example: William Benton Hill's death certificate

1. William Benton Hill, death certificate no. 4702 [1944]. Tennessee Department of Public Health, Nashville. Certified copy in possession of Barbara Renick, 123 Her Street, Brea, California 92800.

Example: A memorandum book that belonged to William Benton Hill in which he wrote the birth, marriage, and death dates of his two wives, three children, and all his siblings

1. "Memorandum Book of William Benton Hill," (Manuscript Source, 1921–1922; Beech Grove, Tennessee), pages not numbered; owned 1978 by his grand-niece, Betty Hobbins (Mrs. John Exeter), Route 1, Box 111, Apache Road, Grantsboro, Tennessee 37800.

Example: William Benton Hill's gravestone in a rural church cemetery

1. William Benton Hill gravestone, New Indian Creek Baptist Church Cemetery, Campbell County, Tennessee (near the intersection of Pine Hollow Road and Shoun Hollow Road); photographed by his great-granddaughter, Barbara Renick, October 1978.

Example: Published book of extracted marriage records

1. Edith Wilson Hutton, compiler, *Campbell County, Tennessee Marriage Records, 1891–1900* (Oak Ridge, Tennessee: Clark Printing Co., 1986), 83.

to whom) and comment on the condition and legibility of the stones. I record directions on how to get to the cemetery and note that Cousin Mark says the road is graded only once a year, right before the Little Cattaloochee Baptist Church reunion in June. I may even take a GPS (global positioning system) reading of the exact latitude and longitude of the grave site. In the heat of the hunt for lost ancestors, it is easy to forget to record all these additional details.

Using a Research Notebook

When I go out to do research, I often take a small, three-ring notebook with me. I use dividers for each section and include some or all of the following:

- To-do lists (printed out by my computer program)
- Analysis chart(s)
- Time line chart(s)
- Blank research log pages
- Printed research logs (printed by my genealogy program)
- My old, hand-typed research logs of
  - Civil searches
  - Church searches
  - Home searches
  - Miscellaneous records searches
- Individual summaries for the people I am researching (printed out by my genealogy program)
- Surname research summaries (kept in my word processor)
- Ancestor charts (and an extra chart or two to give away)
- Family group sheets for each generation back to that ancestral family
- Miscellaneous family group sheets for
  - Other families in that geographic area with that surname
  - Cousins, neighbors, identified family friends
- Copies of my past finds that I may need to consult while searching
- Reference materials
  - List of the alternative spellings for the surname(s)
  - Charts of the jurisdictional histories for their counties of residence
  - Geographical list of all the localities where my ancestor(s) lived (including the time range for their residence in that county)
  - Alphabetical list of all the other surnames I am researching in that area
  - Maps
  - Relationship calculation chart
  - List of state postal codes and other abbreviations I use in my handwritten notes
  - Driving directions to the places I am going
  - The LDS Research Outline for that geographic area (some can be printed online at the FamilySearch Internet site, or check at your local Family History Center for availability of printed versions)

Make it a habit—before you set foot in the cemetery, before you open the book at the library, and before you begin interviewing Uncle Henry—to always write down source details in your research log before you search, interview, or use that source. Once you get involved in the hunt, it is hard to slow down and go back to record your source details. Locate the source, cite the source, *then* search the source. After searching through that source and making copies, go back to your research log and check one more time to make certain you have recorded all the information pertinent to that source (and don't forget to record your source details on your copies, too). Locate, then cite, then search.

Never take any original material or sources with you when you go out to search. Never take anything that you'd hate to lose or can't replace. You wouldn't believe the quantity of original photographs and family documents that pile up in the lost and found box at the Orange Family History Center where I volunteer. Only a small percentage of these items are ever reclaimed by their owners.

The Formula for Citing Sources

Unfortunately, there is no perfect, scientific formula for citing every type of source. Genealogists use many different resources. Each needs different types of information to uniquely identify it. The basic formula is this:

1. Author
    a. Who was interviewed
    b. Who wrote the book
2. Title
    a. Title of the book, manuscript, census record, etc.
    b. Title of an article, followed by the title of the periodical it is in
3. Publication information
    a. Place of publication, name of the publisher, and date of publication or copyright of the book, written in parentheses as (Place: Publisher, Date)
    b. Volume, issue, and page numbers of the periodical
    c. Film and item number for a microfilm, plus the above information about the original if known, written in parentheses as (Author, Title, Publication information)

4. Where you found it (and where it is normally kept, if different)
   a. Repository (such as the Library of Congress or the DAR Library in Washington, D.C.)
   b. Cemetery name and location
   c. Web site name and URL (if you are quoting a Web page at that Web site)
5. Details
   a. Specific page number the information was found on in a book
   b. Entry number and date recorded for a marriage record
   c. Date you found the gravestone, who transcribed the information, and took the picture

The infinite variety of sources, however, means this list is not complete. Add anything you think is needed to clearly and thoroughly communicate how to find that source again.

Always cite what you looked at, while noting what it was originally taken from, if known. For example, don't cite the original marriage record book in the county clerk's office if what you looked at was a microfilm copy in a library or archives. Cite instead the microfilm copy of the original.

The Benefits of Organization

Citing your sources and having a good filing system make it much easier to resolve conflicting information and to untangle the roots of your family tree. Being organized works like fertilizer to help your family tree grow faster.

- Keep thorough research logs.
- Make and keep copies of everything you find.
- Analyze what you find (and record your analysis).
- Always cite your sources.
- Enter your findings in a genealogy computer program (if at all possible).

Chapter 7

More Tools for Taming Family Trees

Paper family group sheets and ancestor charts show at a glance the structure of your family tree. Unfortunately, they provide only a minimum amount of room for event information. They are also woefully inadequate for listing the sources for each name, date, place, and relationship. Therefore, most genealogists quickly outgrow paper forms and move on to genealogy software to keep their findings organized.

Why Computerize?

With typewriters going the way of the horse and buggy, hand-typed forms are now a rarity. This is just as well. During the typewriter era of genealogy, every time you wanted to correct anything on a form, you had to retype it. Every time you retyped it, you risked adding more errors than you were taking out. With computers, you can add or change just one piece of information at a time. I shake my head in wonder each time I push one button and print up-to-date forms and reports with my computer. Even free genealogy programs allow you to easily build big family trees with designated areas for biographical information, source details, and images.

In the typewriter era, you had to fill out two family group sheets for each ancestor: one showing him as a child in a family and another showing him as a parent with his spouse and children. The beauty of using a computer is that you no longer have to do so much work. You simply enter the information for a person once into what is called an Individual Record. That Individual Record is then linked as a child or spouse in any of the families to which he belongs.

The most common mistake made (especially by genealogists new to computers) is to create more than one Individual Record for a person, rather than re-using it in different relationships. They don't understand that their program keeps track of how everyone is linked together and uses those links to print different charts, forms, and reports.

Computers are unsurpassed for keeping track of information. I used to dread getting such enquiries as, "Where did you find George Weston Roberts's middle name? I don't think that's correct. My family told me his middle name was Wesley." Back in the typewriter era of genealogy, it took a great deal of effort to read through my research logs, work sheets, and handwritten copies to find the answer. Today, I can quickly search every scrap of information (if I have entered it) and find the answer in seconds.

Even if you don't own a computer, consider using one at a Family History Center or library near you to record family information. At the Family History Center where I volunteer, I've even done the data entry for people with disabilities who can't type. Most Family History Centers have at least one computer with the Personal Ancestral File (PAF) program installed for patrons to use at no cost. Bring your own floppy disks to save the information you enter, or purchase them there for a small fee.

How It Works

Before you begin evaluating genealogy programs, you need to understand how they help you put together your family tree. After you install the software and at least glance through the manual (yes, it *does* help to read the manual), the first step is to create a new file (also known as a database). Since most programs allow you to create as many different databases as you like, you have some decisions to make.

The first decision is the direction in which you are going to grow your family tree. It can grow in the direction of ancestors, descendants, or both. Choose a starting person based on the direction in which you want it to grow. For example, if you are interested in tracing your ancestry, start with yourself. If, however, you want to keep track of several family tree branches for a family reunion, start with an ancestor and enter information on their descendants. If you are married, decide if you are going to keep your spouse's family tree in the same file as yours.

These decisions help you choose a name for that database. Call it something that reminds you of what is included in that file. For example, I used my husband's initials to name his ancestral database, but I also have a database called Renick into which I put anything I find about that surname.

This extra database works like a junk drawer. I use it to store what I've found during my searches. This keeps my results in a format that is easy to sort, search, and share with other researchers. When I manage to fit some of those Renick pieces onto my husband's family tree, I just export (copy) that information from the Renick research database, import (paste) it into his ancestry database, then attach it to the appropriate record(s)—and never retype a thing.

Recording Event Data

Genealogy programs use two basic building blocks to construct family trees—Individual Records and Marriage Records. They make it easy to link those two types of records together into families, generation by generation, backward or forward along the family tree. They also give you different ways to view and use the information you enter. Typical views include Family View (see Figure 7.1), Pedigree View (Figure 7.2), and Individual View (also known as Name View, or Index View as in Figure 7.3). Some programs even include a Chronology View.

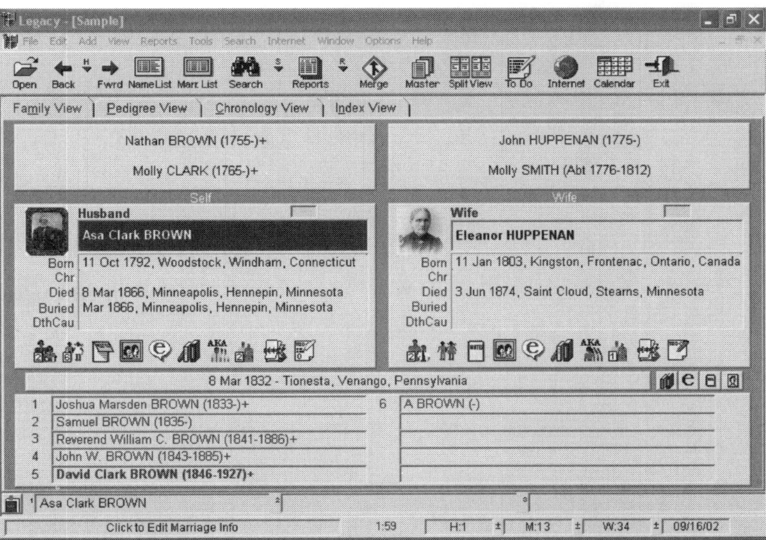

Figure 7.1 Legacy's Family View

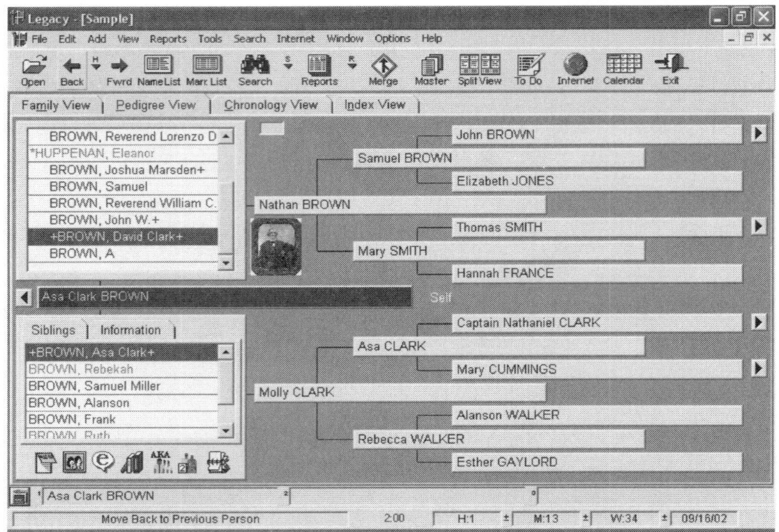

Figure 7.2 Legacy's Pedigree View

RIN	Full Name	Sex	Birth Date	Birth Place	Death Date
1	BROWN, Asa Clark	M	11 Oct 1792	Woodstock, Windha	8 Mar 1866
24	BROWN, Asa Danial	M	4 Jan 1838	, , Pennsylvania	8 Feb 1908
9	BROWN, Au	M	Abt 1840	, , Pennsylvania	
122	BROWN, Charles	M	12 Apr 1803	Charlton, Worcester,	
11	BROWN, Charles	M	Abt 1859	, , Minnesota	
50	BROWN, Charles David	M	5 May 1878	Clotho or Osakis, Do	13 May 194
66	BROWN, Charles W.	M	Abt May 1860	, , Pennsylvania	
92	BROWN, David Clark	M	24 Nov 1846	Deerfield, Warren, P	9 Feb 1927
63	BROWN, Eva Jane	F	12 Mar 1876	, , Minnesota	1956
120	BROWN, Frank	M	20 Sep 1799	Charlton, Worcester,	
59	BROWN, Hattie Mina	F	8 Feb 1875	, , Minnesota	After 18 Jul
17	BROWN, James	M	Abt 1839	, , Pennsylvania	
136	BROWN, John	M	1700		1750
138	BROWN, John Clark	M	1683		1750

Figure 7.3 Legacy's Index View

To add an Individual Record to the family where it belongs, display that family in Family View. Select the position (husband, wife, or child) where you want to add that Individual Record. (This usually involves clicking, double clicking, or right clicking with your mouse, depending on the program.) If there is already an Individual Record attached in that spot (as the husband, wife, or child), that Individual Record is displayed for you to add or edit information. (See Figure 7.4 for an example of an Individual Record.) If there isn't already an Individual Record attached in that spot, a dialog box or pop-up menu appears and asks if you want to

- Attach an Individual Record that already exists in your database
- Create a new Individual Record (if that person doesn't already have one in that file)
- Indicate that the person has not yet been identified (is unknown)

There are other ways to add records and build families in genealogy programs, but this is the most commonly used method.

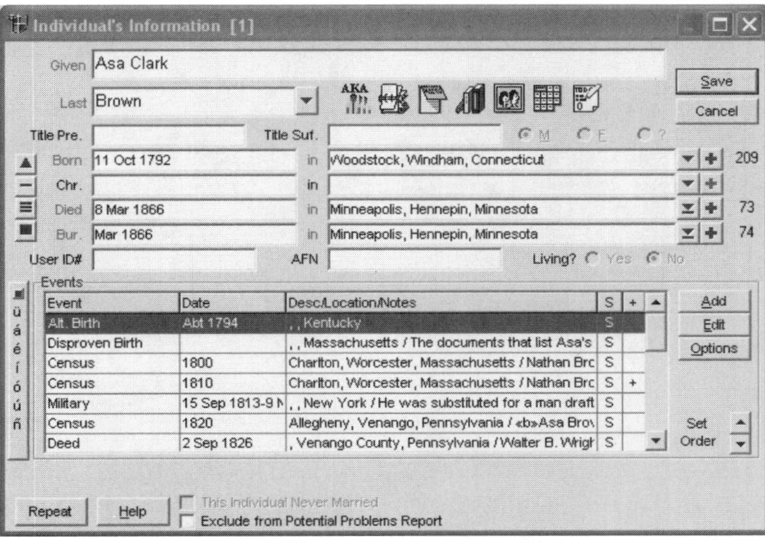

Figure 7.4 Legacy's Individual Record

Each Individual Record has fields (boxes) for you to type in the person's name and event information, plus buttons to attach different types of notes (biographical, medical, etc.) and multimedia files (pictures, video clips, etc.). The standard life events used by most genealogy programs are birth, christening, death, and burial. There are fields for the dates and places of these events, and a button to click to add your sources.

Most programs provide a predefined list of other events to choose from, plus the option of creating your own custom events. Predefined events for an Individual Record include such things as title, nickname, occupation, military service, physical description, and cause of death. Check your program's list of predefined events before taking the time to custom design one.

To add a new Marriage Record to your database, display that family in Family View and click (double click or right click) on the box labeled Marriage, located near the husband's and wife's positions on that screen. A blank Marriage Record appears with fields for you to fill in the date and place (see Figure 7.5). Create customized marriage events as needed for such things as the date of a formal betrothal, when and where banns were posted, or to indicate the type of marriage (church, justice of the peace, special license, etc.).

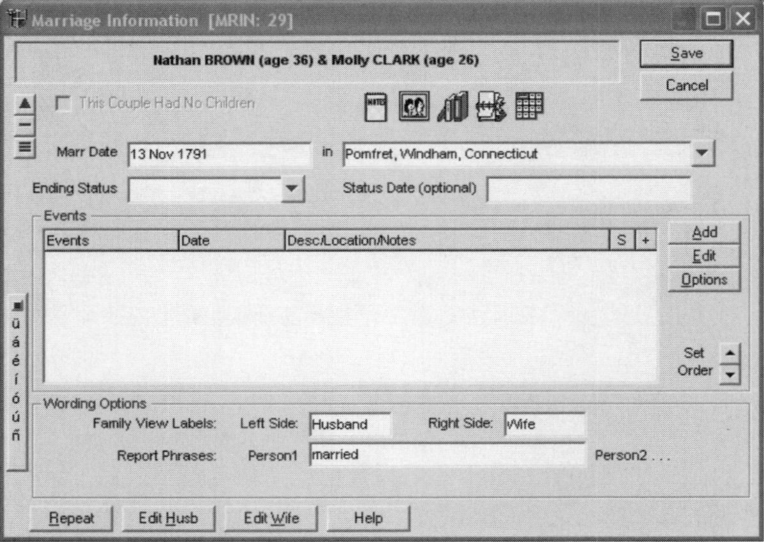

Figure 7.5 Legacy's Marriage Record

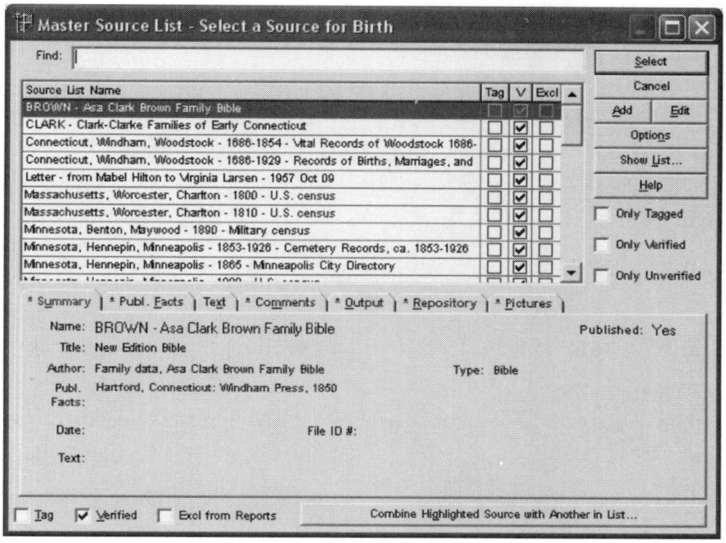

Figure 7.6 Legacy's Master Source List

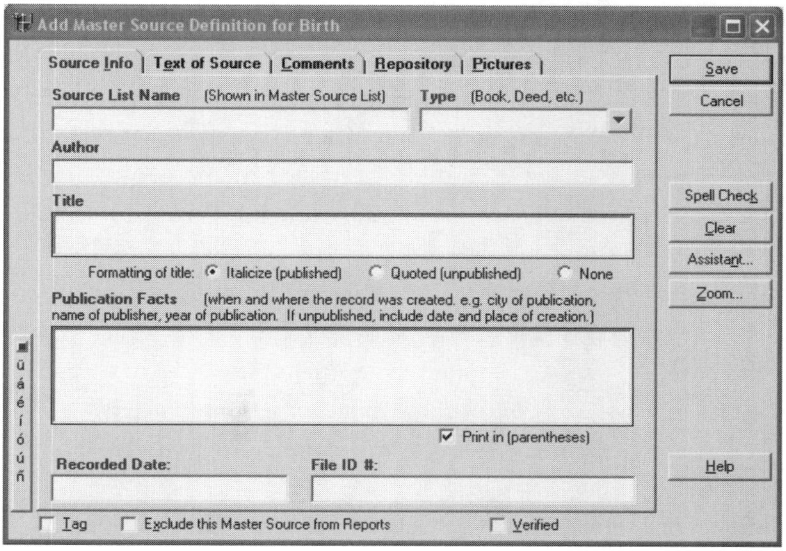

Figure 7.7 Legacy's Add Source screen

Telling Where You Found It

An old proverb says, "Don't try to leap a twenty-foot chasm in two ten-foot jumps." This is certainly true when using a genealogy program. Be sure to cite your sources as you enter your data. Do your data entry and cite your sources all in one big jump. Don't expect to go back months later and add them. See Figure 7.6 for a sample of Legacy's reusable Master Source List and Figure 7.7 for an example of Legacy's Add Source screen.

Completing the Picture

How wonderful it is to attach a scanned wedding picture to your grandparents' Marriage Record, as well as the images of their county marriage license and the church register they signed. You can even attach a sound clip of the song originally played at the wedding, which you recorded at their fiftieth wedding anniversary. All of that is relatively easy to do with current technology. Any genealogy program you choose should make it easy for you to add these finishing touches to your genealogy data.

Does the Shoe Fit? Choosing a Genealogy Program

Before you start chasing dead ancestors, test a variety of genealogy programs. This is a lot like buying a pair of shoes. Genealogy programs vary widely in style, features, and fit. Some programs are particularly good for one type of activity (such as preparing large wall charts with lots of maps and pictures for family reunions), while others are better for other types of activities (such as thoroughly documenting your sources so you can join a patriotic or lineage society).

Ask a dozen genealogists, and you'll get a dozen different opinions about which genealogy program is best. Frankly, no one program is best for every genealogist. It makes me sad to hear stories of computer beginners who bought a particular program only to learn it was too complex for them to master. Conversely, it's a shame for sophisticated computer users to settle for a simple program they'll outgrow in a year or two.

How do you choose the right program? Remember what Mom always told you about buying shoes: "Walk around in them before you buy." You won't be able to tell if a program fits your needs until you practice entering information with it, check out its displays, and print out reports. Even then, you may not notice its limitations until you try to do something unusual, such as printing a bowtie chart or adding more than one digital image to a source citation.

Fortunately, several free genealogy programs can be downloaded from the Internet to try before you spend money. You may even find that one of these free programs meets all your current needs. If not, the commercial versions of most genealogy programs come with a money-back guarantee (typically within thirty, sixty, or ninety days). This makes trying out different programs a fairly painless process.

Criteria for Choosing a Genealogy Program

The first question to ask is whether a program runs on your computer. Mac users have it easy. Only a few programs have been written for the Macintosh. Of those programs, Reunion by Leister Productions, Inc. *(www.leisterpro.com),* is the overwhelming favorite. For more information, check Cyndi's List in her subcategory called Macintosh Information on her Software & Computers page *(www.cyndislist.com/software.htm).*

Currently more programs are available for PC users to choose from. Check the Web site of any program you are considering to see a list of its features. When trying out any software, a basic rule of thumb is this: The more features it has, the steeper its learning curve. Is it going to be worth the cash, time, and other four-letter words you'll spend learning to use it? Consider some of the issues that follow.

Support

If you want a program with more features, you need to consider what types of support are available to help you learn that program. These include the clarity of any manuals or user's guides, the direct support offered by that company (not all companies provide telephone support), and other resources close to home.

There are free e-mail discussion groups (mail lists) about most genealogy programs. In these groups (such as those hosted by RootsWeb at *lists.rootsweb.com/index/other/Software/,* other users share their experience and expertise with you. Ask questions about how to use the software and you are likely to get a quick reply.

If you are a computer beginner, having live help nearby is essential. Find out if there is a local user group for the program you are considering. Find them by checking at that program's Web site. Also check with your local genealogical society. They may have a computer interest group that helps members learn to use one or more of the popular genealogy programs.

Capacity

With current programs, capacity is no longer as much of an issue. Many let you add more than sixty children and dozens of spouses to a family. Most programs allow you to cite multiple sources for any event. Most even allow you to attach multiple images. Only a few programs don't, so watch out for those.

The one area where capacity becomes a problem is if you plan to create very large databases. For example, I have several friends who act as clearinghouses for a particular surname. Their databases have more than one hundred thousand individual records. Not many programs are designed with this capacity in mind.

Efficiency

The ease of entering your names, dates, places, and relationships in a program is very important. As your family tree grows, you will be entering a great deal of information. Check out the number of steps it takes to record one event (like a birth) with two sources. This serves as a good comparison because it is one of the things you do most often.

You also want the process of backing up your data to be easy. Does that program remind you to back up? Does it allow you to back up to different types of media? If this process is easy and you are reminded to back up, you will save yourself a great deal of grief by making regular backups.

Sourcing

This is an area where your program really needs to fit both your needs and your ability level. Putting all the pieces of a source citation into your computer takes time and effort. Some programs make it easier to properly cite your sources. Some even lead you by the hand with templates. Templates tell you what blanks to fill in for that type of source.

I like source templates, as do a great many other genealogists. Several software companies are working on adding this feature to their genealogy programs, although a few already include this feature.

Advanced Features

Different programs offer different advanced features. You may not use all of those features on a daily basis, but they are really important when you do need them. For instance, utilities built into many programs help you maintain your databases. Some allow you to globally search-and-replace a misspelled place name. Others allow you to check the spelling in your notes. Most create a Possible Record Problem report to help you find typos and inconsistencies in your data.

Other advanced features help with your research. Some let you keep a research log right in the program. Most have a date calculator. Some let you spell names using foreign alphabets.

Programs vary widely in their ability to handle multimedia (images, sound files, and video clips). Some give you greater flexibility with placing images in different positions on charts and reports. I remember one program coming out with the option to add Grandma's picture to their fan chart (a type of ancestor chart). Unfortunately, your only option was to put her picture right in the middle of the chart. The branches of your ancestry printed over her face, which many users complained about. The software company had to quickly add the option to change the placement of pictures on that chart.

Publishing

Once you have some information entered, test that program's publishing features. Do you like the look of its standard reports (family group sheets, ancestor charts, etc.)? Do you like the way it lists your source citations on reports? How many different types of reports does it do? How easy is it to custom design charts, forms, or reports?

Most programs will generate a book with a table of contents and a partial index, but some give you more formatting options. For example, does it give you the option to list source citations as either endnotes or footnotes? Does it work with your preferred word processor?

Does that program create good-looking Web pages with the content you want? Does it create Web pages at all? Do you have to post your information on that company's proprietary Web site? Does it allow you to filter out information about living people? I now make it a policy not to include even the parents of someone still living. Privacy issues are a big concern on the Internet.

Merging

Not only will you be typing information into the program you choose, but you will also be importing data from other sources (cousins, the Internet, databases on CDs). When you import information, it often creates duplicate records. In other words, your great-grandmother may end up with two different records in your computer—one you entered and one you imported from your cousin. When you print out an ancestor chart, the information your cousin found won't appear unless you merge it with yours.

Merging duplicates is like performing electronic surgery. You need to test the merging features of any program for its ability to accurately spot duplicate records, the way it displays possible duplicates, and the options it gives you for the merging process.

You want a program that recognizes which records really are duplicates and not just two people with the same name. When the program shows you a possible duplicate for your great-grandmother, does it compare those two records for you? Some programs tell you only that two records are possible duplicates, not which fields are the same and which are different. For example, does it show you that the exact date of birth from your cousin doesn't match the approximate date you had? If the program doesn't do a good job of comparing possible duplicates, it is easy for a vital piece of information to be lost when the duplicates are merged.

Learning

Once the program feels comfortable to you, the next step is to learn to use its advanced features. To extend our earlier analogy, this process is much like breaking in a pair of new shoes. If you chose well, the process is fairly pain-free. Articles in genealogy periodicals, lectures on audiotapes, and instructional videos are available to help you learn the advanced features of popular genealogy programs.

Tutorials are often available online at a program's Web site or on CDs. Some programs also come with lessons built in. For example, when you download the installation program for the Personal Ancestral File, there are seven lessons that you can also download for free.

See the Software & Computers category at Cyndi's List for more information about genealogy programs *(www.cyndislist.com/software.htm)*. See Bill Mumford's Genealogical Software Report Card online for an evaluation of the features in the most common genealogy programs *(www.mumford.ca/reportcard/)*.

Shape Up and Ship Out

If you already have a genealogy program and chafe at its limitations, don't despair. Not all is lost. There are ways to transfer information from one program to another without retyping anything. It's not hard to trade in your old program.

GEDCOM

Each genealogy program stores your information in its own proprietary format, but each also includes an option to copy and export your information in a generic file format called GEDCOM, which stands for GEnealogical Data COMmunication. This makes it possible to share the information you've entered into your database (especially with people using other genealogy programs) or to move your own information into a more full-featured program.

Most programs put their GEDCOM options under menu items called Import and Export. Each of these menu items requires you to choose the type of GEDCOM file. Not all GEDCOM files are the same. Programs are constantly being upgraded, so the GEDCOM standard has evolved, as well. The higher the version number, the more recent the standard.

Older programs can't import GEDCOM files created with the newer standards. If you know your cousin is using an older version of a genealogy program, you need to create a GEDCOM file in a compatible format in order to share your data with her. Conversely, if that cousin sends you a GEDCOM file, you may need to tell your program the name and version number of the program used to create it. Otherwise, you may experience difficulties importing the information.

Another challenge when creating a GEDCOM file is choosing which records from your database to include. It is difficult to select just the branches you want. If you want to send a Hill cousin all your information on the Hills, do you want to include information on their spouses? What about the families their children married into? Do you want to include only ancestors—or descendants, too? Are you going to include information on living people?

When you create a GEDCOM file in most programs, all those multimedia files you attached get left behind. All that is included in the GEDCOM file is a notation of where you stored those files on your computer. Genealogy programs are beginning to improve in this area. Soon you'll be able to easily share your multimedia files with your GEDCOM file.

Be cautious and check the integrity of what you import via GEDCOM. Most of the time, when you import information using GEDCOM, the information and links transfer without problems. On rare occasions, things get lost (like your source citations or notes) or tangled (your grandma's record gets linked as your daughter). When you import a GEDCOM file, verify that everything is there and where it should be.

You have several options for sharing a GEDCOM file. The old-fashioned way is to put it on a floppy disk or CD and mail it. A faster way is to send it as an e-mail attachment. Most e-mail services, however, limit the size of file attachments (most GEDCOM files exceed these limits). Another option is to upload it to an online database or storage site. (I use the free Briefcase feature at the Yahoo! Web site.) These last two options make your GEDCOM files easily accessible to multiple people.

Direct Conversion

Several genealogy programs offer a direct-conversion feature. For example, if you are currently using the older Personal Ancestral File program version 2.31 and want to switch to the Legacy program, do the following:

1. Go to *www.legacyfamilytree.com.*
2. Download the free version of the Legacy program.
3. Install Legacy on your computer.
4. Open the program.
5. Click on File on the menu bar.
6. Highlight Import From.
7. Click on Use Import Wizard to Help with any Import.
8. Follow the Wizard's instructions.

Notice that the Legacy program includes direct-conversion options only for databases from the Personal Ancestral File or Ancestral Quest programs. When you are trying out different genealogy programs, check their Web sites to see which programs they can directly convert. If available, direct conversion is usually the easiest and most accurate method of moving information from one program to another.

Chapter 8
Boot Camp and Beyond

In military boot camp, you learn to be a soldier. For family tree tracers, boot camp means learning to be a genealogist. I teach beginners that genealogy takes place in five phases: Background, Survey, Research, Evaluation, and Preservation Phases (see Figure 8.1). These are repeated over and over again until you feel satisfied that you have constructed a solid picture of that ancestor and his or her family. We will explore the Background Phase of genealogy in this chapter and then move on to the next four phases in the following chapters. Work methodically from generation to generation. Unless you have a compelling reason to work first on just

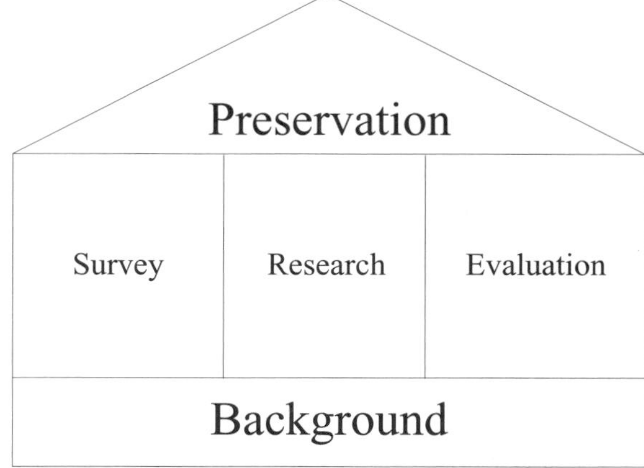

Figure 8.1 The five phases of genealogy

one branch of your family tree, work across your first ancestor chart from left to right by generation. Practice your new skills on recent generations as you build a background of knowledge to tackle earlier generations.

The BEPSC Code

I had a special rubber stamp made to use on my paper ancestor charts. It helps me determine when I have gathered enough information about a particular ancestor and am ready to go on to the next person in my ancestry. It looks like this:

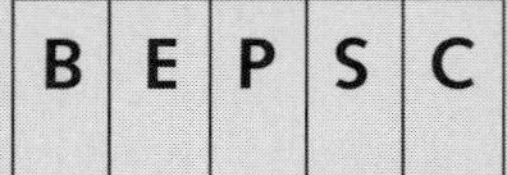

- **B** stands for birth. I color that box when I have fully identified that person's birth (names, dates, places, and relationships).
- **E** stands for extra. I color that box when I have enough extra information about that ancestor's life to be fairly certain I have identified my ancestor and not someone else's. This means I have information about each phase of life.
- **P** stands for parents. I color that box when I believe I have correctly identified that person's parents and siblings.
- **S** stands for spouse(s). I color that box when I have identified all of that ancestor's spouses and marriage information.
- **C** stands for children. I color that box when I have identified all of that ancestor's children and those children's marriages.

The Background Phase

The first phase of family tree tracing is called the Background Phase. It establishes the foundation upon which you build all the other phases. Building a background of genealogical knowledge and skills helps you figure out what records may still exist, where they might be found, and how to read and interpret them once they are found.

One day, as I was working at a local Family History Center, a young patron showed me a large stack of photocopies of the records she had searched for her grandfather's birth. She bemoaned the fact that none of them specifically told her where he was born. She wanted to know where else to look. I suggested we both look through what she had already found.

The first copy I picked up was her grandfather's enumeration in the 1920 U.S. census. She pointed out his name, age, and birthplace (Germany—which was too broad a locality to start searching). I looked across the other columns of information listed for him and asked if she had found his naturalization papers.

She said, "What?!" I explained that the 1920 U.S. census had a citizenship section and pointed to the column in that section that said "na," indicating her grandfather had been naturalized (see Figure 8.2). I further explained that his Declaration of Intention papers (which he would have filled out to become a citizen) should tell her exactly where and when he was born.

She simply hadn't worked with enough census records to recognize all the information they contain. She was, however, tenacious enough to do the searching, find her grandfather's information in many different records, then ask questions when she needed further help. No one knows everything about every type of record in every location.

Family History Centers are staffed by volunteers with varying experience levels. Many Family History Centers keep lists of their volunteers' specialties so that patrons can call or come in when a particular volunteer is there to help them.

Genealogists seeking help in a Family History Center or other library need to be polite but persistent. If the first person you ask doesn't help you solve your research problem, wait a while and ask again. Or politely ask someone else. Remember, I interviewed Aunt Olga five times before she finally pulled out her mother's 1907 steamship ticket.

If you can't wait until your local Family History Center or other library is open, try online genealogy chat groups and e-mail discussion groups for genealogy beginners. Again, be cognizant of the varying experience levels of those who respond to your requests for help.

As you are working with your ancestors' records, follow up on anything you don't understand. Don't look just at the part containing information about your ancestors; study the record as a whole. Find out why that type of record was created and what it typically contains. Then, as radio personality Paul Harvey says, you'll know the rest of the story.

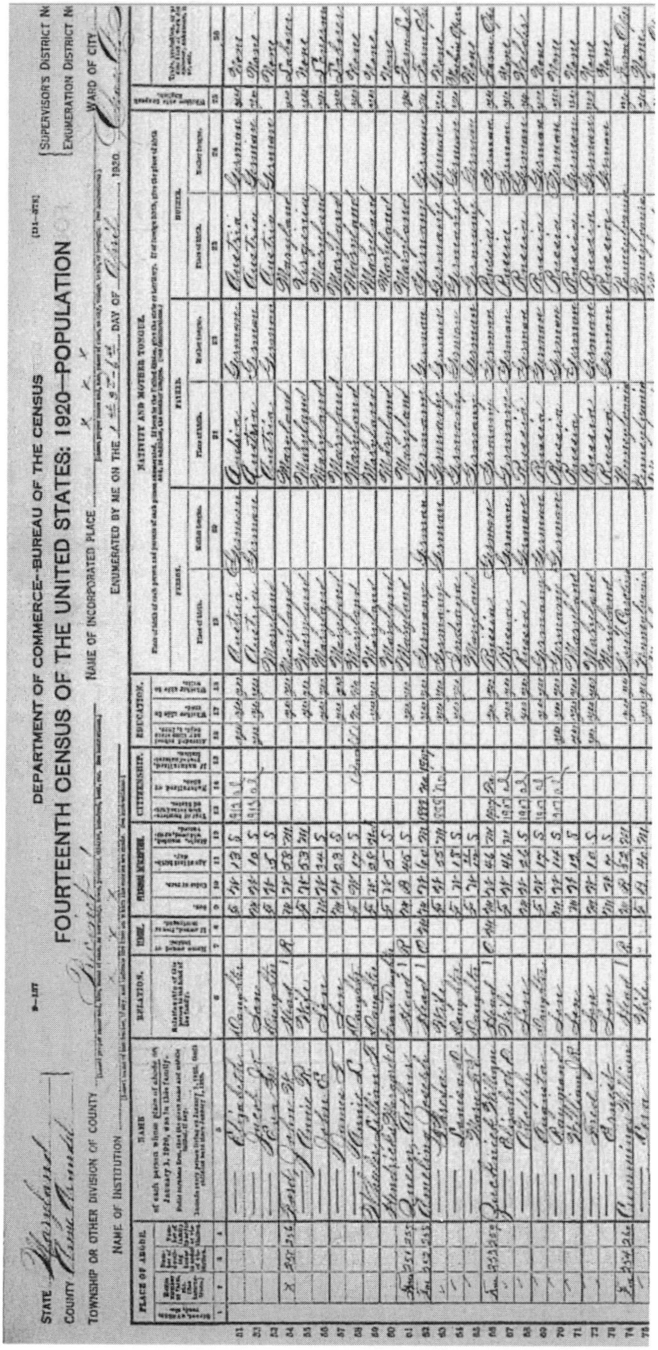
DEPARTMENT OF COMMERCE—BUREAU OF THE CENSUS

FOURTEENTH CENSUS OF THE UNITED STATES: 1920—POPULATION

STATE Maryland

COUNTY Anne Arundel

TOWNSHIP OR OTHER DIVISION OF COUNTY

NAME OF INCORPORATED PLACE

NAME OF INSTITUTION

ENUMERATED BY ME ON THE ... DAY OF April, 1920.

SUPERVISOR'S DISTRICT N

ENUMERATION DISTRICT N

WARD OF CITY

Figure 8.2 Sample of 1920 U.S. census from Ancestry.com online

Seven T's for Successful Ancestor Tracing

Success in family tree tracing depends upon seven T's. You don't have to tackle all these T's at once. As you work back through your family tree, slowly build your knowledge and skills about research in different locations, time periods, and record types.

1. **Timing:** Looking in the right time period is essential to finding your ancestors' information. Sometimes you must look earlier or later than you anticipated.
2. **Targeting:** Identifying all the localities where your ancestors (and their descendants) lived helps you find their records.
3. **Topography:** Geography influenced your ancestors' migrations and lifestyle.
4. **Technology:** It is important to recognize the impact on your ancestors' lives of such things as the Industrial Revolution, changes in transportation, and developments in medical science.
5. **Territory:** Knowing the shifts in political boundaries and jurisdictions for the places where your ancestors lived helps you determine who kept records about them.
6. **Transformations:** One of your biggest challenges is to recognize the different ways your ancestors' names were spelled and written.
7. **Terminology:** Genealogy deals not only with foreign languages, but also has a language of its own.

Timing: How Time Flies

Even if your ancestors stayed put in just one location, things change over time. Research in Kentucky in the twentieth century is vastly different from research there in the eighteenth century. While Kentucky had a statewide registration of births during most of the twentieth century, there was no such thing on the Kentucky frontiers in the eighteenth century when Daniel Boone settled there. To a great extent, the era you are researching determines the types of records you find and use.

One way to judge timing more accurately is to know something about your ancestors' social customs. For instance, many of my Tennessee ancestors married at a younger age than did my German ancestors. In Germany, it was not unusual for a young man to work ten years establishing himself in a profession before marrying.

Sometimes you simply need to look further back or forward. During my Survey Phase, I found my Hannahs mentioned in a county history book. It identified John Jackson Hannah's wife as Martha Ann Simmons, born in 1833. Moving on to the Research Phase, I searched and searched for a record of her death. Unfortunately, I was searching between the years 1900 and 1910. It took me a while to figure out she died in 1920.

Another example is from my search for the first marriage of Edmond, my ancestor's bigamist brother. Edmond lived in a county where early marriage records no longer exist (probably due to a courthouse fire in the 1850s). Edmond's first request for a divorce in 1860 survives, as does his second request in 1870 (which was finally granted), but neither of those cases mentions his original marriage date. It wasn't until I went further ahead in time that I found the answer.

Edmond's daughter Hannah sued her father, brother, and brother-in-law over a land transaction in the 1880s. Depositions made by family members in this court case were replete with details identifying events and relationships that took place before the courthouse fire.

Targeting: Looking for Loved Ones in All the Wrong Places

Targeting the places where your ancestors settled (or paused on their way elsewhere) is a vital step in successful research. Remember the story about my father-in-law hiring a researcher to look for his grandfather in Clinton, Missouri? Because of his lack of knowledge, he ended up having to pay his researcher to determine whether his Roberts were in the county of Clinton or the city of Clinton.

Ancestors who migrated frequently cause all sorts of problems for genealogists. Where did they come from? Why did they move? Who came first, and who stayed behind? Wars, famines, and financial woes all contribute to migrations and create targeting difficulties for genealogists.

If you can't find the place your ancestors came from, try looking at the people who lived around them. Finding out where their in-laws, neighbors, and associates came from may reveal where your ancestors originated. Census records were recorded door-to-door and often reveal your ancestor's neighbors.

Topography: Over the River and Through the Woods

When I started tracing my Wilsons in Pulaski County, Kentucky, I was happy to find a family group sheet compiled years before by another researcher. She had approximated the couple's marriage date, then guessed at their marriage place based on the county where they resided. Since they were my third great-grandparents, I went to work checking her sources to see what I could add to her work.

I checked that county's marriage records—with no success. Knowing that geography plays a role in where people go to get married, I studied topographical maps of the area. I discovered they would have had to cross a stream, go up an escarpment, cross a plateau, go down an escarpment, and repeat the process three times to get to the Pulaski County Courthouse. They weren't dummies. They followed the creek down to the courthouse in the next county to get married. Even today, many people live in one city, work in another, and shop in still another.

When I found their actual marriage date, I noticed it differed from the approximated date by four years. I suspect the original compiler used the 1850 U.S. census and the age of the oldest child still living at home (as recorded in that census) to approximate the marriage date. Additional research in probate and military pension records turned up two older sons who were already married and out of the home by the time that census was recorded.

Does this mean the compiled family group sheet was of little value to me? Not at all. It served as a foundation upon which I was able to build an even more complete picture of my ancestral family. I am very thankful to the person who created it for me to find years later.

Technology: Life in the Past Lane

Changes in technology brought about changes in your ancestors' lives. As a result of the Industrial Revolution, many people moved from rural areas to cities. The history of technology affects where you look for records of your ancestors in other ways, as well.

The principle of propinquity states that your ancestors could only marry someone they could meet. Before the twentieth century, this meant a man and a woman who married usually lived within walking distance of each other. If a man owned a horse (something tax records often tell you), stretch the geographic area in which you search for his bride's family.

When the railroad came to town or a road was built through the area, your focus widens even farther. People who lived on transportation routes (such as canals, rivers, and seaports) or had certain types of occupations (such as sailors, circuit judges, and itinerant preachers) are an exception but, again, one based on the history of technology.

My grandpa's uncle was a railroad conductor. When I couldn't find Grandpa in the

1900 U.S. census, I remembered that family members often rode the trains for free. After tracing the train route and doing some more family interviews, I finally found Grandpa way down in Grayson County, Texas.

Territory: Slip-Sliding Away

I wish I could tell you that researching in Kentucky is the same as researching in Russia, but it isn't. It isn't even the same as researching in Kansas. Each geopolitical area had different laws and created different records.

Knowing the shifts in political boundaries and jurisdictions for the areas where your ancestors lived helps you look in the correct places for their records. You need to know when that state and county were formed and started keeping records (not always the same thing). I chart the jurisdictional history of every county where my ancestors resided—and often for their neighboring counties, too. Figure 8.3 shows a sample of one of my charts.

<table>
<tr><td rowspan="2">Brown Co. 1818 from Michigan Territory</td><td>Crawford Co. 1818 from Michigan Territory</td></tr>
<tr><td>Iowa Co. 1829 from Crawford Co.</td></tr>
<tr><td colspan="2">Milwaukee County was formed in 1834 from Brown County and Iowa County.</td></tr>
<tr><td colspan="2">Rock County was formed in 1836 from Milwaukee County, Wisconsin.</td></tr>
</table>

Figure 8.3 Jurisdictional history of Rock County, Wisconsin

For example, Campbell County, Tennessee, was formed in 1806. Several of my ancestors signed petitions for the formation of that new county. To find records of them before 1806, I have to look in the county that had prior jurisdiction for their community. This was Anderson County, which was formed in 1801. Before 1801, I have to look in Knox County, which was formed in 1792. And the list goes on.

A software program called Animap provides a time-lapse display showing the county boundary changes for states in the United States. See the Gold Bug Web site *(www.goldbug.com)* for more information. *The Handybook for Genealogists* by Everton Publishers, Inc. (Logan, Utah, 1999) is another classic resource for quickly checking the formation date of a county. A standard part of county GenWeb Project sites is the history of a county and its parent counties. (Remember, you can access each county's GenWeb site by going to *www.usgenweb.com.*)

Governmental policies continue to affect a record's location today—if it still exists.

My paternal grandparents were married in Polish Russia. When I began tracing my family tree in the 1970s, there were still Soviet soldiers with machine guns at public checkpoints in Poland. Records tended to stay put because no one wanted to be caught transporting them. My grandparents' marriage record was stored in a stone church with walls three feet thick. Since the Iron Curtain has fallen, those records are now kept miles away in the minister's wooden frame home—more accessible, perhaps, but probably not as safe.

Transformation: Won't You Tell Me Your Name?

If your ancestors' names changed for one reason or another, that event can hold up progress on your family tree indefinitely. It is easy to miss your ancestor's name in a record if it was spelled phonetically or you can't decipher the handwriting. Remember all the different ways Renick has been spelled?

This is compounded when original records are extracted, alphabetized, and then published in electronic formats. If I had been searching for Gordon Mynatt Hill's marriage in an electronic database (published on a compact disc or online), I might never have realized there was a six-month gap in the county records. Fortunately, what I searched was a microfilmed copy of the original records, which were arranged chronologically.

Terminology: It's All Greek to Me

Sooner or later, you'll need some foreign language skills. You usually don't need to be fluent, but you do need a basic knowledge of your ancestor's language (such as the words for *christening* and *grandmother*), dialect (which may indicate where they came from), and alphabet (enough to recognize their name when you see it in records written in that language). For the really gnarly research problems, you can always hire a professional.

Even legal or medical terms in your own language may seem foreign to you. When my hillbilly ancestors sold a piece of land with all its *appurtenances*, I didn't understand what that land record was trying to tell me. So I looked up that legal term in *Black's Law Dictionary*. (Now, I find it faster and easier on the Internet.) I learned that *appurtenances* means things attached to the land, such as the barn, corn crib, and outhouse. I'm not too sure about the still they had hidden up in the woods. I think it was portable.

The older the records, the more archaic the language—and the greater your need for a specialized dictionary. When a doctor's diary, an obituary, or other death record says your ancestor died of dropsy, he didn't just drop dead—or maybe he did. Look *dropsy* up in a dictionary of archaic medical terms.

You will find several categories at Cyndi's List that list Web sites about terminology. Another excellent online resource is Abbreviations and Symbols Used in Genealogy *(homepages.rootsweb.com/scottish/Abbreviations.html).*

Genealogy not only deals with foreign languages and technical terms, but also has a language of its own. I have tried to ease you into the vocabulary of genealogy throughout this book. At the back is a glossary to help you learn some of the common terms used in genealogical research.

Sources for Help: Online and Off

Many resources are available to help you meet the challenges of researching in a particular locality or type of record. The Web provides a plethora of tools and educational opportunities for online genealogists, but you can take many other non-computer routes to acquire the background you need. Most beginners use a combination of books, classes, and the Internet to put themselves through genealogy boot camp.

Research Outlines

Research Outlines, published by the LDS Church, are available for the United States as a whole, each of the fifty states and the U.S. Territories, Canada, each of the Canadian provinces, and many foreign countries. They are free if you print them from the Internet and low cost if you buy them already printed. The LDS Church also publishes a few topical guides, including *African American Records, Handwriting Guide: German Gothic, Jewish Genealogy, Tracing Immigrant Origins,* and *United States Military Records.*

The Research Outlines for each locality cover such things as

- Basic research methods
- Genealogical resources and reference materials
- Types of records kept during different time periods

There are three ways to find the LDS Research Outlines. Check at your local Family History Center, call the LDS Salt Lake Distribution Center at 800-537-5950, or go online:

1. Go to *www.familysearch.org.*
2. Click on the Search tab.
3. Click on the Research Helps subtab.
4. Click on Sort by Document Type in the Options bar on the left side of your screen.
5. Under Document Types, click on Research Outlines to see an alphabetical list.
6. If it says [PDF] after the title, you can print it with the free Adobe Acrobat Reader program that comes pre-installed on many computers. If you don't have a copy on your computer, download it *(www.adobe.com/products/acrobat/alternate.html).*

Libraries and Archives

Every state in the United States has a Web site for its state library and archives. These Web sites are hidden treasures of help. Because genealogists pepper the staff of these institutions with Background Phase questions, librarians and archivists often write articles, essays, and tutorials answering these frequently asked questions. Their writings are often published as flyers, pamphlets, registers, and finding aids. If you ask a Background Phase question, you'll probably be referred to those materials. Sometimes the aids can be purchased on site.

Many facilities now post such helpful resources online. But finding them is often a challenge. Some are posted at that library or archive's Web site, but buried three levels down from the main page. Other helps are posted at sites like the TNGenWeb Project and Cyndi's List. (See the next section for more information.)

For example, the Tennessee State Library & Archives Web site has a Virtual Reference Desk *(www.state.tn.us/sos/statelib/techsvs/vrdesk.htm).* It has a section on preserving your family documents (letters and photos) and a section on Tennessee History & Genealogy. This last section includes instructions on how to request information by mail from the archives.

Often the experts on staff give lectures about topics pertinent to the Background Phase of genealogical research. Flyers about such lectures are posted in the repository, at local public libraries, and perhaps even at Family History Centers in that area. If you are going to visit that facility, check its Web site to see if any helpful lectures have been scheduled during your visit. This is especially true of the Family History Library in Salt Lake City, Utah.

Don't expect the underpaid and overworked staff to do your research for you. Do your homework first. Check their Web site to see if your question has already been answered. Read their list of Frequently Asked Questions (FAQs). If not, keep your questions brief and to the point. Different facilities offer different ways to submit your questions. Most prefer e-mail.

USGenWeb and WorldGenWeb Projects

The USGenWeb Project is a nonprofit, volunteer effort begun in June 1996, and the WorldGenWeb Project followed in October 1996. The WorldGenWeb Project *(www.worldgenweb.org)* covers eleven regions, although not all countries have sites. The USGenWeb Project has a national site *(www.usgenweb.org)* with links to the sites for each state, which have links to the sites for their counties. These projects contain some of the best resources for help with the Background and Survey Phases. Again, this does not mean direct answers to questions about your personal research, but a great many different types of helps are available at these sites.

The goals of these projects are to do the following:

- Help researchers learn more about doing research in a geopolitical area (county, state, country, or region)
- Provide free use and access to public domain genealogical information
- Create online repositories of information with world-wide access

Genealogical and Historical Societies

Genealogical societies are about genealogists helping genealogists. Historical societies have a slightly different focus, but they, too, can be especially helpful during your Background Phase. Both types of societies include members willing to share their expertise in local history and genealogy.

I belong to societies near where I live, as well as ones in the areas where my ancestors lived. I attend meetings at nearby societies for social and educational enrichment.

I look forward to receiving publications from the more distant societies because of the information they contain.

GenWeb Project sites include links to genealogical and historical societies for their areas. Cyndi's List has thousands of links to societies. Find them either in her Societies & Groups category *(www.cyndislist.com/society.htm)* or in subcategories under a specific geographical area. You can also find genealogical societies at the Federation of Genealogical Societies' Society Hall at *www.familyhistory.com/societyhall/*. If you are not online, check in the reference section of your public library for books listing societies in the United States and Canada.

You'll Be Back in the Saddle . . . Again

You'll be returning to these helpful resources—both online and off—again and again. Not only do they help you with your Background Phase, but you'll also need them during your Survey and Research phases.

Chapter 9
Jump Start Your Genealogy

To jump start your genealogy, go find what has already been researched, compiled, and published about any of your ancestral family members. Don't forget to look for information about the families they married into, their friends and neighbors, and even their associates. You may find your family mentioned in their records, too. This is called the Survey Phase.

The goal of this phase is to prevent a duplication of effort—but this does not mean you believe everything you find in print (on paper or electronically published). During this phase, you work mainly with compiled sources. It is easy for errors to slip into anything that is not original. Always analyze what you find; then go out and search for original records to support or disprove your conclusions.

Let me caution you, however, not to get stuck in a rut. Some family tree tracers get so caught up in the Survey Phase that they never move from surveying compiled sources into researching original records. The Survey Phase should be your appetizer and the Research Phase your main meal.

Using PERSI to Pursue Dead Ancestors

Plenty of published resources are available for you to survey. Some online databases contain a billion names. A tremendous amount of information also continues to be published in more classic formats, such as books and magazines. PERSI (the PERiodical Source Index) is an index to journals, magazines, and quarterlies published by genealogical, historical, ethnic, and heritage societies (see Figures 9.1 and 9.2). Most of the indexed publications are from societies in the United States and Canada. Think of PERSI as an index to the tables of contents of nearly ten thousand publications, some of which date back to 1800.

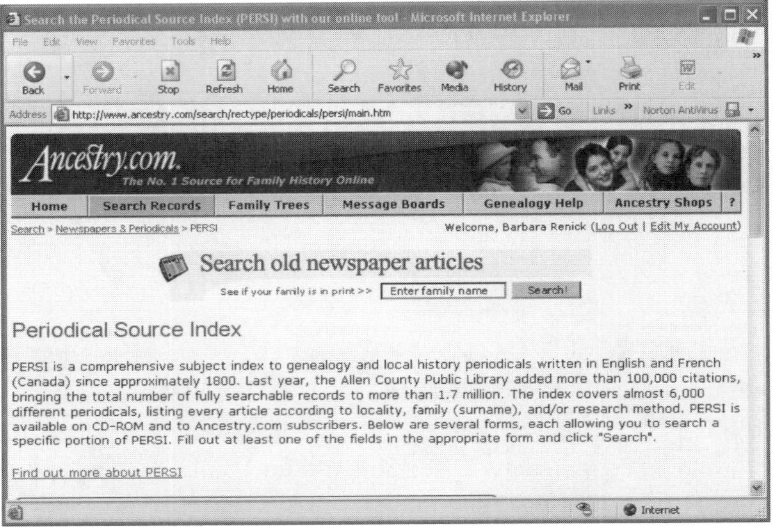

Figure 9.1 PERSI at Ancestry.com

Search Surname Section:
Surname
Article Title Keyword
Search ▸▸

Search PERSI's U.S. Locality Section:
U.S. State: All U.S. States
County
Article Title Keyword
Record Type: Any Record Type
Search ▸▸

Figure 9.2 Search screen for PERSI at Ancestry.com

The Allen County Public Library in Fort Wayne, Indiana, has one of the largest genealogy collections in the United States. The librarians focus on collecting genealogy periodicals, which is what they use to create PERSI. This index currently contains 1.8 million entries indexed by surname, locality, and topic. New citations are being added at the rate of more than one hundred thousand each year, and it is updated semiannually. PERSI is a source you search once, then go back and search again later because so much more has been added. This is what I was doing when I made one of my big finds.

I was looking for the surnames of people who married into my families. The Neals married into my Grosses and Whitmans, but not my Lindsays. Since Whitman and Neal are relatively common surnames, it wasn't until I searched for them together that I recognized an entry pertaining to my ancestry.

By tracking down the original article, I found information recorded back in the 1920s by a gentleman from Arkansas. In his article, he states that his Neal ancestor's mother was a Lindsay. If they were close cousins, this explains why these Neals never married any of my Lindsays. I now have a probable sister to my earliest identified Lindsay ancestor and a whole new avenue of research.

PERSI is indexed three ways (by surname, location, and topic) for a reason. Don't stop with just a surname search. Do a locality search, too. This turned up quite a variety of published records for that county in Arkansas—any one of which might mention these Neals and Lindsays.

Unfortunately, finding a copy of the referenced periodical can be a challenge. PERSI does list some of the major genealogical libraries that also have that periodical, but you may not live near one of those libraries. Rather than chasing around trying to find a copy, it may be more cost effective to use the Allen County Public Library Foundation's copying service. The ACPL houses all the periodicals indexed in PERSI.

Go to *www.acpl.lib.in.us,* click on Genealogy Gateway at the bottom right corner of your screen, click on PERSI, and follow the instructions to print out the order form at *www.acpl.lib.in.us/database/graphics/order_form.html.* You can request up to six articles at a time on one form for a fee of $7.50. Mail the form and your payment to the address provided. They do not accept requests by phone, fax, or e-mail. You are billed twenty cents per page copied, and it takes six to eight weeks. I'd spend more than that in gasoline driving to and from the Los Angeles Public Library (the closest library to me likely to have such periodicals).

There are three versions of PERSI. Older copies are available on microfiche at many Family History Centers. PERSI can be purchased on a compact disc, and is one of the reference CDs I take with me on research trips. The most up-to-date version is available to paid subscribers at the commercial Ancestry.com site.

Survey Again and Again

You'll find yourself repeating the Survey Phase again and again. Each time you trace your ancestors back to a new location or find a new surname associated with your ancestral family, you go back and see what has been published. For example, when I learned my earliest Lindsay ancestor possibly had a sister who married a Neal, I went back through online databases, books, and periodicals looking for the surname Neal in the places my Lindsays lived. I also searched for Lindsays in locations where the Neals lived. I may get lucky and find a county or family history in an Arkansas library with information on my Lindsays. Without making the Neal connection, I would never have thought to look in Arkansas for further information about them.

The article in the Arkansas magazine also noted that the Neals originally came from Washington County, Virginia. The earliest document that I am certain pertains to my William Lindsay Sr. is an 1800 tax list in Carter County, Tennessee. He is probably the son (or grandson) of the Matthew Lindsay who is listed in a 1796 Carter County deed as being a resident of Washington County, Virginia. I have much circumstantial evidence pointing toward an existing relationship between them, but no proof.

This new Neal information provides additional weight toward the conclusion that my Lindsays are related to the ones in Washington County, Virginia. Unfortunately, there appear to be several groups of Lindsays in that area. Extra caution and extra evidence are needed in such cases.

Every time you identify a female ancestor's maiden name, survey what has been published about her surname in that locality. Go back and check in the records you previously searched. You may have already seen records for some of her family members and just not recognized them. They are probably among the witnesses to her marriage, listed on her husband's land transactions, or in the families living next to her and her husband in the census records. For this reason, whenever I find the names of witnesses to an ancestor's marriage, witnesses to land sales, or my ancestor's neighbors in census records, I go back and survey what has been published about those names in that locality.

Another reason to repeat the Survey Phase is to see what's new since you last checked. A growing resource, like PERSI, comes out with regular updates. Many online databases and directories grow regularly. I resurvey these fast-growing resources at least once a year.

When to Repeat Your Survey

Go back and repeat your Survey Phase each time you

- Trace your ancestors back to a new location
- Add a new name to your ancestor chart
- Find the name of someone who married into your ancestral family
- Find the name of someone who was closely associated with your ancestral family
- Find the name of someone who witnessed their marriage
- Find the name of someone who witnessed their land sale
- Find the name of someone who was listed next to (or near) them in a census
- Find the name of someone who was a godparent at their child's christening
- Determine that a year has elapsed since you looked in a growing resource

Where to Get Started Surveying

The Survey Phase is a shotgun approach to family tree tracing. You consult a number of relatively easy-to-use resources, hoping to strike gold. You have already begun surveying if you started interviewing your relatives as mentioned in Chapter 3.

Other types of resources to search in your Survey Phase include books and periodicals. Biographies probably come to mind first. If your ancestors were famous, you'll find them in these types of books. But most of my ancestors were just ordinary folks. To find them in published resources, I focus on a very small geographic area. While my ordinary ancestors aren't mentioned in any national biographical indexes, they are mentioned in quite a few county history books.

There are many different levels of history books to seek out—including city, county, state, and regional. There are histories about ethnic and religious groups, such as the Scots-Irish settlers on the frontiers of colonial Pennsylvania or early Jewish settlers of Southern California. On a more local note, a book about a Baptist church in Anderson County had a whole section on its sister church in Campbell County (the one founded by my two fourth great-grandfathers). It included wonderful biographies of early church members, including my ancestors. This book came along at a time when I was pretty much stuck after doing years of Campbell County research. It opened new possibilities and motivated me to dig further and uncover more of my roots.

The smaller the geographic area covered by a history or biography, the more likely your ancestors are to be mentioned. For example, you're more likely to find your ancestors who lived in Ritchie County, West Virginia, in a history of Ritchie County than in a history of the state of West Virginia.

The best way to find out about such books is by joining the local genealogical and historical societies in the areas where your ancestors lived. They publish some of the best helps for genealogists. PERSI is one tool for surveying these periodicals nationwide, but it does not index every periodical and is not on an every-name level for those periodicals it does index. In other words, it does not index every single name mentioned in every single periodical. It indexes only the major topics and surnames covered in articles in those periodicals.

For the localities where your ancestors lived, you want to look more closely. Many local genealogy periodicals are every-name indexed and frequently include a list of books published about that area and where to buy them.

Genealogy publications tend to fit into three categories:

- General genealogical
- Surname specific
- Geographically oriented

For decades, the most famous genealogy magazine was Everton's *The Genealogy Helper*, published bimonthly. It is now called *Everton's Family History Magazine*. It contains not only articles on how to do research, but also lists of genealogical societies and queries for help. Genealogists pay by the word to publish their queries in this magazine. The advent of personal computers has greatly increased the number of genealogy magazines available today.

Periodicals about a specific surname are more often published by individuals or small family organizations. Only a small number of them have a large base of subscribers from which to draw support. It is not uncommon for a surname publication to be published for only a limited number of years, and fewer copies of such publications are distributed to libraries. This does not diminish their worth, even if they are a bit harder to find.

For example, a quarterly called the *Wilson Warehouse* (published by Charlotte M. Tucker of The Woodlands, Texas, back in the 1970s) published my analysis of the four separate groups of Wilsons, which I identified in Pulaski County, Kentucky, tax lists from 1799 to 1840. This analysis was based on six weeks of work spent extracting all the Wilson entries from those hard-to-read handwritten tax lists. This is a big help to anyone with early Wilsons in that county.

Even though a periodical may no longer be published, seek out past issues to see whether they contain references to your family tree branches. Be aware that not all genealogical or historical publications are every-name indexed, especially those published in the typewriter era. Many societies, aided by computers and indexing software, have gone back and created separate cumulative indexes to their past issues.

There are a variety of geographically oriented periodicals—about one county or one state. Most are published by nonprofit genealogical or historical societies. Some overlap may exist between these publications. For example, Campbell County families may be mentioned not only in the *Campbell Countian* (published by the Campbell County [Tennessee] Historical Society), but also in regional publications like the *Pellissippian* (published by the Pellissippi Genealogical and Historical Society) and *Tennessee Ancestors* (published by the East Tennessee Historical Society).

Lineage and patriotic societies often publish magazines with genealogically useful queries and articles. For example, the National Society Daughters of the American Revolution (NSDAR) publishes a magazine called *American Spirit*, which contains helpful articles, queries, and lists of proven patriots. For years, local chapters of the NSDAR have sought out and transcribed genealogical records (often rare, original records) that are published by each state organization in books by the Genealogical Records Committee. Each book produced by these committees has a different title, so they are generally referred to as GRCs. These are now beginning to be every-name indexed by some of the state organizations.

Remember that records migrate. The records found by a DAR chapter in Arkansas may be about your Virginia family. Don't overlook books and periodicals published by lineage and patriotic societies.

Where to Find Books and Periodicals

Libraries are your best resource for finding books and periodicals, but there are many different levels or types of libraries to consider. Geographically, there are city, county, regional, state, and national libraries. Each has its advantages and disadvantages for your Survey Phase searches. Most libraries in the United States have Web sites that feature a variety of useful details about researching in their facilities, as well as online catalogs to search.

State libraries are typically larger, with more resources than local libraries, but the local library where your ancestor lived may have a book the state library lacks. Many local genealogical and historical societies lack resources to maintain libraries of their own, so they work out an agreement with a local public library to house their collections. There are exceptions, such as the New York Genealogical and Biographical Society, which maintains its own research facility in New York City.

State genealogical and historical societies (and larger antiquarian societies) usually maintain their own research facilities (libraries). I have found state library Web sites to be a gold mine of resources and reference materials. They usually maintain fact sheets about each county in their state, including information about genealogically significant records and publications. They are a resource for maps, information about that state's land record system, and vital records availability. I've even found extremely helpful histories of the state's court systems.

Once, I was working on a term paper in the library at California State University, Fullerton. I was shocked to find a book for which I had traveled all the way to Utah. There it was—only fifteen minutes from my home. Don't overlook university libraries. Many have historical and biographical collections, as well as research tools (like a microfilmed index to obituaries in the *New York Times*), that are useful to genealogists. Their online catalogs facilitate your survey of their resources from near or far.

Religious organizations frequently publish newspapers (with information about their members) and biographical works about their early history and their pioneer preachers. Such materials are often housed in the libraries of the religious universities founded by those churches. Some churches even maintain archives of their historical

Tips on Using Library Catalogs

- A library may have more than one catalog:
  - Older card catalog
  - Newer electronic catalog
  - Newest online catalog
- A large city or county may have more than one library—each with different resources.
- A university may have more than one library:
  - Main campus library
  - Satellite libraries on satellite campuses
  - Law library
  - Medical library
  - Specially endowed library for special collections (including historical)
- Patriotic or lineage society libraries often have unique resources:
  - Hanging files
  - Microfilm collections
  - Analytical card catalogs
  - Special manuscript collections
- Ask about materials or collections found only in that library.
- Always ask if all the library's holdings are in their electronic catalog.
  - Many institutions have not had the funds to retro-catalog resources acquired prior to computerization.
  - Manuscript collections are often listed in separate registers.

collections. Micajah Wilson's brother, Jonas Durman Wilson, was a pioneer Baptist preacher in Missouri. I found fascinating biographical and autobiographical material about him (and his ancestors) in a Missouri Baptist Archive—even though his early years were spent in Virginia and Kentucky.

Speaking of unique resources, many ethnic, patriotic, and lineage society libraries contain unique resources for genealogists. The DAR Library in Washington, D.C., has what is called an analytical card catalog. DAR members volunteer to create indexes for resources without indexes (such as large, eleven-hundred-page, county histories). The entries are typed onto 3 x 5 cards and kept in this special card catalog only in that library.

Lastly, there are private libraries, such as my own collection of books and periodicals from the counties surrounding the Cumberland Gap. While these collections are harder to find, they also offer unique research opportunities. For instance, I have complete series of genealogical periodicals from those counties, which is something you rarely find in most libraries.

Knowing the breadth of historical and biographical resources in the Family History Library in Salt Lake City, Utah, I traveled all the way there to work on a history paper. I was reaching for a biography of a South Carolina politician when I saw right next to it a book titled *The Progeny of Christopher Brunk*. Knowing my ancestor's brother married a Brunk, I just had to pull it off the shelf and survey it. It had a whole section on my Whitmans. I hadn't taken the time to survey for published works about my ancestor's brother's wife's family—but there it was right in front of me.

Many of the resources of the Family History Library are available on microfilm or microfiche through your local Family History Center—this one was not. This published work was available only as a book, and books don't circulate to the Family History Centers.

Queries Here, There, and Everywhere

Queries are a classic survey tool. You place queries hoping other people will see them and share their research with you. You also look for other people's queries about your names in your areas of research, so you can share with them. The periodicals described earlier in this chapter are the classic venue for distributing queries. See Figure 9.3 for a typical query in a genealogy periodical.

Any query you post should contain your contact information plus the basic elements of genealogical identification: names, dates, places, and relationships. A query asking for help finding your Mary Jones isn't likely to get many responses. A query asking for help finding your Mary Jones born between 1806 and 1810 possibly in Wilkes County, North Carolina, to Dorothea Guinn and an unidentified Jones is more likely to get responses.

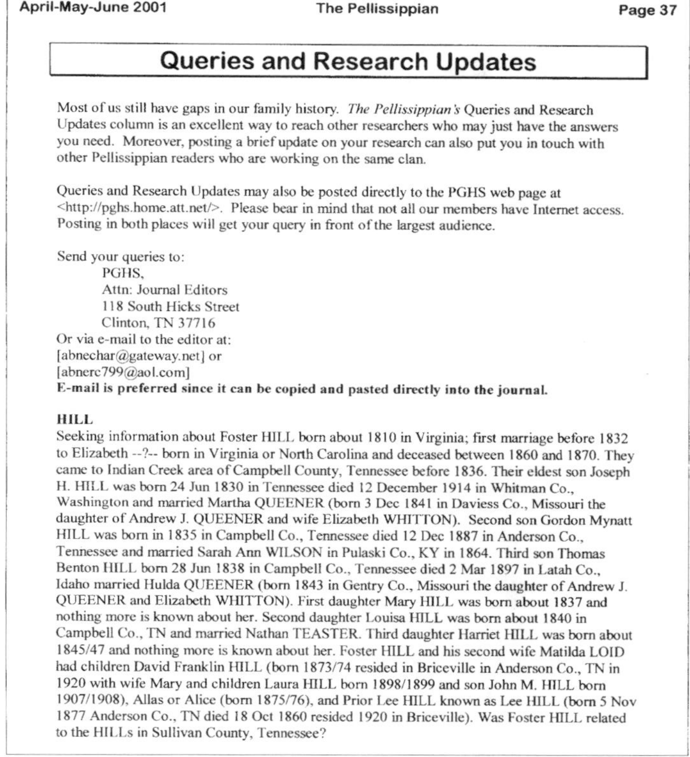

April-May-June 2001 The Pellissippian Page 37

Queries and Research Updates

Most of us still have gaps in our family history. *The Pellissippian's* Queries and Research Updates column is an excellent way to reach other researchers who may just have the answers you need. Moreover, posting a brief update on your research can also put you in touch with other Pellissippian readers who are working on the same clan.

Queries and Research Updates may also be posted directly to the PGHS web page at <http://pghs.home.att.net/>. Please bear in mind that not all our members have Internet access. Posting in both places will get your query in front of the largest audience.

Send your queries to:
PGHS,
Attn: Journal Editors
118 South Hicks Street
Clinton, TN 37716
Or via e-mail to the editor at:
[abnechar@gateway.net] or
[abnerc799@aol.com]
E-mail is preferred since it can be copied and pasted directly into the journal.

HILL
Seeking information about Foster HILL born about 1810 in Virginia; first marriage before 1832 to Elizabeth --?-- born in Virginia or North Carolina and deceased between 1860 and 1870. They came to Indian Creek area of Campbell County, Tennessee before 1836. Their eldest son Joseph H. HILL was born 24 Jun 1830 in Tennessee died 12 December 1914 in Whitman Co., Washington and married Martha QUEENER (born 3 Dec 1841 in Daviess Co., Missouri the daughter of Andrew J. QUEENER and wife Elizabeth WHITTON). Second son Gordon Mynatt HILL was born in 1835 in Campbell Co., Tennessee died 12 Dec 1887 in Anderson Co., Tennessee and married Sarah Ann WILSON in Pulaski Co., KY in 1864. Third son Thomas Benton HILL born 28 Jun 1838 in Campbell Co., Tennessee died 2 Mar 1897 in Latah Co., Idaho married Hulda QUEENER (born 1843 in Gentry Co., Missouri the daughter of Andrew J. QUEENER and Elizabeth WHITTON). First daughter Mary HILL was born about 1837 and nothing more is known about her. Second daughter Louisa HILL was born about 1840 in Campbell Co., TN and married Nathan TEASTER. Third daughter Harriet HILL was born about 1845/47 and nothing more is known about her. Foster HILL and his second wife Matilda LOID had children David Franklin HILL (born 1873/74 resided in Briceville in Anderson Co., TN in 1920 with wife Mary and children Laura HILL born 1898/1899 and son John M. HILL born 1907/1908), Allas or Alice (born 1875/76), and Prior Lee HILL known as Lee HILL (born 5 Nov 1877 Anderson Co., TN died 18 Oct 1860 resided 1920 in Briceville). Was Foster HILL related to the HILLs in Sullivan County, Tennessee?

Figure 9.3 Typical query in a genealogy periodical

Queries are often limited in length. It may not always be possible to add such details as Mary's two marriages, the names of her children by each husband, her places of residence throughout her life, and the probable location of her death; but such details greatly increase your chances of being contacted by someone related to your Joneses.

I make it a policy to search queries as far back as I can go in each publication, though some of the people who posted them are no longer living. The queries themselves have value as a compiled record and may lead me to a branch of descendants who are also researching my ancestral families. (A great many Internet resources are available to help you locate living people.)

Most locality-specific and surname-specific periodicals require you to pay a fee to be a member of that society and receive their publications. As a member or subscriber, you get to place queries in their publications. Most online resources are free, and distribution is world-wide. Despite online advantages, I still place my queries in both venues.

There are so many places to put your queries online that it is hard to choose where to start. Web sites specifically designed to handle genealogical queries are called *message boards.* They are available for localities, surnames, and genealogical topics. My favorite places to find message boards are at GenForum *(genforum.genealogy.com)* and at Ancestry.com *(boards.ancestry.com).* They are free, have very high traffic (so more people are likely to be exposed to your queries), and have search capabilities. Use not only the Queries & Message Boards category at Cyndi's List, but also her Surnames, Family Associations & Family Newsletters category to look for Web sites that handle queries about surnames.

Geographically focused Web sites are the specialty of the USGenWeb and WorldGenWeb Projects. These sites allow free queries, but only if they pertain to that county or state. In other words, a query posted about your North Carolina Joneses at the Delaware GenWeb Project site is erased if it doesn't mention a connection to Delaware. Search past queries placed at these sites, too.

There are two types of free e-mail discussion groups for genealogists: mail lists and newsgroups. Mail lists forward your e-mailed queries to all subscribers, whereas newsgroups store your messages online where subscribers go to read the posted messages. There is no charge for subscribing to either type of group.

There are 177,000 free Collaboration E-mail Lists hosted at the FamilySearch Internet site (under the Share tab at *www.familysearch.org).* The RootsWeb site *(www.rootsweb.com)* is the other major host for genealogical mail lists (more than 25,000 of them). I recommend using both sites during your Survey Phase of research.

Electronic Databases

Many different kinds of genealogical databases have been published both online and on compact discs. Some online databases are free of charge and others require a subscriber fee, but even the commercial sites provide many free services and resources. Cyndi's List has two pages specifically for databases. Databases—Lineage Linked *(www.cyndislist.com/lin-linked.htm)* contains links to Web sites with family data linked together, much like you see in your genealogy software. Databases—Searchable Online *(www.cyndislist.com/database.htm)* has links to Web sites with databases of information, such as vital records, census records, and military records.

One of the newest and most rapidly growing genealogical databases published on CDs is the Pedigree Resource File. This database has grown to fifty-five million names on fifty CDs, which cost five dollars each. These CDs are often available for patrons to use for free at Family History Centers. The master index to the Pedigree Resource File can be searched in the Search for Ancestors section at FamilySearch Internet. To submit a copy of your records to the Pedigree Resource File (via a GEDCOM file), go to the Share My Genealogy section under the Share tab at FamilySearch.

One of the original collections of GEDCOM files published on CDs is the World Family Tree by Broderbund. (Family Tree Maker is the full-featured genealogy program that automates the search in the World Family Tree index.) This collection is now up to ninety-six volumes. Their master index is also searchable online by paid subscription at the Genealogy.com Web site. Some libraries and genealogical societies have these resources for their patrons' use. For example, the Orange County California Genealogical Society has a collection of the World Family Tree CDs for members to use for a small extra membership fee in their Family Tree Maker Users Group.

Online Database Searching

Again and again I hear stories about a genealogy beginner who goes to the Search for Ancestors section at FamilySearch Internet, fills in all the boxes, finds nothing, then thinks this is a lousy resource—even if it does have nearly a billion names. This is a classic example of why the Background Phase is so important. You must learn how to best use that resource so you get the most from it. In this case, if you fill in all the boxes, you are, in effect, telling the computer to show you those records that match *all* those pieces of information.

When I use Search for Ancestors, the first thing I do is judge whether or not I am searching for a common name. If I'm searching for Zucknicks, the only thing I fill in is the last name. Doing so recently brought up sixty-five matches on the results page. To save time on its initial results page, FamilySearch Internet displays only the first twenty-five matches from each of its record collections. But the Sources Searched box on the upper right side of the screen said there were over twenty-five matches in the IGI Germany collection. I clicked on the IGI/Germany link (in the Sources Searched box) and saw the full results from that record collection, which had sixty matches on that surname.

Great-grandpa W.B. Hill, however, has a common last name. Entering just his surname isn't going to be nearly as useful because of the large number of matches I'd get.

You need to provide more specific information to pare down your results when searching for a common name. Since Search for Ancestors is free, I try different combinations of the search fields and compare the results I get.

To get an overview of the instructions in the Search for Ancestors section, click on Help in the upper right corner of your screen. For more specific help, click on the underlined link that says Tips on How to Search for Your Ancestor. You'll be amazed at how much more you can find in this database if you know how to search it.

Other Internet Resources

There are so many different types of genealogically valuable sites on the Internet, no one research tool lists them all. Genealogy-specific directories, such as Cyndi's List and the Web Sites directory at FamilySearch Internet (under the Search tab), are good places to start surveying the Internet for your names and localities, but don't stop there. Also use large Internet search engines such as Google.com to search for your ancestral names and places.

One of my students complained that when he used search engines to search for his last name, Mallard, all he found were sites about duck decoys. He was thrilled to learn that many search engines have advanced search options where he can specify that matches not include the words *duck* or *decoy*. If you have a common surname like Jones, pair it with other search terms—like the locality where your Joneses lived—for more effective searching with search engines.

The Internet is just like any other form of publishing, only more ephemeral. A Web site you find today may be gone tomorrow. Always make copies of anything you find online, as you would with any other find, and don't believe that the things published online are any more accurate than those published in paper formats. The next book in the NGS series, *Online Roots,* explores this concept more fully.

CHAPTER 10
Combing for Clues

THIS CHAPTER IS ABOUT HOW TO FIND AND SEARCH ORIGINAL RECORDS in the Research Phase of genealogy. Sometimes computers can help you find and search original source material, but most of the time you have to do this the old-fashioned way. You look at microfilmed records, write requests for copies, go on location to search the originals yourself, or hire someone to search them for you.

Preparing to Sleuth

It is amazing how the most esoteric bits and pieces of knowledge become important to genealogists. Just one summer trip exploring weed-covered rural cemeteries convinces most genealogists it is better to pursue such endeavors in the late fall (when chiggers and ticks aren't out, snakes and bears are less active, and poison ivy is bright red and easier to avoid).

It is just as important to know when and where to search as it is to know what to search. I frequently hear stories of genealogy beginners who travel all the way to Europe to search records in the areas in which their ancestors lived, only to be told they must go to an LDS Family History Center to look at the microfilmed copies—something they could have done at home.

On research trips, I take the CD version of the Family History Library Catalog and my laptop computer. This way I can determine if a record is available from that library and not waste valuable travel time on resources I can access nearer to home. For instance, many of the most genealogically significant records from U.S. county courthouses have been microfilmed and are available either in that state's library and archives system or through the LDS Family History Library system (or both). Many states and countries have laws mandating that county records of a predetermined age be sent to a specified state repository. Unless you do some background checking, you will not know where to find those records and could show up at a county courthouse and be disappointed.

Setting Goals

Genealogical research is a simple ten-step process:

1. Choose an individual or family to research by looking at your ancestor (or descendants) chart.
2. Identify what you already know about them in your computer or on your paper forms.
3. Set a goal. What specific piece of information do you want to find?
4. Decide which type and time period of record is most likely to contain that information.
5. Locate the record (or a microfilmed copy, if the original is not accessible) and write a description of it (the source details) on your research log.
6. Search the record.
7. Copy pertinent information, if any is found.
8. Analyze and evaluate what you have found.
9. Record the results in your genealogy program or on your paper forms.
10. Set your next goal.

If you do not find what you are seeking on your first try, choose another source to search and repeat Steps 4 through 9 until you meet your goal.

Help! I Need Somebody's Records

Helping you decide which type of record to search next is the forte of the LDS Research Outlines (previously mentioned in Chapter 8). They contain very concise

Record Selection Tables. For example, the table in the *United States Research Outline* (see Figure 10.1) says in effect: If you need a birth date, look first in vital records (government-issued birth certificates), church records (for infant christenings), and Bible records; then search cemeteries, obituaries, and census records. This Record Selection Table lists twenty-three typical U.S. research goals and their most likely solutions.

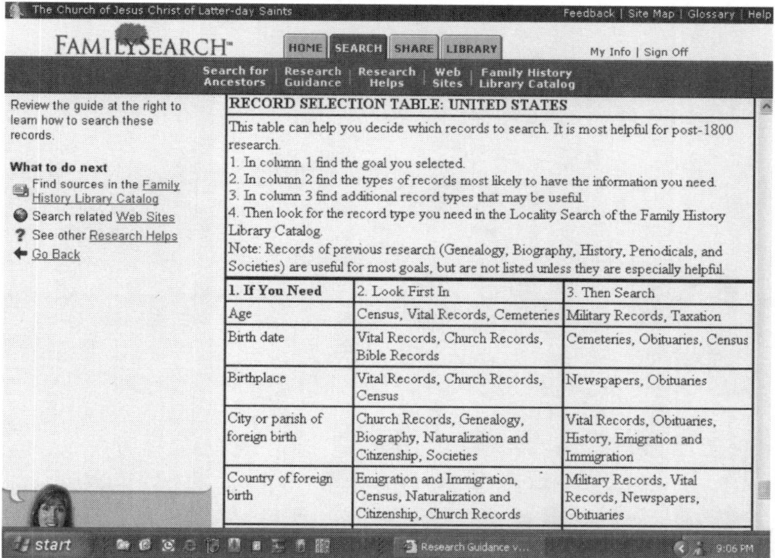

RECORD SELECTION TABLE: UNITED STATES

This table can help you decide which records to search. It is most helpful for post-1800 research.
1. In column 1 find the goal you selected.
2. In column 2 find the types of records most likely to have the information you need.
3. In column 3 find additional record types that may be useful.
4. Then look for the record type you need in the Locality Search of the Family History Library Catalog.
Note: Records of previous research (Genealogy, Biography, History, Periodicals, and Societies) are useful for most goals, but are not listed unless they are especially helpful.

1. If You Need	2. Look First In	3. Then Search
Age	Census, Vital Records, Cemeteries	Military Records, Taxation
Birth date	Vital Records, Church Records, Bible Records	Cemeteries, Obituaries, Census
Birthplace	Vital Records, Church Records, Census	Newspapers, Obituaries
City or parish of foreign birth	Church Records, Genealogy, Biography, Naturalization and Citizenship, Societies	Vital Records, Obituaries, History, Emigration and Immigration
Country of foreign birth	Emigration and Immigration, Census, Naturalization and Citizenship, Church Records	Military Records, Vital Records, Newspapers, Obituaries

Figure 10.1 Record Selection Table from the LDS *United States Research Outline* (Reproduced by permission. Copyright © 1999–2002 by Intellectual Reserve, Inc.)

After using the *United States Research Outline* for general guidance, read the research outline for the state where your ancestor's life event probably occurred. This gives you specific help on what, where, and how to search in that state. The online versions of these LDS Research Outlines contain active links to the Web sites of the resources mentioned (government offices, libraries and archives, state vital record departments, etc.). Figure 10.2 shows a page from the *Alaska Research Outline.*

In just the last few years, the LDS Church has developed interactive Research Guidance at its FamilySearch Internet site. This free service helps you to

- Determine what types of records were kept for the geopolitical area and time where your ancestor's birth, marriage, or death occurred

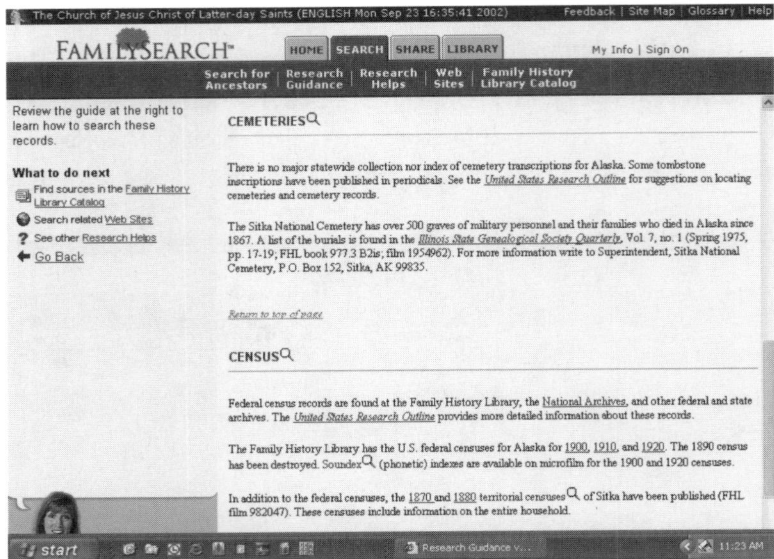

Figure 10.2 Online version of the *Alaska Research Outline* with active links (Reproduced by permission. Copyright © 1999–2002 by Intellectual Reserve, Inc.)

- Find those records in the Family History Library Catalog, from a government agency, or through a Web site indexed in the Web Sites directory at FamilySearch Internet
- Understand the typical contents of such records and how to analyze them
- Decipher the language (foreign or technical) used in such documents with FamilySearch Internet's Glossary (a multilanguage genealogy dictionary)
- Link to other online resources pertinent to your research goal

Layers of research guidance hide under nondescript tabs called Historical Background, For Beginners, and Search Strategy (the default view). Just as their names imply, these levels of guidance serve as a background to your Research Phase. Research Guidance at FamilySearch Internet is like an onion—layers within layers of advice, tips, background information, and Internet links. Geographically, guidance is available for the United States as a whole, each of the fifty states, Canada, all the Canadian provinces, and most of the major countries in Western Europe.

If you don't have an Internet connection or there isn't a Research Outline or

Research Guidance Section about your research locality, you have to determine record availability in a more traditional fashion—by reading books, taking classes, and listening to lectures about that specific area, time period, or record type. Even with the LDS research aids, it is a good idea to build your background knowledge and skills. The LDS resources can't possibly cover everything available.

Free research guidance is available at FamilySearch Internet:

- Go to *www.familysearch.org*.
- Click on the Search tab.
- Click on the Research Guidance subtab.
- Choose a locality (like Alaska, Baden, or Denmark).
- Click on a time period for one event in your ancestor's life (birth, marriage, or death).
- Research Guidance then comes up with multiple levels of advice on how to achieve that research goal.

Whistle (or at Least Chant) while You Work

I teach beginners a little chant to help them remember the seven common categories of records for U.S. research—in descending order from most accurate, complete, and accessible to least. The chant goes like this: "Civil, church, family, single, multiple, census, and probate."

Civil refers to a government-recorded birth, marriage, or death. These records include

- Birth certificates and birth registers
- Marriage bonds, licenses, certificates, and registers
- Death certificates and coroner's reports

Civil records are usually, but not always, the most accurate type of record for the event they document. For example, Great-aunt Menny's death certificate gave her birth date as 1887. However, when I looked in the 1900 U.S. census, she was listed as born in April 1881, age 19 years, married, with two of her four children still living—which makes an 1887 birth date quite unlikely. Death certificates are usually the most accurate source for death information, but other information found on them is often less accurate.

Unfortunately, civil registration is not uniform throughout the United States. It was not required in most states until the early twentieth century. You often find a town clerk recording all the births in a small New England village back to the 1600s, only to be frustrated by the lack of a recorded birth certificate for a cousin born in Tennessee in 1952. (Yes, you read it right. The midwife failed to report the birth of my cousin. By the time her family realized this, the best they could do was to estimate the date. Even as recently as the twentieth century, we are not free of such problems.)

Civil registration of births, marriages, and deaths began at different times in foreign countries. See the appropriate LDS Research Outline for information about a foreign country's civil records.

Church refers to a written church record associated with the christening, marriage, or burial of an individual. Churches seldom record the birth of a child, but infant christening records can be used in lieu of a birth record if, for any reason, you can't obtain one. Since the state of North Carolina didn't keep birth records in the 1880s, I could look for a church christening record for Aunt Menny. If she was christened in 1881, that shows she was born before 1887, the birth date listed on her death certificate.

In many countries, church records predate civil registration of births, marriages, and deaths. But church records may be difficult to locate or no longer exist, like those from my great-grandmother's village church, which burned down during World War II. While most christenings were done as soon as possible after the birth of a child, there are cases where two or three children (and even adults) in a family were christened at the same time. Delayed christenings occur for a number of reasons. The family may have changed faiths, or there may have been no church of their faith nearby. In Polish Russia, if there wasn't an Evangelische (Lutheran) church available, my ancestors had their children christened in the nearest Catholic church.

Another problem—especially in America—is a blending of religions in one family. For example, Aunt Menny's father was Methodist, but her mother was Baptist. The Baptists in North Carolina in the 1880s didn't do infant christenings, but the Methodists did. The research challenge is to determine which Methodist church her parents might have attended, then locate those records.

Many people will tell you that records from Baptist churches contain little or nothing of genealogical value. There are, however, enough exceptions to make searching those records worthwhile. I purchased a church history book with a whole section about the Baptist church founded by two of my ancestors. There were only two memorials written into the minutes of this church, and one of them was about my great-great-grandfather.

Church records can be hard to track down. They may still be at the local church your ancestor attended, or they may have migrated to another state with the clerk who kept those records. Copies may be filed at church headquarters, or they may have been microfilmed and made available through the LDS Family History Library system. Some church records may even have been published in books, as was the case in the Baptist church history book I bought.

Church records vary by denomination and era. Many churches created records of infant christenings, marriages performed, and funeral memorials given by the minister. Some religious ordinances are generally performed at a certain age. The date of first communion, bar/bat mitzvah, or confirmation found in church or synagogue records help you approximate a birth date.

Family records are third in order of desirability, but they migrate with families, which makes them hard to track down. Some families leave behind a richer legacy of written records than others. If your ancestors never learned to read or write, like some of mine, they could not leave behind much in the way of written family records. They had to depend on their neighbors, itinerant preachers, or local officials to record life events for them.

Sometimes you find valuable information in the most unlikely places. Search between the pages of books you inherit. You may find old family letters, an obituary clipped from a newspaper, or even a wedding invitation. I found the birth dates for my mother's family written on the back of an envelope in grandma's cedar chest. There are many different types of written family records.

One of my most valuable family finds was a cross-stitch sampler. As a young girl, Dora Lee, daughter of George Hill, stitched a priceless record of her father's family—including all their birth dates.

Dora's grandfather, Gordon Mynatt Hill, joined a cavalry regiment during the Civil War. According to his invalid pension application, he contracted tuberculosis during his service. He was denied a pension for lack of proof (he was treated by the unit's veterinarian, not a regular surgeon). Even though it was denied, it is important because it contains his age and birth place, but no exact birth date. Other than that, I have not found any records created by Gordon during his life.

Gordon, his wife, and their youngest daughter all died of tuberculosis and were buried in unmarked graves. Their oldest surviving son, George (Dora's father), took care of his siblings until they were grown. He then married and raised his own large family.

The only way to determine where Gordon was buried was to interview his surviving grandchildren. Oscar Harris, a grandson of Gordon, was in charge of the Beech Grove Baptist Church Cemetery where Gordon's wife and youngest daughter were buried. He told me the church kept no records of where people were buried, but he remembered that the graves of his grandmother and youngest aunt were graded over when the road was widened, so all he could give us was an approximate location.

It wasn't until I took two of George's grandsons to meet their cousin Oscar that we managed to figure out where Gordon Mynatt Hill was buried. The grandsons remembered their grandfather George telling them he pulled his father's body on a sleigh up the side of a snowy mountain for burial. Oscar realized the only place that could be was Swag Baptist Church (named for its location on the swag in the mountain). We didn't find a gravestone for Gordon in that church cemetery, but I now feel reasonably certain I know where he is buried. If your family lacks written records, your interviewing skills become even more important.

Here is something important to keep in mind when copying information from a family Bible: Always include a copy of the Bible's publication page. If the family data goes back to the 1700s, but the Bible was published in 1940, you know the information was not recorded in that Bible when the events happened.

Single refers to any other single written source giving all the pieces to identify an event in your ancestor's life (name, date, place, and relationship). This might be an obituary in a newspaper, a military pension application, or a ship's passenger manifest.

Single sources rank fourth because they vary widely in content and accuracy. When my father died in a boating accident, I gave the information to three different newspapers. Each spelled our last name differently, even though I spelled it out—not just once, but twice—to each newspaper's reporter. Grandmother's steamship ticket spelled her married name wrong, as did the alien passenger manifest taken by the immigration officer. Even my first-grade teacher taught me to spell it wrong. Just because something is written down doesn't make it accurate or true.

Multiple refers to using several sources to put together the pieces of an ancestor's identifying event (birth, marriage, death, etc.). Using multiple sources ranks fifth in probable accuracy because none of those sources is a complete record in and of itself. An example of putting multiple sources together to document a person's death is when you use family interviews to establish where the person died and was buried, coupled with a name and death date from the gravestone.

Census refers to both federal and state census records. These are one of the most commonly used tools for putting together family trees. Genealogists often consult them first since they are so readily available and many are indexed. Because they contain so many errors, however, they should be used only as a stepping stone.

For years I searched census records for an Isaac Lindsay. Isaac left Campbell County, Tennessee, in 1848. I could not find him listed anywhere in the 1850 U.S. census. One day, as I was researching a different branch of my family in Monroe County, I stumbled across Isaac's will, dated 1861. It specifically mentions two of his sons as still living in Campbell County, so I knew I had the right Isaac Lindsay.

This motivated me to search the 1850 U.S. census again—only this time I focused on Monroe County. I found an entry for a household containing an elderly Isaac and Mary with no last name recorded. This couple was enumerated two houses away from Isaac Lindsay's youngest son. Through serendipity, I had finally found him.

Census records sometimes mangle names a little (Edmond D. Gross listed as E.D. Goose) or a lot (Ludwig Diem listed as Louis Team). Sometimes a portion of a name is entirely missing (given name or last name) or ditto marks are used incorrectly, leading you to extrapolate the wrong last name for a person. Your male ancestor may even be listed as a female. All sorts of errors creep into census enumerations.

Despite these common errors, one of the first things most genealogists do is find every member of each ancestral family in every federal and state census in which they could have been enumerated. You should search every one of these censuses, whether indexed or not. In other words, if you have to search the whole county page-by-page and line-by-line, do it. You'll be glad you did because of all the clues you'll pick up about family and friends who lived in that neighborhood. You never know when Grandpa, Grandma, or other family members might be living with the family next door or just down the road.

Probate records rank seventh on my chant. They are usually more accurate than census records, but a great deal less accessible. Not everyone had an estate that needed to be probated, nor do wills and probate records always include detailed information about family members—or even mention all of them. They may not mention children who died young or without heirs. Isaac Lindsay's will is an exception because it states where his children resided at the time he recorded it.

If your ancestor died intestate (without a will), there may still be plenty of probate records to search. Great-grandpa W.B. had a brother, Joseph Alfred Hill. Joseph and his wife never had any children, and his wife died before him. About the time he died, the state built a road through his farm. Joseph didn't have a will, but his estate was still probated in the local chancery court. The money from the sale of his farm, combined with the compensation from the state road department, was divided among his living siblings and the descendants of his dead ones. The result is that most of the descendants of Gordon Mynatt Hill (Joseph's father) are mentioned in this estate record.

Another added benefit is that copies of the probate papers were kept not only in the chancery court vault of the courthouse, but also at the state highway department. Probate cases generate many different types of records that end up in surprisingly different locations.

A Pyramid of Sources

Generally speaking, the quantity of material you find from these seven categories forms a pyramid. At the base are your home sources. You'll probably find lots of help at home on your first few generations of ancestry. The next layers are civil and church records. The smallest number of records providing exact names, dates, and places usually comes from miscellaneous sources (the single, multiple, census, and probate portions of my chant).

The farther back in time you go, the more inverted this pyramid becomes. By the time you are researching back in the 1700s, the largest segment comes from church and miscellaneous records, with the quantity of civil and home resources dwindling away at the tip.

Climb Every Mountain, Ford Every Stream

Genealogists and family historians work back in time from the known to the unknown. All too often, you encounter difficulty finding one or more of the key events or relationships in an ancestor's life. This is like trying to guess the picture on a jigsaw puzzle with only some of the pieces put together.

In such cases, carefully and methodically work through each stage of that ancestor's life. Fill out a timeline of the life events you have documented. Work backwards in time (burial, death, later life, child-rearing years, spouses and marriages, childhood years with siblings, christening, birth, and parents). Look for such diverse details as

- Businesses they were involved with in any way
- Each and every census they would have been enumerated in
- Education they acquired in any form (both formal and informal)
- Emigration
- Engagement and marriage patterns
- Graduations and ceremonies
- Hobbies and crafts they enjoyed
- Holidays celebrated
- Everyone who ever lived in their home
- Hospitalizations or illnesses
- Military service
- Naturalizations and citizenship
- Neighbors who may possibly be related by blood, marriage, religion, or ethnicity
- Occupations
- Organizations or societies to which they belonged
- Places of residence
- Property owned, leased, or rented
- Religious events in their lives, such as
    - Confirmation in the Lutheran church
    - Bar/bat mitzvah in the Jewish faith
- Slang words they used or the dialect they spoke

Putting these life elements together helps you be sure you have the correct ancestor.

As for my great-grandmother in eastern Europe, I still hope to find a record of her birth with her parents' names, even though the local church burned down. From interviews with my aunts Olga and Gussie, I know she was married three times and the third husband's name was Julius Draeger. By placing queries about him, I may find more information about my great-grandmother. The more I come to know about an ancestor, the people involved in her life, and the way she lived, the more likely I am to accurately move back another generation.

You Can Go Your Own Way

There is not a single, always correct, order in which to search different types of records. In other words, there is no one formula on how to do genealogical research. There are various types of records that are likely to contain the information you are seeking, but accessibility is often an issue. You must balance the probable content and accuracy of a record against the amount of time and effort it will take to find and search it.

Some of the records you find during the Research Phase were recorded by eyewitnesses at or near the time the event occurred. Others will be a great deal less reliable since they were recorded later or were based upon hearsay or inference. These types of records are still valuable as clues to find more accurate records. An example is using a census record to calculate someone's birth date, thus narrowing down the span of years in which to search for a birth certificate or christening record.

Be a Joiner

Join the genealogical and historical societies (referred to in Chapter 8) in the localities where your ancestors lived. Many genealogical societies publish transcriptions of local records in their periodicals. The publication of such resources has been greatly accelerated by the advent of personal computers.

Always look through society periodicals when they come in the mail. Once in a while, you'll get lucky. As I glanced at the East Tennessee Historical Society's *Echoes*, which had just arrived in the mail, I saw transcribed entries from a local physician's diary. This diary included James W. Monday's cause of death, exact death date, and the amount charged for the three days of care before his death. I knew from probate records that he had died early in 1858, but now I had exact information from a source I might never have thought to check—and certainly would have had difficulty accessing. As mentioned in Chapter 9, a locality search with PERSI is a good way to find such unique resources.

Check for indexes and research aids to original records in the following resources:

- All levels of libraries and archives in that area
- All levels of societies (genealogical and historical) in that locality
- The appropriate county and state GenWeb Project pages (accessible from the USGenWeb site at *www.usgenweb.org)*

Don't go out blindly to do research at libraries, archives, universities, and government agencies. Do your homework first on the Internet and in published information about those repositories. Save your money and eventually, when you are as prepared as you can be, take your trips to the places your ancestors lived and the localities where their records are kept.

Putting the Pieces Together

My father-in-law, Phil, hired several different researchers to find the ancestry of his grandfather George W. Roberts. Phil's grandparents were divorced, and he had never seen a picture of his mother as a child. When I married into the family, he turned this research project over to me.

Survey Phase. One of the first things I did was subscribe and place queries in the *Roberts Register*, a periodical about the surname Roberts. Eventually, I was contacted by Al Roberts, who had seen my query. He was also a grandson of George W. Roberts, but from his second marriage.

Research Phase. Al's branch of descendants had inherited the family photos—including a picture of Phil's mother and her sister at their father's knee. Al graciously allowed me to have copies made. (They made a great Christmas present for my father-in-law.)

Background Phase. I noticed the word LeRoy stamped on the front of one of the photos. I had traced George W. Roberts from Missouri to Wisconsin. In Wisconsin census records, his parents (Jeremiah and Harriet) were listed as born in New York. But where? I eventually learned that LeRoy is a town in Genesee County in the northwest corner of New York.

Survey Phase. At that time, there was no genealogical society in Genesee County, but there was a historical society. I wrote to that society, asking if I could put a query in their newsletter. They wrote back and suggested I send five dollars to the LeRoy town clerk for a copy of the Roberts probate file.

Research Phase. What I received from the clerk included complete birth dates and relationships for Jeremiah Roberts's parents and family. England was listed as the birth place for Jeremiah's parents (James and Agnes) and their four oldest children. I gleefully shared this with Al, who promptly went out and found a book of early alien registrations in the state of New York. This book listed the family as arriving in New York on 12 April 1800 from Lancashire, England.

Background Phase. I contacted the friend of a friend who specializes in British Isles research. He recommended that I check *Boyd's Marriage Index*. He cautioned that it was not complete for all marriages in all of England, but it was easy to use.

Research Phase. I was lucky and found an entry for the marriage of James Roberts to Agnes Lord (at about the right time) in Newchurch-in-Pendle of Whalley Parish in Lancashire, England. I knew the birth dates of the four oldest children from the probate records in LeRoy. Since they were all born before the family's arrival in New York, I checked the Family History Library in Salt Lake City, Utah, to see if they had a copy of the christening records for this parish in England, then searched their microfilm copy.

Evaluation Phase. I found the christenings of the four oldest children, confirming I had the right people and locality. I had managed to trace my husband's Roberts ancestry back two generations from Missouri to Wisconsin, then across three counties in the state of New York, and finally over the ocean to Lancashire, England.

As you see, there are no penalties for not finding your ancestors' information on the first try. You simply try again. Even the most fruitless searches teach you something—where the answers aren't. This helps you rethink your goals and brings you a step closer to realizing where your ancestors *were* listed in records. Often the Evaluation Phase (covered in the next chapter) is the key ingredient in turning perceived failures into stepping stones for success.

Chapter 11

Tallying the Score

If genealogy is like putting together a puzzle or playing a game, then the Evaluation Phase is where you tally the score. As with any game, a variety of rules affect the scoring.

A *source* is anything containing information about an ancestral family or family member. *Evidence* is the information the source contains. *Proof*, on the other hand, is a thought process by which you arrive at an assertion of fact. What genealogists do is assemble the best evidence available, in a sufficient quantity, for a thorough (and, one hopes, low-biased) analysis. Later, as more evidence comes to light, a genealogist must be prepared to reevaluate previous conclusions.

Is This the Right Person?

In the chapters leading up to this one, I introduced some of the mistakes commonly made when tracing your family tree. I explained the dangers of researching a common name, such as John Smith, or an unusual name that may be common in one county, such as Amon Gross or Isaac Lindsay. By identifying all the members in a family, you build a stronger case for identifying *your* ancestor and not someone else's.

One of my errors in evaluation resulted from an ambiguous census entry. I was looking in the 1870 U.S. census for my second great-grandparents, Gordon Mynatt Hill and Sarah Ann Wilson (see Figures 11.1 and 11.2). Sarah's father, Micajah Wilson, was also listed in this household. Directly below Micajah's entry was one for

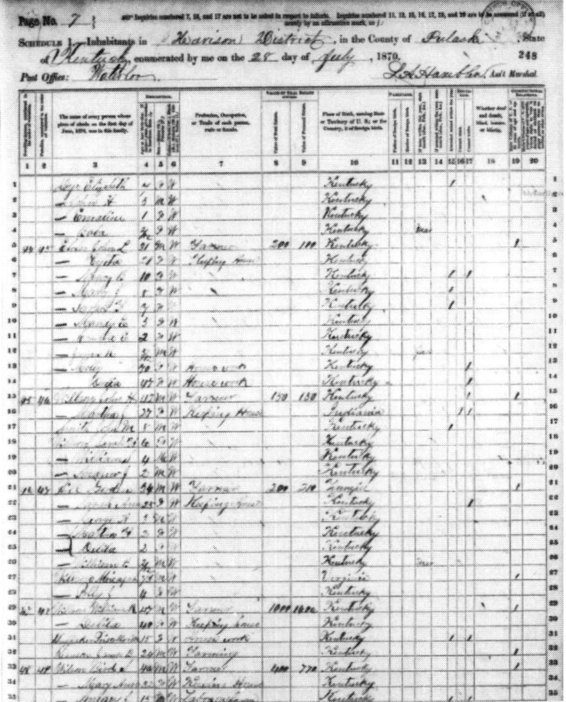

Figure 11.1 1870 U.S. census, Pulaski County, Kentucky, for Hill/Wilson family, from Ancestry.com online

a Polly J., age four. In front of her given name was a dash, which I assumed meant her surname was Wilson, like the entry immediately above hers.

For years I typed and distributed family group sheets for the Hill family without a mention of this Polly. It wasn't until I found my great-grandpa's memorandum book listing Pollie Jane Hill as his oldest sibling that I realized my error. I cannot get back all the incomplete family group sheets and GEDCOM files I shared over the years. Undoubtedly, those who find my earlier work will continue to leave poor Pollie Jane out of this family until they, too, discover this error.

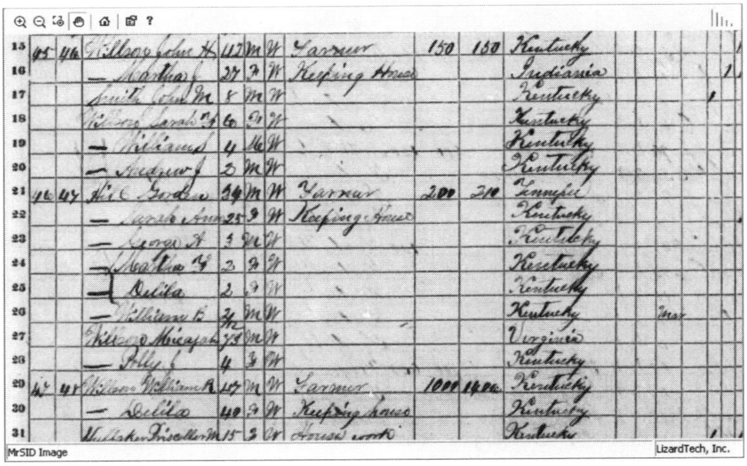

Figure 11.2 Closeup of 1870 U.S. census, Pulaski County, Kentucky, for Hill/Wilson family, from Ancestry.com online

Evaluating Compiled Sources

To err is human. This especially applies to compiled genealogies. By their very nature, they contain errors. The bigger the compilation, the more errors it is likely to contain. Genealogists, therefore, need rules by which compiled sources can be evaluated. If three or more of the following rules are broken, you are out of luck and need to do more research to ensure the correctness and completeness of the compiled information. I call it "Three Strikes and You're Out of Luck." More exacting researchers always seek original records to support or refute compiled sources.

Take the information you find in a compiled source and copy it onto a paper family group sheet (or type it into your computer program and print it out). This organizes the information so it is easy to see what you have—and what you don't. Next, apply the following seven questions to the information on that family group sheet:

1. What sources are quoted, if any?
2. What is the relationship of the compiler to that ancestral family?
3. Has standard usage been followed? Did the compiler enter names, dates, places, relationships, and sources in a consistent and clear fashion?
4. How complete are the fields in this record?
5. Is the family structure incomplete or inconsistent?
6. Are the migration patterns realistic?
7. Did the author have anything to gain by stretching or obscuring the truth?

I go over each family group sheet with a red pen, circling anything I have questions about. I put the form aside for a day or two, then repeat the process all over again. I repeat this red inking a third time before deciding what needs to be done next. It is amazing how much more I find to question each time I review the same family group sheet.

What Sources Were Quoted?

There are three specific questions to ask about the sources quoted in a compiled record. First, consider the number of sources. How many were quoted for the family as a whole? How many for each family member? A disproportion signals a strike against this compiled source. If at all possible, you want information about all the branches of a family—not just one person in a family.

The compiler of the Wilson/Dick family group sheet (see Figure 11.3) was a descendant of the wife's brother. Her best sources document only the wife in this family. You'll see why this was a dangerous thing as I apply the seven questions above to this compiled work.

Sheer numbers of sources don't in and of themselves make the compiled record accurate, but they do reflect a greater effort to complete the information. If no

FAMILY GROUP SHEET

HUSBAND	WILSON, Micajah		
Born	(55-1850) 1795	**Place**	Pulaski County, Kntc
Marr.	Abt 1825	**Place**	of Pulaski County, Kntc
Died		**Place**	
Bur.		**Place**	
Husband's Father		**Husband's Mother**	
Husband's Other Wives			
WIFE	DICK, Nancy		
Born	8 June 1800	**Place**	Chester County, S-Cr
Died		**Place**	
Bur.		**Place**	
Wife's Father	DICK, John	**Wife's Mother**	WYLIE, Margaret
Wife's Other Husbands			

SEX	CHILDREN	WHEN BORN	WHERE BORN County, State		DATE OF MARRIAGE To Whom	WHEN DIED
1.M	WILSON, John	(24-1850) 1826	Plsk	Kntc		
2. M	WILSON, Samuel	(16-1850) 1834	"	"		
3.M	WILSON, Turner	(14-1850) 1836	"	"		
4. F	WILSON, Margaret	(13-1850) 1837	"	"		
5. F	WILSON, Elizabeth	(11-1850) 1839	"	"		
6.F	WILSON, Sarah	(5-1850) 1845	"	"		
7.M	WILSON, Henry	(3-1859) 1847	"	"		

Sources of Information	Other Marriages	Necessary Explanations
1. Census Oulaski Co., Kntc. 1840, 1850, 1870. 2. "The Roy Family of Virginia & Kentucky" by Nancy Reba Roy (GS #929.273, R812r) 3. "Annals of Platte Co., Mssr"(GS #977.8135, H2p) 4. Pension rec of Wife's parents, Gen Serv ADmin, National Arch & Rec Serv		

Figure 11.3 Old Wilson/Dick family group sheet

sources are quoted or only other compiled sources are quoted, then the reliability of that compiled record is much lower.

The second question to ask is, Did all the quoted sources come from the same original source? If you used a letter from Barbara Renick, a family group sheet found at the Pulaski County Historical Society prepared by Barbara Renick, and a family group sheet prepared by Jane Doe quoting Barbara Renick as her source, it looks like you have lots of sources—until you stop and realize it all comes from Barbara Renick (and are all compiled sources to boot).

The last source question is about the quality of the sources quoted in that compilation. If they were original sources, like a pension application, then you need to know if they were created by an eyewitness who recorded the information soon after the event occurred. Or was it created years later by someone who was not an eyewitness? These two extremes create a sliding scale on which you judge their quality. (See the "Evaluating Original Records" section later in this chapter.)

Your evaluation of a source's quality depends on how directly it pertains to that individual or family. On the Wilson/Dick family group sheet, a Revolutionary War Widow's Pension Application is quoted. This sounds like a good source—until you realize it was not made by Micajah Wilson or his wife, Nancy Dick. The application was made by the wife's mother. When I obtained copies of the original from the National Archives, I found it contained only a birth date for Nancy and nothing about Nancy's husband or children. It is a good source for Nancy's parental family (Dick/Wylie), but an incomplete one for the Wilson/Dick family.

The old-style paper family group sheets had only a small box with space for just a brief listing of the sources consulted. An unintentional misrepresentation, like the one that occurred with Nancy's mother's pension application, was therefore common in the typewriter era of genealogy. Few beginning genealogists took the time to use superscripted numbers to tie their sources to the details they represented. With computers and modern genealogy programs, it is easy to attach as many source citations and images as you have to each detail.

How Is the Compiler Related?

It is not always true that the closer the compiler is related to the ancestral family, the harder she works to make an accurate record—but this is most often the case. Diagram the relationship of the compiler to the family recorded in the source. Notice the number of generations separating them, the number of removes separating them, or the lack of a blood relationship between them (if they are related only by marriage). The left part of Figure 11.4 diagrams my relationship to the Wilson/Dick family. The right part of that figure diagrams the relationship of the Wilson/Dick family group sheet compiler to that family. In general, the greater the separation, the more chances there are for assumptions and errors to creep into the work. In this case, even though more generations separate me from that family, my relationship is direct while the family group sheet compiler's relationship is indirect.

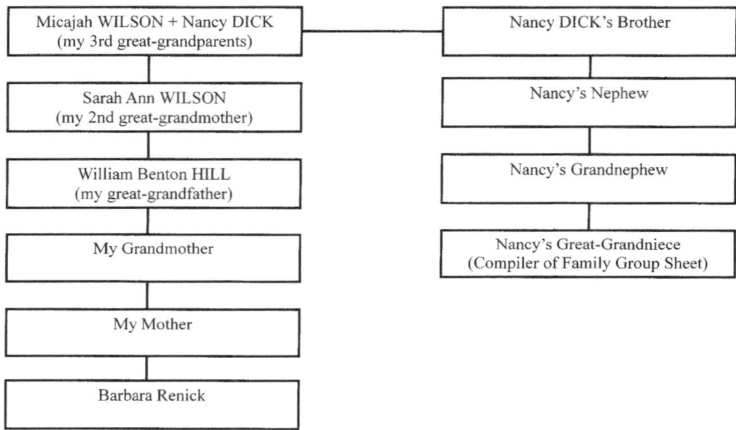

Figure 11.4 *Left:* Diagram of my relationship to the Wilson/Dick family. *Right:* Diagram of compiler's relationship to the Wilson/Dick family.

When some people begin tracing their family trees, they don't see a need to record their sources. They blithely add anything they find to the family tree, creating more of a fairy tale than a pedigree. When they encounter conflicting information—as they will sooner or later—they become frustrated. They have no way to evaluate which piece of information is more accurate. A feeling of close kinship often motivates a researcher to build his family tree on a firmer foundation by quoting his sources and evaluating each piece of information in each source he finds.

Has Standard Usage Been Followed?

A genealogist who consistently follows the rules of standard usage for recording names, dates, places, relationships, and sources has obviously had some training. Such training helps you avoid the common pitfalls of compiling a family tree.

The standards for recording genealogical information have changed over the years.

Watch out for the older system of removing the vowels in place names, like Kntcky for Kentucky. Another abbreviation system used the first four letters of the state name followed by a period, like Tenn. for Tennessee. We see IA as the abbreviation for Iowa, but many of our ancestors used it to refer to Indiana. Be extra cautious when working with abbreviations.

Remember the story of the family group sheet with Mary Unk? The use of abbreviations (including using Unk. for the word *Unknown*) is dangerous. I had to remove all the Unknowns I typed into my early computer files. Modern genealogy programs give you an option to specify that an ancestor's name is unknown.

Common names, or names that are common in just one area, also raise a red flag of caution simply because it is too easy to claim the wrong person as one's ancestor. I want to see specific proof that the Mary Jones born in one state is really the one who married and had children in another state. I watch out for her family, friends, and associates in the records I search. Some of the same people living in Mary Jones's birthplace should also be associated with her in the places where she married and had children. People rarely dropped all family connections and moved elsewhere (unless they were fleeing for a reason like avoiding legal punishment, a war, social stigma, or a feud). If they did, they usually reestablished those connections again later in life.

Beware of dates entered as all numbers. They lead to confusion and mistakes (as explained in Chapter 5). Exact dates are usually more accurate than calculated dates, but not always. For example, I have only one source with a full birth date for my ancestor William Lindsay. This full date came from a regional history book. Even though this compiled source directly states he was born on 4 July 1762, it seems too early when compared to all my other indirect evidence (evidence from which his age can be implied, but is not directly stated). I consider this full date to be wrong. See Figure 11.5 for my analysis of William Lindsay's birth date.

If He Was Born . . .	4 July 1762	About 1779
First appears in 1800 tax list in Carter Co., TN	age 38	age 21
1830 U.S. Census age 50 to 60		born 1770—1780
1840 U.S. Census age 60 to 70		born 1770—1780
First child born in 1806	age 44	age 27
Last child born in 1829	age 67	age 50
Attained rank of Major by 1819	age 57	age 40
Died in 1848	age 86	age 69

Figure 11.5 My analysis of William Lindsay's birth date

Calculated dates are usually more accurate than approximated dates, but not always. If the birth date is calculated from just one census record, you may have a problem. Ages, as listed in census records, tend to experience an accordion effect. They are most accurate for young children, tend to lengthen in early adulthood, shorten in midlife, and lengthen again in a person's later years. Figure 11.6 shows an example of this with my third great-grandmother, Elizabeth Noland.

Source	Age	Calculated Date
Marriage record 31 April 1829 (date as recorded)	15 to 20	1809/1814
1830 U.S. census with one child age 0 to 5	15 to 20	1810/1815
1850 U.S. census	38	1811/1812
1870 U.S. census	60	1809/1810
1880 U.S. census	78	1801/1802
1900 U.S. census	100	May 1800
Gravestone		May 1804

Note: She and her husband have not been found in the 1840 or 1860 U.S. censuses.

Figure 11.6 My analysis of Elizabeth Noland's birth date

On the Wilson/Dick family group sheet (Figure 11.3), the husband's birth date is calculated as being 1795 (taken from his age in the 1850 U.S. census). This calculated date was only one year off (he was actually born 24 June 1796). His approximated marriage date of 1825 was probably based on the age of the oldest child in that family's census enumeration. Further research revealed the date was off by four years. This approximation of the marriage date contributed to the two oldest children being missed—children who were already married and on their own by 1850.

Places can also be approximated—based on a place of residence when a specific life event occurred. This is usually designated by the use of angle brackets around the place name, as in <Pulaski County, Kentucky>. Another way to designate an approximated place is by putting the word *of* in front of the name of the place, as in "Of Pulaski County, Kentucky." The use of a question mark, as in "Pulaski County, Kentucky?" is a third method of showing uncertainty.

It is better to approximate dates and places than to leave those fields blank—so long as you clearly designate them as approximated. A family group sheet for a Micajah Wilson with no dates and places isn't much help when evaluating who goes where on your family tree. One for "Micajah Wilson, born about 1795, <Pulaski County, Kentucky>" would be much more helpful, if it weren't for some obvious errors in this birth information.

On the family group sheet in Figure 11.3, Micajah Wilson's birthplace is an obvious mistake because that county wasn't formed until 1798—several years after his birth. If it didn't exist when he was born, it couldn't have created any records about his birth. If you do much research in a county, you really need to know when it was created.

Micajah's birth place is listed as if the compiler had definite proof he was born in Pulaski County, Kentucky. The compiler used neither angle brackets nor the word *of*

Finding the Creation Story for Your States and Counties

It is important to know the creation story for your ancestor's states and counties of residence. Many genealogically significant records were kept at those jurisdictional levels. You need to learn when the county was formed, the geopolitical unit(s) it was formed from, and when the various types of county records were kept. Such a study is basic to the Background Phase of research in that area and time period.

The first place most genealogists turn for such information is *The Handy Book for Genealogists*, tenth edition (Logan, Utah: Everton Publishers, 2002). This book has been a mainstay for genealogists for longer than I've been doing genealogy. Actually, the first edition was published in 1947 (according to the foreword in the ninth edition).

One of the many things this book does for genealogists is to give a brief history of each county in each state, including when it was formed, its parent counties, the address and telephone number for the county offices, and the location of that county on the included state map. Also included is a brief summary of the genealogically significant records that county has and the time periods they cover. *The Handy Book* lists even more types of information for each state and includes information about counties that no longer exist in each state.

Genealogists with Internet connections have even more resources at their fingertips for information about counties and states. My two favorite resources have been mentioned in previous chapters: state library and archives Web sites, and the state and county levels of the USGenWeb Project.

with the place name. No question mark is used. Despite the positive way the birth place was stated, I had doubts about its accuracy—especially since that birthplace didn't exist in 1795.

When I evaluated the sources used to compile this family group sheet, I noticed Micajah's age and place of birth had not been compared in all the census enumerations done during his lifetime. I did my own comparison and found that half the censuses listed his birth place as Kentucky, the other half as Virginia.

I next searched through tax lists in Pulaski County, Kentucky, which made it clear Micajah's family first paid tax there in 1800, but not in 1799. This focused my next Survey and Research Phases on Virginia. With a bit more work, I was able to determine that Micajah was probably born in the Bent Mountain community of Montgomery County, Virginia, where his family was living in 1796.

Are the Fields Complete?

On the Wilson/Dick family group sheet, no death data is listed for any member of the family. No marriage information is listed for any of the children. Too many incomplete or empty fields of information on a family group sheet are an obvious strike against its probable accuracy and completeness. It shows that the compiler did not take the time to locate all the major identifying events for family members.

A distinct disadvantage to the old-style paper family group sheets is that they lack spaces for the children's marriage places. Knowing the children's marriage places provides rich ground for hunting descendants. It is a tragedy that these marriage places can be so hard to find today, when the compiler quite possibly knew those details and more.

Is the Family Structure Incomplete or Inconsistent?

When I look at the members of a family, as reported in a compiled source, I look for gaps in the children's ages. It was common for a married woman to bear a child every two or three years for twenty to thirty years after her marriage. If there are gaps in the children's ages, consider why. Was the husband away at war or prospecting out West? Is there a child who died young but is not yet identified?

The Wilson/Dick family group sheet shows obvious gaps in the children's ages. I suspect that more than one child died young, never living long enough to be enumerated with the family in a census. This is a good reason to search other types of records, not just census records. As mentioned previously, I identified the two oldest sons from Micajah's Civil War Dependent Father's Pension Application and the oldest son's probate records. He and his wife had no children, so their estate was divided between his surviving siblings and hers. The more types of sources you use, the more likely you are to fill in gaps in the family's structure.

I still have quite a few gaps in this family to fill. I sure wish I could find a family record passed down through the generations. That is the most likely source to fill in these gaps for a family living in that locality and time.

I arrived at that conclusion because I know Kentucky tried several times during the nineteenth century to initiate a state-wide registration of births and deaths, but was unsuccessful until 1911. Only a few years of these nineteenth-century vital registrations exist for Pulaski County, and those are probably not complete. No birth registrations exist for the years when Micajah's children would have been born, so that eliminates civil records. The family was probably Baptist since Micajah's brother was a pioneer Baptist minister in Missouri and Micajah's son was the Baptist minister who married sister Sarah Ann Wilson to Gordon Mynatt Hill. Baptists don't do infant christenings, so that most likely rules out a church record. This leaves a family record as the next most likely source of enlightenment on the structure of this family.

When evaluating compiled sources, consider the ages of the spouses

- At the time of their marriage
- When their first child was born
- When their last child was born
- At their deaths

You'd be amazed how many family group sheets claim children were born to women who were in their sixties and seventies. While this might occur in a woman's forties, it is rare for a child to be born to a woman in her fifties, much less in her sixties and seventies.

Check the number of years between the couple's marriage date and the birth of their first child. When Micajah's actual marriage date was identified as 1821, I realized there was a six-year gap between his marriage and the birth of his first child—as listed on that compiled family group sheet. Actually, there was plenty of room for the two older sons who had been missed.

Look at the birth dates of all the children in a family. Micajah's two oldest sons had gravestones listing their birth dates as 26 January 1822 and 22 August 1822—just seven months apart. In my computer files, I list the dates from their gravestones with the notation that they are impossibly close together. Other evidence indicates the second son's birth was probably in 1824 (even though his descendants adamantly insist his gravestone is correct).

Occasionally, dates that seem a bit stretched are proven to be accurate. Gordon Mynatt Hill's mother died during the 1860s. Gordon's father, Foster Hill, was sixty-one years old in 1871 when he married Matilda Loid, who was twenty-one. Foster fathered at least three more children before he died. While there is a large difference in Foster and Matilda's ages on their county marriage record, those ages are supported by all my other evidence.

As a genealogist, I dream of finding descendants from his second marriage. They may have Foster's family Bible containing his parents' names (something I haven't yet found). In return, I have a picture of Foster and Matilda on their wedding day that I would love to share with them.

If you find a really large family with more children than seems probable, consider whether two families were combined. Many women died in childbirth, and the husband, with small children to care for, usually remarried soon afterward. Hints that two families may have been inadvertently combined include

- A noticeable difference in the spouses' ages
- Gaps in the children's ages
- Step-children with a different surname

In addition, conflicting information about the following facts may indicate that more than one marriage was involved:

- Spouse's name (if a man had two different wives, it's not surprising to find records mentioning two different names)
- Couple's marriage date (here again, two different marriages mean two different dates, sometimes just a few years apart if the wife died in childbirth)
- Spouse's death information (more of the same)

Another important clue is who is buried next to whom. For example, Edmond (the bigamist) wasn't buried next to his brother Isaac. That seems a little unusual until you learn that Edmond and Isaac's wives were sisters. Buried next to Isaac were his wife Martha and her sister Mary (Edmond's first wife). Edmond and his second wife were buried at the opposite end of that cemetery. Small things like who is buried next to whom can be big clues.

Check every source, compiled or original, for inconsistencies in recorded information. Most genealogy programs generate Possible Record Problem reports, listing a wide variety of possible errors. You'd be amazed at the number of compiled records that show an individual died before he was born. Watch for typographical errors giving the wrong century (typing 1980 instead of 1880) or transposing numbers (typing 1745 rather than 1754).

Are the Migration Patterns Realistic?

Look at all the event places in the compiled record. Is the pattern of places a typical one? Were all the children born in Tennessee, except for one born in Massachusetts? This didn't happen very often; it is more often a case of someone grabbing a name from somewhere else without proof.

Each state had its own unique settlement and migration patterns. These shifted with time and technology (as mentioned in Chapter 8). The only way you'll know whether a family's migration pattern was typical is if you do a thorough job during the Background Phase (including asking experts).

In an online database called the Ancestral File, the computer merges what it recognizes as duplicate records. Back in 1979, I submitted to this database a record of my ancestor, James Wylie, who died in 1806 in South Carolina and had a wife named Sarah. Unfortunately, that same year in New York another James Wylie died who also had a wife named Sarah. The computer read these as the same man and merged the two families.

I contacted the submitter of the information on the James Wylie from New York. She and I compared notes and quickly concluded that these were two different families that had been merged in error.

Genealogists sometimes make the same mistake. They think they have found the last will and testament of their South Carolina ancestor—way up in New York. While this does occasionally occur, more often it means the researcher grabbed someone else's ancestor by the same name. Such unusual combinations of event places and migratory patterns need to be researched further.

Was There a Reason to Obscure the Truth?

Would the author benefit monetarily by claiming descent from a particular ancestor? Was she trying to join a prestigious lineage society? Is there is a famous person being claimed as an ancestor? Are there historical inconsistencies on the compiled family tree? Anyone who claims to be descended from President George Washington has a problem. President Washington had no (historically documented) children of his own. It is only human to want to be related to a famous (or sometimes infamous) person. Researchers may not be as careful or as critical as they should be in these circumstances.

When family members are reluctant to talk about a particular member of the family, there is usually a good reason. Perhaps that person served on the wrong side of a war or spent time in prison. Dates in family Bibles may have been stretched or left out if there was an irregularity. For example, the marriage date may not be recorded if the first child was born too soon.

Be aware of past stigmas from a mixing of races, minority religions, illegitimacy, illegal immigration, children born with birth defects, persons with certain medical conditions, or if a family member practiced what was considered an undesirable occupation (like being an executioner). While you may be avidly interested in the truth, others may be trying to hide what they consider embarrassing situations. Be sensitive to their feelings. Besides, few events occur in such secrecy that no one else knows. You can usually find someone willing to talk about members of your ancestral families.

Evaluating Original Records

Even original records can contain errors. Evidence should always be weighed as it would be in a court case. This is what makes citing your sources so vitally important.

Today's genealogical standard is to document in each ancestral family

- Every name
- Every date
- Every place
- Every relationship

In the past, genealogists referred to sources as being either primary or secondary. A primary source was one recorded by an eyewitness close to when the event occurred. A secondary source was recorded at a later time by someone who may not have been an eyewitness. But problems occurred with the use of these terms. A death certificate, for example, would be a primary source for the death information, but not for the birth. Therefore, the basic rule for judging original records is to never take them at face value and to consider separately each piece of information they contain.

If at all possible, go back and look at the original version of anything you find. If you use a published book of extracted records, try to find the original to see if it was extracted correctly and if the original source contains more clues.

Test for Credibility

There is a series of questions that work as a credibility test for original records. These questions help you determine the authenticity, accuracy, and probable completeness of any piece of information found in an original source. As mentioned above, credibility is not applied to a document as a whole, but to each detail on a case-by-case basis.

The first question to ask is if that source was recorded by an eyewitness—a court clerk, a clergyman, or a close relative. These are generally the people who would have been involved in your ancestor's major life events. They are also the ones who usually created the original records (civil, church, and family sources). When was it recorded? Was this close to when the event occurred or years later when someone's memory may have faded?

How were the facts recorded? Under what conditions was the record created? Was it testimony given under oath or written by an eyewitness in a diary? In a court of law, both are considered reliable sources. On the other hand, a statement made in an application for admission to a lineage or patriotic society has less credibility.

What details best describe that source? Was the handwriting sloppy? Did you find a copy of the original record or the original? Has the copy been altered in any way? An example is a county clerk typing a copy of your ancestor's original marriage record, rather than photocopying the original.

Can you identify your ancestor's handwriting? I compared copies of W.B. Hill's handwriting to the writing in his memorandum book to assure myself that the names, dates, and places were written by him. If you are looking at a will recorded in chancery court records, you are not looking at the original. The handwriting is that of the court clerk or his assistant. Wills were transcribed into the court records during probate, and transcription errors sometimes crept in.

Records Have Histories

Is the record historically consistent with similar records from that location and time? An example is finding a purportedly original marriage certificate with the blank fields typed in—before the invention of the typewriter. This could be a later clerk's copy of an original record, but not the original itself. Other examples are an early nineteenth-century Bible with family events recorded in ball-point pen and an 1803 divorce record purportedly granted by a county in South Carolina. At that time, South Carolina was divided into districts (not counties) and divorces were granted by the state legislature. Putting effort into your Background Phase helps you spot such inconsistencies.

Do you know the history of the record you have found? How many metamorphoses has it undergone? For example, are you looking at an original will or at a copy of a copy? Computer databases, searchable on CDs or online, are never original. They have gone through several stages to get from their original form to this electronic format. Consequently, they make great research tools, but are never considered original source material.

What were the biases of the original recorder? Or did the recorder get the information from someone who was biased? Was the recorder or the person supplying the "facts" prejudiced about the situation or the persons involved? For example, one might report that a relative was institutionalized when, in fact, he was in prison.

You have to know the historical, religious, and cultural background of that area and time to understand the strengths and weaknesses of its original records. Again, a thorough Background Phase helps you analyze what you find.

Chapter 12
Publish . . . or Perish the Thought

A family tree doesn't come together instantly. It takes time, cash, and work to put together the pieces. The more widely you disseminate your findings, the more likely it is that at least one copy will survive. In the meantime, chances are greater that someone with corrections or additions will see your work. The more formats in which you publish (books, newsletters, online databases, and Web pages), the broader your audience.

The objective of the Preservation Phase is to preserve and disseminate your findings, conclusions, and documentation—in other words, all the information you compile about your family tree. The technological wonders of the twenty-first century make this phase easy and relatively inexpensive. There is no excuse not to do it.

A Sad but Common Story

I had a friend who worked for a bank. One day, she called me and said her department was handling the estate of an elderly woman who had died and left everything to two grand-nephews living in the Midwest. As my friend was helping them go through the woman's effects, they came across a dozen large boxes filled with handwritten genealogical research. The heirs were not interested in taking these boxes of genealogy back with them.

My friend was aghast at the thought of so many years of research being tossed out.

She told them she knew a professional genealogist who might know what to do with this genealogy. The heirs carelessly agreed.

I tried to contact them the next morning, but they were no longer in California. When I finally managed to reach them, I learned that I was too late. They had thrown all the boxes into a dumpster before flying home.

If that material had been entered into a genealogy program and backed up onto CDs or if the woman had published it in a book, her nephews might have been motivated to keep it. It certainly would have been easier for me to find it a home. In my own will, I have provided for the disposition of my genealogy collection, along with a bequest to cover its shipping and processing.

More than a decade ago, I created several family history manuscripts (unpublished books). I used my genealogy program to print out everything I had for several of my surnames. I placed copies in repositories in the localities where those ancestors lived. I also donated copies to the Family History Library in Salt Lake City, Utah, where they were microfilmed for circulation to Family History Centers.

These are not perfect works. In fact, the ones from my first decade of research are somewhat embarrassing. They contain some errors (which I've since corrected) and my prolific (but messy) source notes. These manuscripts do, however, provide a great deal of help for anyone researching those names in those areas. If they contact me, I have even more to share with them now. I hope to do similar books for the rest of my surnames. This time, I'll include images of my unique, one-of-a-kind sources (now that I have learned to use a digital camera and scanner).

Don't wait until you have perfected your genealogy to publish. It will never happen. Publish now and preserve what you have done—even if it is just giving handwritten family group sheets to the local genealogical society in the areas where your ancestors lived.

Make More Than One Copy

I rarely teach a genealogy class without mentioning the importance of backups. One of my students is an engineer and works with computers for a living. He spent eighteen months putting all his genealogical information into his home computer. One day, he admitted to me that his computer's hard drive had crashed. Because he hadn't made backups, he lost all his computer files.

I asked if he had submitted his information to the Pedigree Resource File (published on CDs). If so, he could recover all his data, notes, and sources without having to retype them. He sheepishly admitted he had not, but said he would do so as soon as he reentered his information from his paper printouts. (At least he had those!)

Here is how to submit your genealogy to the Pedigree Resource File:

1. Use your computer and genealogy program to create a GEDCOM file of the information from one or more branches of your family tree. (Remember to include your notes and sources. You might be the one who needs them in the future.)
2. Jot down the name you gave the GEDCOM file you just created and where your genealogy program stored that file on your computer.
3. Go online to *www.familysearch.org*.
4. Click on the Share tab.
5. Click on the Share My Genealogy subtab.
6. Sign in if you have previously registered, or click on I Need to Register in the options bar on the left side of your screen.
7. Complete the free registration process (your information is kept strictly confidential).
8. Read the information provided by clicking on the items in the options bar on the left side of your screen:
   a. About Share My Genealogy
   b. How do I submit my genealogy?
   c. What will be done with my genealogy?
   d. I am ready to submit
   e. Check the status of a submission
9. Follow the outlined steps to send your GEDCOM file to be mastered onto CDs.

The master index to the Pedigree Resource File is published on CDs and is also available under the Search tab at the FamilySearch Internet site. This master index is updated regularly. Your submission is indexed in the next update and mastered onto a Pedigree Resource File CD that is sold for a nominal cost. A copy is also stored on a special CD in the LDS granite mountain vault.

To look at these Pedigree Resource File CDs (with all the notes and sources and information not included in the master index), check in your local genealogical society's collection or at your local LDS Family History Center. They often purchase copies for their patrons to use. The Pedigree Resource File CDs can be purchased (singly or in sets) online at FamilySearch Internet or by calling 800-537-5950.

Make Copies on More Than One Type of Disk/Disc

On the wall of my office hangs a cartoon of a female genealogist sitting at a computer with her hands thrown up screaming, "Eeek! Pacman is eating my genealogy!" It is there to remind me to back up what I have done.

Every time I make changes in my computer files, I back them up. This includes my genealogy databases, word processor files, and images. I use a revolving system to back up my daily work:

1. I have three CD-RW (rewritable) discs labeled X, Y, and Z.
2. Today I back up onto disc X.
3. Tomorrow I back up onto disc Y.
4. The third day I back up onto disc Z.
5. The fourth day I back up onto disc X again.

By using a revolving system, if anything gets scrambled (or infected with a computer virus), I have a previous version that (I hope) does not have a problem. I also print updated family group sheets and place them in the corresponding surname notebooks on my shelves.

When I have a very valuable resource, such as a copy of an 1855 photo of my third great-grandparents, I save the image on a CD-R (record once) disc. A CD-R disc can't be overwritten by mistake.

Periodically, I back up all my computers to an external hard disk drive. I store this removable drive in a heavy, metal safe. Yes, I admit to a certain amount of paranoia about having thirty years of research stored on a computer, but I am consulted all too often about how to recover work lost in a computer disaster.

Don't make copies of your genealogy files onto just floppy disks. Floppy disk drives can get out of alignment and make your disks unreadable. Nor should you back up onto just compact discs (CD-Rs or CD-RWs)—they do wear out eventually. Both these types of media can also be easily damaged if you leave them in your car on a hot day or someone accidentally steps on them. To minimize your risks, use more than one type of storage medium.

Free and low-cost storage sites are available on the Internet. This is a great way to back up your most important computer files, and it is the fastest and easiest way to share files that are too big to send as e-mail attachments.

Free and Low-Cost Storage Online

Yahoo! offers 30 MB of free storage in its Briefcase area. If you rent an additional 100 MB of space, you can mark your files for public access. This makes them easily accessible (at *briefcase.yahoo.com/yourusername*) to other genealogists and members of your family.

The Genealogy.com Web site gives genealogists free Web home pages. This space allows you to store and share GEDCOM files, photos, and word processor documents. To create your own genealogy home page on the Internet:

- Go online to *www.genealogy.com*.
- Click on the Community tab.
- Click on Create or Edit Your Home Page.
- Read the agreement and then click on Create Your Own FREE Home Page.

Make Copies in More Than One Format

At least once a year, I do a generic backup of my irreplaceable files—and not just my genealogy databases:

1. I make a generic GEDCOM file of each of my genealogy databases.
2. I save important e-mail messages as plain-text files. This is in addition to the paper printouts I have already made and filed in my correspondence hanging files.

3. I export a copy of my Web browser's bookmarks (or favorite places list) to a storage site on the Internet *(backflip.com)* and make a generic HTML backup, too.
4. I print my address book on paper and put it in a three-ring notebook for quick reference when my computer is turned off.
5. I save my research logs and other word-processor documents in a plain-text format.

In the future, I or one of my heirs can use any of a variety of programs to open these generic files. The last time I had my desktop computer upgraded, I forgot to back up my browser's Favorites list. I had to use my generic copy to restore my bookmarks to my new hard drive. In the last twenty years, I have been infected with computer viruses four times. So far, I haven't lost anything (other than my time)—thanks to my backups.

Store Your Copies in More Than One Location

My generic files are copied onto CD-R discs and sent to out-of-state relatives who store them for me. By saving my work in different locations with different formats, not only is my work extra safe, but I hope that one of my cousins, nieces, or nephews will someday pick up where I leave off. I have been contacted twice by cousins enquiring if I still had a copy of their GEDCOM files previously shared with me—one cousin's house flooded and another had a hard disk crash on his computer.

The more widely you disseminate your findings, the more likely it is that at least one copy will survive you. The more formats in which you publish your work, the broader the audience it will reach. These are important concepts to consider when looking for a final resting place for your research.

The LDS Church publishes a guide titled *Donations to the Family History Library.* It covers the types of materials the library accepts, what it does not accept, and where to submit them. View and print it online (from the Research Helps section under the Search tab at FamilySearch Internet) or order it from the Salt Lake Distribution Center at 800-537-5950.

Other types of repositories that accept genealogical materials include genealogical societies, historical societies, archives, and libraries. Check with the different levels or types of these repositories (city library versus university library, etc.), as mentioned in Chapter 9.

Repositories in the areas where your ancestors lived are more likely to accept your materials than are those in other areas—unless they have a special collection focused on something that pertains to your ancestor's life. For instance, if your ancestor was a steamship captain, his biographical and genealogical information might be of interest to the Steamship Historical Society of America Collection in the Langsdale Library at the University of Baltimore.

The Manuscript Repositories Section of the Society of American Archivists has a helpful brochure titled *A Guide to Donating Your Personal or Family Papers to a Repository* at its Web site *(www.archivists.org/catalog/donating-familyrecs.asp).*

Give Your Family Tree Longevity and Accessibility

Another way to preserve your genealogy is to submit your GEDCOM files to large, online databases. Some (like the Pedigree Resource File) maintain not only your data, but also your notes and source citations—if they are included in your submission. Through these sites, your data becomes accessible to researchers all over the world. Hundreds of thousands of people access online genealogy databases each day. The likelihood that some of those people are researching some of your ancestors is very high. One of my students found two thousand of her Teters in the index at Gene Stark's GENDEX Web site *(www.gendex.com)* and spent the next six months organizing and evaluating that information.

These online databases range from small and specialized to large and world-wide. They are compiled by individuals, organizations, and commercial enterprises, but even the commercial genealogy sites provide many free services. For example, the Ancestry.com site accepts GEDCOM files for inclusion in its Ancestry World Tree database. Searches of this database are always free, whereas you have to be a paid subscriber to see your search results in most of its other databases. Ancestry.com adds an average of three new databases each business day. Currently, more than one billion names can be searched on its Web site.

Other commercial database services include Genealogy.com, HeritageQuest.com, Everton.com, and MyTrees.com (a Kindred Konnections Web site). Cyndi's List has

Guidelines For Publishing Web Pages on the Internet

Recommended by the National Genealogical Society

Appreciating that publishing information through Internet Web sites and Web pages shares many similarities with print publishing, considerate family historians

- Apply a title identifying both the entire Web site and the particular group of related pages, similar to a book-and-chapter designation, placing it both at the top of each Web browser window using the <TITLE> HTML tag, and in the body of the document, on the opening home or title page, and on any index pages
- Explain the purposes and objectives of their Web sites, placing the explanation near the top of the title page or including a link from that page to a special page about the reason for the site
- Display a footer at the bottom of each Web page that contains the Web site title, page title, author's name, author's contact information, date of last revision, and a copyright statement
- Provide complete contact information, including at a minimum a name and e-mail address, and preferably some means for long-term contact, like a postal address
- Assist visitors by providing on each page navigational links that lead visitors to other important pages on the Web site, or return them to the home page
- Adhere to the NGS "Standards for Sharing Information with Others" (see page 177) regarding copyright, attribution, privacy, and the sharing of sensitive information
- Include unambiguous source citations for the research data provided on the site, and if not complete descriptions, offering full citations upon request
- Label photographic and scanned images within the graphic itself, with fuller explanation if required in text adjacent to the graphic
- Identify transcribed, extracted, or abstracted data as such, and provide appropriate source citations
- Include identifying dates and locations when providing information about specific surnames or individuals
- Respect the rights of others who do not wish information about themselves to be published, referenced, or linked on a Web site
- Provide Web site access to all potential visitors by avoiding enhanced technical capabilities that may not be available to all users, remembering that not all computers are created equal
- Avoid using features that distract from the productive use of the Web site, like ones that reduce legibility, strain the eyes, dazzle the vision, or otherwise detract from the visitor's ability to easily read, study, comprehend, or print the online publication
- Maintain their online publications at frequent intervals, changing the content to keep the information current, the links valid, and the Web site in good working order
- Preserve and archive for future researchers their online publications and communications that have lasting value, using both electronic and paper duplication

two categories with links to information about large genealogy databases:

- Databases—Lineage-Linked *(www.cyndislist.com/lin-linked.htm)*
- Databases—Searchable Online *(www.cyndislist.com/database.htm)*

Another way to preserve and disseminate your genealogy is to post your family tree on your own personal Web pages, then register your Web site with genealogy directories and popular search engines. Most genealogy programs can create Web pages about individuals, families, lines of ancestry, or lines of descent. (I find it trickier to upload these Web pages to rented Web space than it is to create them with genealogy software.)

The Winner and Still Champion

If I were to bet on which type of medium will still be easily readable one hundred years from now—a book, a floppy disk, or a microfilm—I'd bet on the book. Figure 12.1 shows some advantages and disadvantages of publishing a book. Good-quality, acid-free paper lasts a long time. Gordon Mynatt Hill's pension application was more than one hundred years old when I found it at the National Archives in Washington, D.C. Many books published more than two centuries ago are still readable.

One reason things printed two centuries ago last longer than things printed today is because our paper now has a higher acid and lower rag content. This means today's paper literally eats away at itself. When printing something you want to preserve, use acid-free paper and, if possible, a laser printer, which burns the ink onto the page. Typesetting is an even more durable (but more costly) form of printing.

Advantages	Disadvantages
Paper lasts a long time.	Although easy to create from a genealogy program, adding biographical material, images, and finishing the index takes time.
Can be read without help one hundred years from now.	Costs money to print and bind.
More readily accepted by repositories.	Need to register for copyright and ISBN.
Easier to store than handwritten files.	Takes up more storage space than electronic files.

Figure 12.1 Advantages and disadvantages of publishing a book

While a properly stored microfilm copy should still exist one hundred years from now, it takes special equipment to read it. As for floppy disks, how many of you still have computers that can read the old 5¼-inch floppies? While it takes time, work, and cash to publish a book, that is still the preferred way to preserve your genealogy.

A second reason books are the preferred method of preservation is that so many more institutions and individuals are willing to accept a copy of a book. Boxes of handwritten genealogy notes have a harder time finding a permanent home.

Publish a Newsletter

To reach family members who have not computerized, consider publishing a family newsletter. This lets you distribute family information in small, easy-to-digest bites with images of photos, gravestones, and documents. Include personal histories, family histories, and transcripts of your interviews. Newsletters motivate other family members to share. Personal computers make this an easy and fun method of preservation.

Your newsletter can be about

- Just your family
    - Immediate family (your brothers' and sisters' families)
    - Extended family (your living ancestors plus aunts, uncles, cousins, nieces, and nephews)
- All the ancestors or descendants (or both) of one of your ancestors
- All the ancestors or descendants (or both) of a particular ancestral couple
- Just your immigrant ancestor and his or her immediate family
- A particular surname
    - Just one surname with all its spelling variations in all localities
    - Just one surname with all its spelling variations in just one locality

Cautionary Note

Avoid publishing information about living people in material that goes out to the general public. If you do publish names, dates, places, or relationships about living family members (in a family newsletter, for instance), be sure you have their permission to do so. As mentioned previously in this book, privacy and security issues are a major concern these days.

When creating a generic GEDCOM file or Web page on your computer, be sure to select the option to exclude information about living people. See the NGS Genealogical Standards Committee's recommendations in its "Standards for Sharing Information with Others" (page 177 and *www.ngsgenealogy.org/comstandsharing.htm).*

Other Items for Sharing

Don't forget to share copies of family photos and digital images of family mementos—objects significant to your family's history, such as Grandpa's straight-edge razor or Grandma's handmade quilt. These types of artifacts can be in only one place at a time, so at least take pictures of them to share.

Preserving Photos

There are several things to keep in mind when handling irreplaceable photos, documents, and memorabilia. Never deface an original photograph or document by writing on it. Make a copy and write only on your copy.

If you feel you must write identifying information on a photo, do so on the back. Gently write on the edges using a soft number-two lead pencil. Ballpoint pens leave a furrow that may break the emulsion on the picture side, causing the photo to deteriorate faster. In addition, most inks eat away at your photo.

Pencil stays legible far longer and under more adverse conditions than ink. If your photo has a slick finish, you may not be able to write on it with pencil. In that case, look for an archival quality fiber-tipped pen. Do not write in areas where important details are located on the picture side of the photo.

I have done research in the photographic collection of the National Archives in Washington, D.C. They store their historic photographs in acid-free containers. Researchers use special cotton gloves to handle them because the acids in skin are hazardous to these irreplaceable items.

Take care how you handle, display, and store your family's treasures. Preserve your treasures from bugs, careless handling, fire, heat, humidity, sources of light, and water damage.

Scrapbooks are a great way to get people interested in your ancestors, but they are not the best way to preserve your family tree. Scrapbooks are not easily copied and, if you don't buy archival supplies, can eat up your photos and records almost as fast as a computer disaster. I have seen archivists, whose jobs center around preservation, cringe when scrapbooks are mentioned. With the advanced capabilities of computers and digital imaging, preserve copies of your family photos and artifacts in your newsletters and books.

Bev Kirschner Braun wrote an article called "Play It Safe." You'll find it at the *Family Tree Magazine* Web site *(www.familytreemagazine.com/articles/apr02/archival.html).* In the article, Braun lists important considerations when choosing materials for storing your priceless family treasures. (*Family Tree Magazine* is an excellent genealogy magazine, and its Web site hosts one of the few genealogy meta-search engines on the Internet.)

Pass on memories of loved ones to future generations, and preserve the legacy that is your family. Make the time—or your thoughts and your ancestors' thoughts may perish.

Standards for Sharing Information with Others

Recommended by the National Genealogical Society

Conscious of the fact that sharing information or data with others, whether through speech, documents or electronic media, is essential to family history research and that it needs continuing support and encouragement, responsible family historians consistently

- Respect the restrictions on sharing information that arise from the rights of another as an author, originator or compiler; as a living private person; or as a party to a mutual agreement
- Observe meticulously the legal rights of copyright owners, copying or distributing any part of their works only with their permission, or to the limited extent specifically allowed under the law's "fair use" exceptions
- Identify the sources for all ideas, information, and data from others, and the form in which they were received, recognizing that the unattributed use of another's intellectual work is plagiarism
- Respect the authorship rights of senders of letters, electronic mail, and data files, forwarding or disseminating them further only with the sender's permission
- Inform people who provide information about their families as to the ways it may be used, observing any conditions they impose and respecting any reservations they may express regarding the use of particular items
- Require some evidence of consent before assuming that living people are agreeable to further sharing of information about themselves
- Convey personal identifying information about living people—like age, home address, occupation, or activities—only in ways that those concerned have expressly agreed to
- Recognize that legal rights of privacy may limit the extent to which information from publicly available sources may be further used, disseminated, or published
- Communicate no information to others that is known to be false, or without making reasonable efforts to determine its truth, particularly information that may be derogatory
- Are sensitive to the hurt that revelations of criminal, immoral, bizarre, or irresponsible behavior may bring to family members

CHAPTER 13

Overcoming Culture Shock

SOONER OR LATER, MOST GENEALOGISTS TRACE THEIR FAMILY TREES back to an immigrant ancestor—the one who came to America. When this happens, the best advice I can give you is to find every single piece of information you can here in America before even thinking about researching over there—wherever "there" might be. Here's why:

- Records here tend to be in English, whereas records "over there" tend to be in a language you may not read fluently, if at all. Even if you speak that foreign language, the records may be written in an archaic form of handwriting using archaic terminology.
- Depending on your ancestor's age upon arrival in the United States, and how long he lived afterward, he may have generated more records here than in his country of origin. Records here are often more accessible than those in a foreign country—unless they were microfilmed and are, therefore, available through Family History Centers. Of course, the records on microfilm will still be in their language of origin.
- Family sources, both here and overseas, often play a key role in solving your questions about your immigrant ancestor. Start by interviewing as many of your relatives as you can find here to learn about those living overseas.

Don't assume all your answers are in foreign records. My paternal grandmother was born in 1873 in Russia. She came to America in 1907, but she already had a brother and uncle living in Wisconsin. Grandmother died in 1952, having spent the greater part of her life here in America.

My father's Wisconsin cousins were the ones who actually began compiling information about our family tree. When I started doing genealogy, I was very happy to learn that those cousins existed. They had answers to many of the questions I was researching—and they lived right here in the United States. Two of those cousins had already made a trip behind the Iron Curtain and reestablished contact with some of the European branches of our family. As a college student, that was something I couldn't afford to do.

If I had had to rely solely on the written records generated by my immigrant grandparents, I would probably still be searching for their marriage record. I have not found any American records mentioning where they were married. It was Grand-uncle Henry's memory of his sister's marriage that made finding my grandparents' marriage record possible.

If your immigrant ancestor didn't leave any records telling you where she came from, maybe one of her relatives did. If you can't find any relatives in the United States, try investigating the origins of your ancestor's friends and associates. Few people move to a place where they know no one.

The More Things Are Different, the More They're the Same

The good news is that all the basic principles covered in this book still apply to identifying and tracing the origins of your immigrant ancestor in another country. You'll still be using, and reusing, the same five phases: Background, Survey, Research, Evaluation, and Preservation. The bad news is that making a correct connection overseas is often a major challenge.

Correctly connecting your John Smith who married here in the United States to the Johann Schmidt born in another country is often a bigger hurdle than connecting the John Smith who married in Tennessee to the one born in North Carolina. To meet this bigger challenge, you need to add a few more search strategies, look in a few more types of records, and be downright critical of what you find. The Evaluation Phase is especially important in foreign research. You don't want to be the genealogist who spends years researching the wrong Johann Schmidt.

In foreign countries, you'll encounter the same types of records you find here in the

United States—compiled, original, and those derived from the original (transcribed, extracted, abstracted, or indexed). Original records still fall into the same categories (civil, church, family, etc.), though you may encounter different types of records in these categories.

Bastardy bonds are a good example. In centuries past, a woman who had a child out of wedlock was brought before a civil or church official and required to identify the father of her child (as in *The Scarlet Letter* by Nathaniel Hawthorne). Whoever was judged to be the father was required to post a bond guaranteeing that he would see that the child never became a financial burden on the community.

In England, the Anglican Church kept these records in its local parish Poor Law Records until the early 1800s, when the government took over this function. The bastardy bond for an illegitimate birth in North Carolina in 1800 was posted in the local county court. This is an example of different jurisdictions (church versus civil) keeping the same records in different localities.

The period covered by a particular type of record varies from country to country. For example, nationwide registration of births in England started in 1837, but in some parts of Germany, civil registration began as early as 1803.

As mentioned in previous chapters, Research Guidance (under the Search tab at

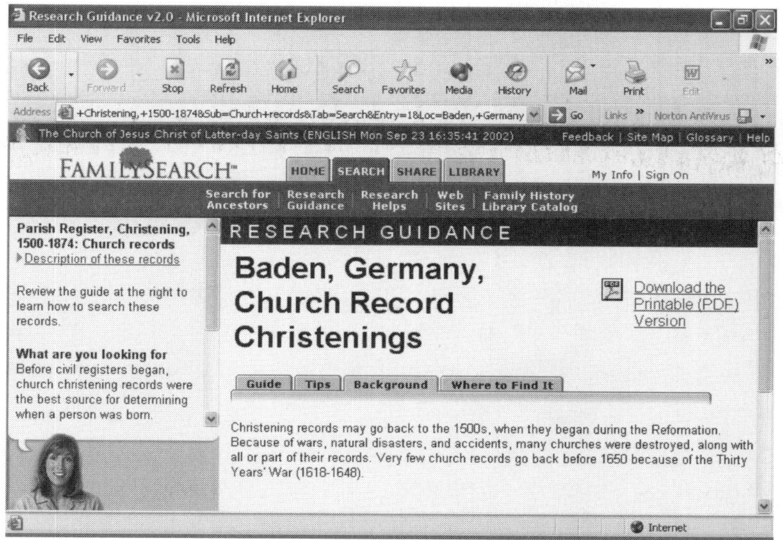

Figure 13.1 Information about record availability in Research Guidance at FamilySearch (Reproduced by permission. Copyright © 1999–2002 by Intellectual Reserve, Inc.)

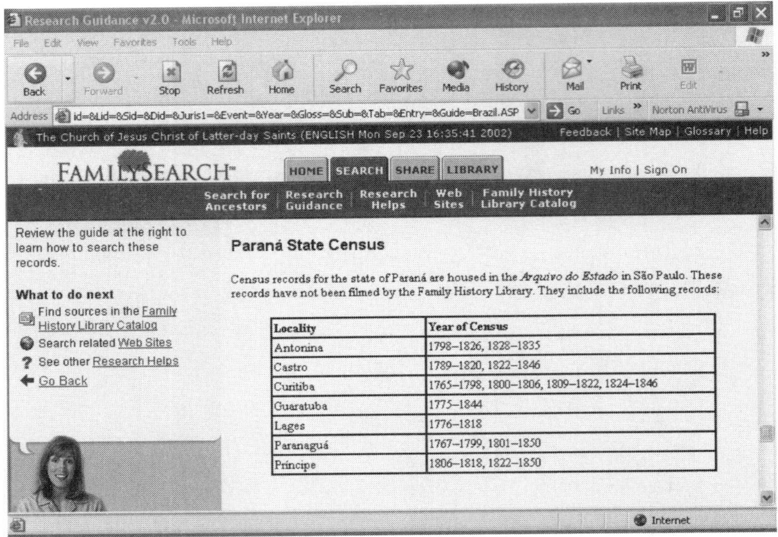

Figure 13.2 Table of record keeping in Research Outline in Research Helps at FamilySearch (Reproduced by permission. Copyright © 1999–2002 by Intellectual Reserve, Inc.)

www.familysearch.org) has helpful background information. (See Figure 13.1 for an example of such research guidance.) The Research Outlines for many countries (available at Family History Centers and in the Research Helps section under the Search tab at *www.familysearch.org)* include tables listing the years certain records were kept. (See Figure 13.2 for an example of such a table.)

The Key to Older Generations

Determining your immigrant ancestor's birthplace (as opposed to all the places she lived before coming to the United States) is the key to correctly identifying her ancestry. Remember, her last place of residence before coming to the United States may be her

- Birthplace in the birth country
- Last place of residence in the birth country (but not the birthplace)
- Last place of residence in a country other than the birth country

This means that when you find a source showing your immigrant ancestor came from Hohenhausen, Prussia, you need to stop and think about which of these three possibilities applies.

Putting the Pieces Together

It took me nineteen years to correctly identify my immigrant grandfather's birthplace. Most U.S. records identified his birthplace as Koflof—but there was no town called Koflof anywhere in Germany, Poland, or Russia. It wasn't until his marriage record was found that his specific birthplace was identified as the small village of Biernatowizna, near the larger village of Kuflew. Koflof turned out to be a phonetic spelling of Kuflew.

The only problem was that the church in Kuflew burned down during World War II. That left me with family as the next best source for clues to my grandfather's ancestry. I went back to interviewing my relatives here in America.

I asked about the structure of grandfather's immediate family. My father's two older sisters, Olga and Gussie, remembered that their father had only one sister, Augusta, who died from appendicitis at age twelve. Aunt Olga remembered that her father's mother had been married three times, but had only those two children from her first marriage. This meant that my grandfather had no known surviving siblings.

I again asked my father what he knew about his father's ancestry. He remembered his father, Wilhelm, explaining that there were four generations of Wilhelm Zucknicks in a row, ending with my father (whose nickname was Bill). Grandfather said his grandfather dreamed of going to sea, so he ran away from home and became a cabin boy. He eventually worked his way up to the position of captain. No ship name. No details to prove or disprove the story. Just this vague story that seemed of little help at the time.

I went back to my aunts Olga and Gussie with this story, then asked them, "Didn't your father have any other relatives?" Suddenly, Aunt Gussie perked up and said, "Why, yes. He had that handsome cousin, Wilhelm Herzog, who came to visit us here in Maryland." She also remembered he had left for home on a ship the very week the *Lusitania* was sunk in 1914. Because World War I was being fought in Europe, she had always wondered if he made it back home. They never heard from him again.

With four small children in my own home, I didn't have the time or energy to dig through port records. Nor did I have a strong enough background in this type of research. Besides, Herzog is a fairly common surname in Germany and I didn't even know which U.S. port he had used. I saved up my money and hired the same firm I had used to obtain my grandparents' marriage record in Poland. I gladly turned the Herzog research over to them.

Baltimore and Philadelphia port records turned up nothing. In New York City, there were three likely passengers named Wilhelm Herzog. One was from Hungary and could be immediately ruled out. The second was from the wrong part of Germany. The third was from Tschulschitz, the German spelling for the town of Czulczyca in Polish Russia—something only someone specializing in eastern European research would recognize. The specialist also knew that this town was practically in the backyard of the village where my grandparents were married. Bingo!

Since this firm had several clients with eastern European ancestry, we all pooled our money to cover the expense of sending the firm's specialist to Poland once again. In the church records for Czulczyca, he found the marriage of an Emilia Zucknick to Ferdinand Herzog. Her marriage record listed her father as Wilhelm Zucknick, a ship captain by occupation.

The pieces began to fit, and the puzzle I had worked on for twenty years was finally solved. Those seemingly vague bits of information my grandfather told my father, together with my aunts' memories of one cousin's visit, helped us finally put together my Zucknick ancestry—from the marriage of my grandparents in 1892 in Polish Russia back to the birth of my fourth great-grandfather in 1733 in Prussia.

By talking to relatives here in the United States, I found the clues that allowed the eastern European specialist to find Emilia Zucknick's marriage record. The corroborating evidence between what my father and aunts remembered and what was found in that marriage record anchored all our further research on my Zucknick ancestry.

You Can't Find Them If You Don't Recognize Their Name

Even looking in the right place isn't going to work if you are looking for the wrong name. Suspect a name change for each immigrant ancestor, until proven otherwise. Suspect that both people and place names were spelled phonetically by American record takers.

Build up a body of evidence to support your hypothesis about a name change. I suspected the Louis Team in Wisconsin records was really the same person as my great-grandmother's brother, Ludwig Diem. Since I had done my homework, I recognized the

Help finding and using U.S. immigration records is available at FamilySearch Internet:

- Go to *www.familysearch.org*.
- Click on the Search tab.
- Click on the Research Helps subtab.
- Click on Sorted by Subject in the options bar on the left side of your screen.
- Click on E for Emigration and Immigration. Check the titles for your locality. In particular, look at
  - United States, Immigration Records, 1820 to 1943.
  - United States, Immigration Records, 1600s to 1900s.

See also the LDS Research Outline *Tracing Immigrant Origins:*

- Go to *www.familysearch.org*.
- Click on the Search tab.
- Click on the Research Helps subtab.
- Click on Sorted by Document Type in the options bar on the left side of your screen.
- Click on Research Outline in the list of document types.
- Scroll down and click on Tracing Immigrant Origins Research Outline.

If you don't have an Internet connection or prefer to have a printed copy, you can order the LDS Research Outline by telephone at 800-537-5950, but remember the online version has active hyperlinks to the resources mentioned.

names of two people from Louis Team's later life who were listed next to a Ludwig Diem in an earlier record. In addition, I knew the German pronunciation of the surname Diem sounds exactly like the English word *team*. In other cases, you work by a process of elimination, as with the three Wilhelm Herzogs listed in New York port records.

The risk is high that you will accept someone else's ancestor as your own if you fail to track down each place your ancestor lived in this country, then each place he lived in foreign countries, working your way back through his life events. This process helps you differentiate between the Ludwig Diem who came to America in 1887 and the one who came here in 1904.

I knew my Ludwig Diem worked in Detroit from 1887 to 1889 until he earned enough money to bring over his wife and two oldest children. They moved to Wisconsin shortly before 1900. Therefore, I could prove that the other Ludwig Diem who arrived in the United States in 1904 was not my great-grandmother's brother but, instead, another person with the same name. Genealogists often have to use a process of elimination like this one.

As Time Rolls By

Your ancestor's date of arrival is pivotal. Not only does it tell you to look in U.S. records after that date, but it also indicates what types of emigration and immigration records were kept about his move from there to here.

For the United States, arrival after 1880 means more records were kept, first by immigration officials, then later in the naturalization system if your immigrant ancestor applied for citizenship. After 1906, naturalizations were indexed nationwide. Before 1880, you are probably going to have a much harder time proving a specific place of origin for your immigrant ancestor. Before the Revolutionary War, fewer accurate connections can be made overseas because of the small number of records still in existence from that time.

An **emigrant** is one who exits a country or region in order to live in another. Your ancestor is an emigrant from a place.

An **immigrant** is one who enters a country or region with the intent to live there. Your ancestor is an immigrant to a place.

Your ancestor also left records behind when he came to the United States. In many countries, he had to register with the local police before leaving the area. He may or may not have applied for a passport or visa. Port records included listings of emigrants, as well as immigrants.

Unfortunately, some countries have a scarcity of emigration records. Most of the passenger lists created before 1890 in England were destroyed in 1900. In Germany, there were two major ports of emigration to the United States: Bremen and Hamburg. The nineteenth-century port records for Bremen no longer exist, but the Hamburg Passenger Lists are a major source for genealogists with German ancestors coming during that period. The Hamburg Passenger Lists are available on microfilm through the Family History Centers.

Genealogists with Danish ancestry benefit from the Danish Emigration Index *(www.emiarch.dk),* which has been taken from several different types of emigration records and made available on the Internet. So your success at finding an emigration record for your ancestor depends on where he came from and when he came to the United States.

Studying the topography and migration patterns in foreign lands helps you know where to look for your ancestors, just as it does in the United States. In northern Europe, migration patterns were from west to east, as opposed to the typical east-to-west pattern in the United States. During earlier times, a general migration occurred from southern Europe to northern Europe.

Foreign Places: Somewhere Out There

You need a specific place to start searching in a foreign country. Knowing just the country isn't enough because it's too general. Knowing the province in a country usually isn't narrow enough, either. You usually have to get down to the town or village level to successfully locate your ancestor's records. Your first goal is to find a source that tells you specifically where to start looking in your ancestor's country of origin. An exception to this occurs when there is a national index to vital records for that period in that country, such as the civil registration indexes for England and Wales after 1837.

Be aware that there are likely to be quite a few places within that country with the same name. (Remember all the places named Laurel in the United States?) My grandparents were married in Ludwinow. That is a nice fact to know, but in 1892 what country was it in? Was there more than one town by that name at that time? Using MapQuest on the Internet shows twelve towns by the name of Ludwinow in Poland today, which indicates that I need to check a historical gazetteer to determine how many places called Ludwinow existed in that area in 1892.

The LDS Research Outlines at FamilySearch Internet are a good resource for ways to find historical gazetteers for your ancestor's country of origin. WorldGenWeb sites also include lists of historical gazetteers for their areas. For example, the Help Me!

page at the PolandGenWeb site *(www.rootsweb.com/~polwgw/helpme.html)* contains information about Polish place names, maps, and historical gazetteers to locate places that no longer exist.

Political boundaries shift over time. Sometimes it is a result of wars, other times it is simply a change in governmental policies. In 1892, Ludwinow was in Polish Russia. After World War I, the country of Poland was reorganized and Ludwinow was in Poland, not far from the Russian border. From 1975 until 1999, when Poland once again restructured its provinces, Ludwinow was in the *powiat* (province) of Lubelskie (or Lublin, as it is listed in the Family History Library Catalog). Today, it is in the province of Chelm. The town didn't move, but the political boundaries changed.

I was lucky. When I started tracing my family in eastern Europe, my grandmother's brother Henry was still alive. He was present at her wedding in their tiny village of Ludwinow. He told me this village was between the bigger towns of Chelm and Cycow. He knew that the nearest train station was in Vladislov (my phonetic spelling for Wladyslawow) and that their family later moved to Ruda-Huta to work in the glass factory.

If you are not so lucky as to have living relatives who were born overseas, you have to dig deeper. There are many possibilities for finding your ancestor's exact place of origin. Optimally, you want to find family records (a Bible, letters, diaries, etc.), citizenship papers, a passport, a ship's passenger list, an obituary, a newspaper article, a christening certificate—anything that specifically states where your immigrant ancestor came from. Even postcards from relatives left behind in the old country can give you clues by the picture on the front, the postmarks, or the people and places mentioned.

The Ties That Bind

It is important to clarify relationships of all kinds in your immigrant ancestor's life—relationships by blood, marriage, occupation, religion, neighborhood, or other affiliations. The more pieces you put together from her life, the more likely you are to spot her in the records you search—even if her name is spelled differently.

Relationships often turn out to be the detail that solves your immigrant's ancestry. If you can't trace your own immigrant's ancestry, but can trace the ancestry of a known relative, you may be able to work around your problem (as my Wilhelm Herzog story illustrates).

Your immigrant ancestor's religious affiliation is an important detail. Churches recorded many of our ancestors' important life events much earlier than civil registration in most countries. In parts of Asia, family or clan records may be the most common source of information about your immigrant ancestor. Other important details about your immigrant ancestor's life include the following:

- All his relatives living here in the United States
- Family members still in his country of origin
- All his relatives who may have migrated to other countries. (For example, many German families splintered, with branches going to Argentina, Brazil, Canada, and the United States.)

Find out as much as you can from family stories and traditions:

- The geographic features of your ancestor's homeland
- The towns in the vicinity of his home in that country
- The train station nearest his home—or the nearest major transportation route
- Where he shopped when he went to the big city (these details help you sort out places with the same name)
- The occupations of the various family members you have identified and the places where they worked
- The language and dialect your ancestor spoke, which helps place him within a geographic region

Doing the Two-Step

When making that challenging initial connection of your immigrant ancestor back to his or her country of origin, your Research Phase needs to be a two-step process. First, you want to use records here to specifically establish where your immigrant came from—down to the village level, if possible. Next, search in the records of that foreign country to confirm that you have the correct ancestor in the correct locality.

If you have difficulty with this first step (determining where your ancestor came from), check to see if you have covered all the levels of records available here in the

United States. Have you searched in the city, county, state, and federal levels of civil records? Have you searched in the different levels at which your ancestor's church saved records (typically, congregation, parish, diocese, then regional or national organization)? In your family, have you considered your relatives' additional marriages, step-relationships, adoptions, and foster parents or guardians?

Even if you don't find your ancestor's exact point of origin within U.S. records, this first step is still useful. Along the way, you learn vague and seemingly unimportant tidbits about your ancestor's life and relationships. These clues help you correctly put together your ancestor's origins when you have to resort to foreign tools and finding aids.

Tools and Finding Aids

A growing number of tools and finding aids are available to help you locate your immigrant ancestor in his place of origin. But you should be cautious when using them because they are not original records. They can be used successfully—if you use them with corroborating evidence. Finding aids point you in the direction of the correct locality and help you find your way back to original records.

An example of this was my use of *Boyd's Marriage Index* to find the marriage place of my husband's Roberts ancestor in Lancashire, England. Successfully finding that marriage record in the *Index* did not end my project. I verified my results by finding the children's records in that same parish. Only then could I conclude that I had found the right Roberts family.

When using indexes, get a feel for how common your immigrant ancestor's name is in that area and time. Note the spelling variations for the name. Work down through international, national, regional, and local indexes. This is especially important if you don't have someone like my Uncle Henry to clearly identify all the localities surrounding the places where your ancestor's life events occurred.

These types of tools are easy to find for many foreign countries if you have access to the Internet. Cyndi's List is just one example of a tool for finding other tools on the Internet. The FamilySearch Internet site is filled with tools to help you, as are the WorldGenWeb Project sites. Much can also be done in your local Family History Center by way of microfilms of foreign records, finding aids and indexes, and reference books.

Weigh the Evidence

When you finally identify what you think is a record of your immigrant ancestor in his purported original locality, evaluate it carefully and critically for credibility. You may even want to play devil's advocate and make an effort to disprove the connection, as did the Swedish genealogist my husband hired. She analyzed what we gave her. She became skeptical about what had been previously compiled when she realized only one type of record had been used. By searching both local death records and christening records, she proved we were barking up the wrong family tree. (See Chapter 3 for more on this story.)

Ask yourself the following questions to make sure you have located the correct ancestor:

- Did that person die before your ancestor came to the United States? If so, he can't be your immigrant ancestor. You'd be amazed how many genealogists fail to check the death records in a locality where they think their ancestor came from.
- Are there inconsistencies in the births of his supposed children?
  - Are the children's births too close together? A Johann Schmidt with a child born in January shouldn't be having another child born three months later. If so, you probably have two or more couples with the same names.
  - After your ancestor emigrated, were there still children being born in that location to a parent with your ancestor's name?
- Do you find your ancestor's name in the records of that foreign locality after the date your ancestor emigrated?
- Can you find any of your ancestor's family, friends, or neighbors in that foreign locality's records? Failure to do so may indicate you have the wrong locality.

Try, Try Again

Sometimes you just have to try, try again until you successfully locate your ancestor's records in her country of origin. An example of this was the quest for my grandparents' marriage record.

The first thing I did was to write to the Polish National Archives asking if they had a record of my grandparents' 1892 marriage in the village of Ludwinow near the city of Chelm. I waited six months for their reply (normal for Iron Curtain countries at that time). They wrote back to say they had the record and the amount of money to send for a copy. I immediately replied and waited another six months. No response. I wrote them again, thinking my payment had been lost or stolen. They again replied that they had the record and to send payment. I did so, again, and waited another six months. No reply.

I didn't know why the Polish National Archives hadn't sent me the record I had paid for twice, but I did know I really wanted that record. So I hired a genealogy firm with an eastern European specialist to get the information for me. He had to obtain permission ahead of time to research in the Polish National Archives. After arriving there, he had to wait several days while his permit was authenticated. When he was finally able to enter the archives, he checked the catalog, which said they had the book for the year needed. But that book was missing from the shelves. It wasn't found anywhere in the archives.

My specialist went on doing research in Poland for his other clients. Toward the end of his trip, he was in the Lutheran diocese offices looking up someone else's records. While there, he found a duplicate copy of the book with my grandparents' marriage record. He wasn't able to obtain a photocopy (no copy machines could be found anywhere in that building), but he did photograph the page with his camera.

As he was leaving Poland, he was stopped at the border checkpoint while his luggage was searched. Suddenly, the Soviet soldiers pointed their machine guns at him and one of them began pulling out the plastic storage containers holding all his film, which they confiscated. My luck this time was good, however, because they neglected to look in his camera. It still had film in it—including the pictures of my grandparent's marriage record.

Do what you can, here and abroad, to trace your immigrant ancestors. If they prove especially difficult to find, you can always hire professional help just as I did.

Chapter 14

Guns for Hire: Working with Professionals

As mentioned earlier in this book, genealogy involves a great many four-letter words, such as *cash, time,* and *work.* When you encounter some of these four-letter words, you know it is time to hire professional assistance.

You Can't Put Time in a Bottle

I hired a research firm to tackle my recalcitrant Simmons family when I had four children under the age of six. I had neither the time nor the energy to do all the research myself. I continued to do what I could in libraries in my area, but I turned over to them the major planning and on-location research in Tennessee and North Carolina.

If the Internet had existed then, I could have done a great deal more at home—but not all records and resources are available online. Even today, when you lack the time to go on location and research thoroughly, consider hiring professional help.

Do You Know the Way?

Both of my paternal grandparents spoke German, so I thought I would be researching their ancestry in Germany. During the era B.C. (before copiers, computers, and children), I spent three years learning the basics of German research. Then Uncle Henry stunned me with the information that my grandparents were married in Polish

Russia. That's when I knew it was time to hire someone who not only could read the languages, but also had the background knowledge and was willing to go behind the Iron Curtain.

If you lack the special knowledge or skills needed to do research in a particular geographic region, time period, or type of record, consider hiring professional help.

When You Can't Boldly Go

Many times you'll find you need to do on-location research, but simply can't take a trip. Both of the examples above resulted from my travel limitations. I simply couldn't abandon my responsibilities at home. Many genealogists have responsibilities at work and only limited leisure time to pursue their genealogy. Still others have physical conditions that limit their ability to travel. As mentioned in the previous chapter, you can probably do a great deal to trace your family tree from home. Do as much as you can, then consider turning your biggest ancestral questions over to a professional.

It Takes Cents but Makes Sense

Sometimes it is best to hire someone on location to do the looking for you. Not only does this save you the time and expense of traveling, but that professional is already there, is familiar with the local records and repositories, and often has access to records you do not.

For some types of records, you fill out a form and pay a small fee, and the local clerk tries to find that record and send you a copy. This works for only a few types of records—such as government registrations of births, marriages, and deaths. For a small fee, librarians, archivists, and volunteers in local genealogical or historical societies may do limited searches in other, less commonly used types of records. But for a thorough search, you have to either hire a professional or go yourself.

Sooner or later all genealogists encounter a challenging situation on their family tree. When you find yourself butting your head against a brick wall, just remember that two heads working together are often better than one. If your usual contacts can't help (like the staff at your local Family History Center or friends from your local genealogical society), consider hiring a professional to analyze your findings or advise you on where else to look.

The Results of a Cannon Consultation

My Cannons are now and have always been a challenge. My great-grandparents were married in Jackson County, North Carolina, where courthouse fires destroyed many of the early records. And two groups of Cannons hail from that area. One group was in the oil business, and the other included a superior court judge who owned gold mines (mentioned in his will).

During my third or fourth Evaluation Phase on these Cannons, I realized I hadn't checked the witnesses to my great-grandparents' marriage. John W. Cannon and Julia Ann Hannah were married in the home of an A. M. Parker, who also served as a witness. By researching him, I learned that three months before my great-grandparents' marriage, an Alfred M. Parker married Lula A. Cannon—daughter of the superior court judge with the gold mines. Now I had circumstantial evidence that my Cannons were related to the group with the gold mines. But my efforts to find descendants of the gold mine Cannons failed, so I was stuck again.

Finally, I hired a professional genealogist for a consultation. I paid for a few hours of her time to look over my Cannon research logs and read my research summary. She was impressed with the long and varied list of resources I had searched, but noticed I had not searched any North Carolina newspapers.

I followed her advice and made a pilgrimage to North Carolina. With the help of a librarian at the North Carolina State Library, I found a newspaper obituary for Judge Cannon of Jackson County. He was born in 1822 in Buncombe County, North Carolina. As my luck goes, this was also a county where the courthouse burned down, but at least I had a new place to search.

I placed a query in the Old Buncombe County Genealogical Society's periodical. A descendant of John W. Cannon, through another of his marriages, contacted me. She knew of descendants from his other marriages who lived in Ohio. They knew where John W. Cannon was buried in Knox County, Tennessee. Their family stories also claimed that the Knox County, Tennessee Cannons often visited relatives in Buncombe County, North Carolina. Sometimes all it takes is one good piece of advice about where to look next.

What Kind of Help Do You Need?

Professional genealogists tend to specialize in a particular type of research service. These include ancestral research, descendant research, and record searches.

With a Little Bit of Luck: A True Research Story

I traveled to Tennessee and met my cousin Gaylord and his wife, Marion, who were both from Ohio. Our goal was to get into the chancery court vault in the courthouse of the county where our ancestors lived. We had previously viewed microfilms of the court minute books, but hoped to find the original depositions in those cases mentioning our ancestors' surnames.

We arrived at the courthouse and found our way to the clerk's office. At the counter, we saw a junior clerk (younger) and a senior clerk (older) seated at desks. To our left was the steel vault, with its twelve-inch-thick door wide open.

The senior clerk kept her head down and continued working, so the junior clerk got up and came to the counter. I asked if we could see deposition numbers such-and-such, as recorded in the microfilmed court minute books. She looked over at the senior clerk who, without looking up, shook her head. The junior clerk told us those records were not available. I asked if we might look at other records in the vault that would tell us more about the family we had come all this way to research. She again looked at the senior clerk, who again vigorously shook her head.

Just at this moment, a most unkempt-looking man staggered into the office. His suit looked like it had been slept in and he obviously hadn't shaved in several days. He had one of his hands in his pocket and was mumbling in a slurred voice that he was going to shoot the blankety-blank preacher who had married his daughter to that so-and-so. The junior clerk said to us, "If you'll follow me . . ." and headed into the vault, leaving the senior clerk to deal with the situation. We gladly followed.

It was immediately clear why that office did not allow public access to the records kept in the vault. The junior clerk had to move the kitchen supplies (paper plates, napkins, etc.) off a short filing cabinet, climb onto it, turn around, and reach up to the top shelf where the narrow, metal boxes of depositions were stored. These depositions were not filed in numerical or chronological order. The junior clerk simply pulled a box off the shelf and began hunting through the packets, which were folded and tied with string. Each time she found one mentioning our surnames on its cover, she asked if we wanted to see it. Our answer was always, "Yes, thank you."

We carefully unfolded each brittle packet of papers. Marion and I transcribed them by hand while Gaylord stood guard at the vault's door. Luckily, it took the senior clerk more than half an hour to get a bailiff to come and remove the disturbed gentleman. Since we were already in the vault and were being so careful with the papers, she allowed us to remain there the rest of the morning.

It was in those depositions that we learned, in Edmond's own words (remember Edmond, my ancestor's bigamist brother?), how he had to return his first wife's dower upon their separation of bed-and-board in 1860. He mentioned that his daughter, Hannah, was widowed during the Civil War and lived with her mother on those dower lands until her mother's death. Hannah then inherited her mother's property. Edmond went on to relate how he had asked to see the deed to Hannah's lands—to make certain everything was in order—then somehow lost it. Hannah brought suit in that chancery court when Edmond tried to sell the property to her brother and brother-in-law.

Sometimes it takes not only time, cash, and work to get to the records you need, but also a bit of luck. A local genealogist who had gone to school with the senior clerk, or one who had a relative who was an elected official in that county, might be able to get into the vault on a regular basis. Sometimes, however, an opportunity simply presents itself and you just need to take it.

Ancestral Research

If you need ancestral research assistance, your best choice may be to hire a professional genealogist to work on one of your ancestral families or to extend your pedigree. This is complex research because it often includes different localities and time periods, which require a variety of knowledge and skills. You need this type of assistance when you want to discover exactly where your immigrant ancestor came from, join a lineage or patriotic society, or pursue your pedigree under challenging circumstances, such as

- Ancestry in a difficult locality (for example, where major records have been destroyed by fire, flood, or war)
- Ancestry during a difficult period (for example, early American research when record keeping was sparse on the frontier)
- Irregularities in your ancestry (if your ancestor was an only child, orphaned, adopted, lacked legitimate parents, etc.)

- If your ancestor was from a minority (like Native American, African American, or less common religious and ethnic groups)

Descendant Research

Hire a professional genealogist to track the descendants of one of your ancestors or an ancestral couple if

- You want to contact descendants to share information about your joint ancestry
- You want to form a descendants' organization to preserve family history
- You need to find missing heirs for an inheritance
- You have genetic medical reasons

Tracing descendants often includes research in the twentieth century, which is different from research in earlier centuries, so look for a professional who specializes in that period.

Record Searches

A professional record searcher specializes in records from a specific locality, a specific type of record (such as military, immigration and naturalization, or land records), or a specific repository (like the Library of Virginia). You hire that professional to focus on finding just one record in her locality (such as just one marriage record) or to look in any records in that locality for your family names. Such research, however, is not usually as broad in scope as an ancestral or descendant research project.

Additional Services

The following may or may not be included as part of ancestral research, descendant research, or record searches:

- Consulting about a research problem
- Translating records written in archaic handwriting, a foreign language, or where symbols or abbreviations (or both) were used

- Creating and giving lectures or multimedia presentations specifically about your family tree, genealogy in general, or related topics—at family reunions, to surname society meetings, etc.
- Entering and organizing genealogical research in a computer database and word processor (for those who cannot type or don't have a computer)
- Helping to write and publish a personal history, a family history book, or a family record (like an ancestor's diary that needs transcribing)

Free Lookups

Local genealogists sometimes volunteer to do free, limited lookups in a specific type of resource. Keep in mind that these volunteers range in experience from beginner to professional. Remember, too, that these lookups are necessarily narrow in scope. The following are places to find volunteers:

- Random Acts of Genealogical Kindness *(www.raogk.org)*
- GenExchange Look Up Volunteers *(www.genexchange.org/ISearch.CFM)*
- USGenWeb Project on each county's Web site (go to *www.usgenweb.org,* then click on the desired state and follow their links to the county GenWeb Project site)
- Local genealogical publications
- LDS Family History Centers
- E-mail discussion groups (called mail lists or collaboration lists)

Types of Professionals

Just like doctors, professional genealogists tend to specialize or generalize. Even those who generalize still have some specialties and some limitations. Unlike doctors, however, anyone can simply hang out a shingle as a professional genealogist. This definitely creates a situation of *caveat emptor* ("Let the buyer beware!"). The level of skill and training you need in the professional you hire depends largely on the type of research assistance you need.

Do you need a generalist or a specialist? If you are expanding your pedigree into earlier generations, you need a generalist who can evaluate the situation and plan a research strategy. When records are not readily available, he will then travel to that locality and do the research himself or subcontract it to be done by local record searchers and specialists. The generalist regularly provides you with concise reports on his progress and helps you identify likely future areas of research.

Not every professional genealogist functions as a generalist. The wide range of knowledge, experience, and managerial skills needed in ancestral and descendant projects means you may pay more for the services of such a skilled professional. These types of projects also tend to be larger and more complex, and they require more hours to complete.

Back in the 1980s, I had a problem finding the parents of my great-great-grandmother, Martha Simmons, so I decided to hire professional help. I simply couldn't find her in the 1850 U.S. census. I knew from her death certificate that she was supposedly born in North Carolina in 1833 to Abe Simmons and Mary Jones. From the birth dates of her children, Martha probably didn't marry until after 1850, so she should be listed somewhere in that census as a young woman with her parental family.

One year in my Christmas newsletter, I bemoaned my lack of success with this Simmons family. Mark Hannah (Martha's grandson, the retired park ranger) wrote back to me with one new piece of information. He remembered Martha had a half-brother named Tom Raines. With four small children at home, I had no way to take advantage of this new clue, but I felt an urge to pursue this branch of the family tree while Martha's elderly grandchildren were still alive to give me further clues. This fueled my decision to seek professional help.

It was a large and difficult job, so I hired a genealogy research firm. Working together, we quickly found Martha in the 1850 U.S. census in Cocke County, Tennessee, with her mother, siblings, and half-siblings—all listed with the last name Raines. As you can imagine, this opened all sorts of research possibilities. We decided to send a researcher back to that area.

Because Cocke County had a courthouse fire in 1876 that destroyed many genealogically significant records, the researcher had to look in other places for records. In the Stokely Memorial Library in that county, he found two unpublished manuscripts about this joint Raines and Simmons family, their ancestors, and descendants. The research in these manuscripts had been done in the 1960s by a woman in Texas who descended from the Raines side of the family. Like any compiled genealogy, much of it was supported by further evidence, while some of it merely raised more questions.

One manuscript included a 1922 affidavit made in Texas by Martha's half-sister, Amanda, stating that their mother, Mary Jones, was the daughter of Dorsie Guinn, who married a man by the name of Jones and moved to North Carolina. It mentioned Mary's two sisters, including their husbands' and children's names, and a brother (who got lost while hunting and was found dead in a cave). The affidavit also claimed that Dorsie was the daughter of Betsie Hill of Dublin, Ireland, who married William Guinn.

This was a tremendous amount of information from just one affidavit. I was thrilled with the progress this firm had made on the first Simmons research project, so I decided to hire the firm again to find out more about Martha's mother, Mary Jones. Meanwhile, I was doing as much research as I could in libraries near my home.

When the firm reported back to me, their second researcher had found little new information. I felt he had not done a particularly good job since I had managed to find the 1798 will of a Peter Gwyn in Wilkes County, North Carolina, giving his cattle, horses, and household furnishings to William Hill, Elizabeth Hill, and Dorothy Hill. I thought the researcher should have thought to look in that county—especially since that is where Martha's husband's family originally came from. I still don't know if Elizabeth Hill is the same as the Betsie Hill of Dublin, Ireland, who supposedly married William Guinn, but it sure is a coincidence.

Fortunately, this research firm has a review committee. When they considered my questions about the work done in their second research unit, they agreed with my assessment and did additional research at no additional charge.

Finding and Working with a Professional

When you deal with a reputable individual or firm, you are more likely to get what you pay for—professional research. So how do you find and choose a reputable professional?

Step 1: Determine What You Need to Have Done

First, you need to have a specific research goal in mind. Just telling a professional you want to know more about your great-great-grandmother, Martha Simmons, isn't enough. Setting a specific, short-term goal and a more general, long-range goal brings better results. For my first Simmons research project, my short-range goal was to find Martha in the 1850 census. My long-term goal was to prove her parents were Mary Jones and Abe Simmons, as claimed on Martha's death certificate.

List, in writing, what you specifically want that research project to accomplish. The more clearly you state what you want, the more likely you are to be pleased with the outcome. My short-range and long-term goals in the paragraph above are examples of written goals.

Save yourself money by doing as much as you can before hiring someone. Remember my father-in-law's Clinton, Missouri, problem? He could have saved time and money if he had determined his Roberts ancestor lived in the town of Clinton, and not the county of Clinton, in Missouri.

Once you have hired a professional, continue to work from home on supporting evidence. Write letters and e-mail messages, and interview your relatives and any of your ancestor's friends, neighbors, or associates who are still living. You may glean further clues that help your researcher meet your research goals. For example, by interviewing relatives I learned my ancestor Krystyana Diem had a frail older sister. This knowledge helped my eastern European specialist find more records in Poland, which documented Krystyana's father's migration from Württemberg to Polish Russia.

It is not unusual for a researcher to review and analyze what you have found. With her expert knowledge and experience, she may notice something you did not in the records you searched. Remember how I noticed the "na" on the 1920 U.S. census for the patron researching her German grandfather? Your professional may need to re-do some of your searches to look for additional clues.

Step 2: Organize Your Files

Organize what you already have so your researcher spends less time reviewing what has been done and deciding what remains to be searched. Your source citations and research logs really pay off here. Materials your researcher is likely to request include

- Your ancestry or descendancy charts
- Your family group sheets with source citations. She may also request a GEDCOM file (generic copy) of your genealogy database, if you have one.
- Copies of your research logs (also known as research calendars or to-do lists)

- Copies of the records you found pertaining to the families being researched
- Summaries of your family stories, traditions, and interviews
- Your preferred method of contact. You will be working with that professional—not just hiring her—so you will be communicating back and forth.

Step 3: Find Professional Genealogists

If the scope of your project is broad or you need a highly paid specialist, it is particularly important to contract with a professional who adheres to a code of ethics and has a known history of performance in this field. I recommend you look for a researcher through one of these three professional organizations:

- The Association of Professional Genealogists (APG), *www.apgen.org*
- The Board for Certification of Genealogists (BCG), *www.bcgcertification.org*
- The International Commission for the Accreditation of Professional Genealogists (ICAPGen), *www.icapgen.org*

The APG does not have a testing procedure for its members. Anyone may join by paying dues and signing the APG Code of Ethics. It does, however, have a Professional Review Committee, which mediates complaints involving its members. In cases when the Code of Ethics has been flagrantly broken, the APG Board of Directors votes to expel that member.

Postnomial	Title	Organization
CGRS	Certified Genealogical Record Searcher	BCG
CG	Certified Genealogist	BCG
CLS	Certified Lineage Specialist	BCG
AG	Accredited Genealogist	ICAPGen

Figure 14.1 Postnomials used by genealogy professional organizations

Both the BCG and ICAPGen test and credential professional genealogists based upon their geographic specialization and the types of research they perform (see Figure 14.1). This helps to ensure the competence of the professional you hire. Both the BCG and ICAPGen also have a professional review process to handle complaints.

Mailing Addresses of Professional Organizations for Genealogists

Association of Professional Genealogists
P.O. Box 745729
Arvada, CO 80006-5729

Board for Certification of Genealogists
P.O. Box 14291
Washington, D.C. 20044

ICAPGen
P.O. Box 970204
Orem, UT 84097-0204

If your project is small and inexpensive, you have several options for finding a professional genealogist to assist you. APG, BCG, and ICAPGen all list record searchers.

In addition, you can request from a local library, archive, or genealogical society a list of researchers who accept clients and are familiar with the records in that facility or geographic area. These lists usually include a disclaimer, but it is common practice to remove a researcher's name from the list if complaints about his or her work are received. The researchers on these lists may or may not be credentialed and may do one or more types of research (ancestral, descendant, or record searches).

Genealogy periodicals often include advertisements placed by genealogists who accept clients. It is especially important to evaluate a candidate for your project found in such a manner. Be sure to verify his qualifications.

Step 4: Evaluate Your Candidates

Contact several researchers who specialize in the type of research you need. A professional genealogist should already have a résumé that covers most of the information you want to know about her and her standards. Evaluate your list of possible professionals based on the following criteria:

- Their experience solving your type of research problem. Are their research specialties appropriate to your needs?
- Their experience with the geographic area and time period of your project. Do they have access to the records that need to be searched? Will they need to travel to those records or subcontract a local record searcher?
- Their availability. Experienced professionals are frequently booked up months in advance. Can they reasonably complete your project in a time frame that is acceptable to you?
- Their credentials. Be sure to verify they are currently in good standing with any credentialing organization they claim on their résumé or advertisement.
- The general research strategy they propose. Is it likely to meet your goals? At this stage, do not expect a free, detailed list of what they plan to do. If you engage them in a lengthy telephone discussion about your project, be considerate and pay for their time spent consulting with you, whether you hire them or not.
- The types of reports you will receive at the conclusion of your research project (or at various stages during a lengthy project).
- Their proposed costs and schedule of payments. Never contract for unlimited research. It is always wise to start with small research units first and, if you are pleased with their work, invest in larger projects later. Always set a limit on what you are willing to spend.
- How interested they seem in taking on your project.
- Their timetable. Will they complete your work in an acceptable length of time and maintain contact with you during that time?

No reputable genealogist promises positive results for even the simplest research project. Guaranteeing results indicates the person is either an inexperienced researcher or a charlatan. All that should be promised is that competent searches will be made and the results evaluated. Too often, unforeseen roadblocks or missing records complicate even the most straightforward projects.

Compare the proposed project costs from several professionals. Be suspicious of any that seem too high or too low. If necessary, ask for a further breakdown to make certain you are comparing like to like. For example, if one researcher says he hopes to solve your problem in just four hours, but another says it will take a minimum of ten hours, you need to determine whether the first has easier access to the needed records than the second or whether the second recognizes a difficulty that the first one doesn't.

Step 5: Pay and Provide

The rates you are charged depend on several factors. Highly trained and experienced genealogists tend to be in great demand and, therefore, may charge a higher hourly rate for their services. Specialists with unique skills—such as minority or ethnic group research, foreign language expertise, or experience with research in difficult localities—also tend to charge more. Unfortunately, it is not just a case of picking out the most expensive researcher to get the most skilled professional. Many competent genealogists research for moderate rates. A higher fee doesn't always mean a better job. There needs to be a reason for a high fee.

The more complex or specialized the job, the more it will likely cost. Larger projects are often done in units, where you contract for a set number of hours to be applied to meet your goals. If you are satisfied with the work performed, you then contract for additional hours of research until either your goal is met or you reach a point of diminishing returns (where the likelihood of success is no longer worth the cost of the remaining search options).

Many professionals will not contract for anything less than a minimum unit ranging from ten to twenty hours of time spent on the project. Contracting for additional research units with the same individual or firm is more efficient because the initial review and analysis of your problem has already been done.

Typically, on the first unit of your research problem, one-third of your paid hours are for a review of what has already been done, an initial analysis, and strategy planning. One-third should be spent on the actual research and photocopying of pertinent records. The last third should be spent on the evaluation and report writing. If you have a complex problem on which a great deal of research has already been done, your whole first unit may need to go to evaluation, analysis, and report writing.

Check to see whether your unit hours cover

- Review and analysis of previous research
- Development of a search strategy
- Travel and record-access expenses

- Record searching and copying
- A research log of all the sources searched—whether anything was found or not
- Evaluation of what was found and not found
- Report writing (plus data entry or publication, if you request those services)
- Preparation of billing statements showing how their time was spent (some researchers include this under "report writing")

Step 6: Get a Written Agreement

In all but the smallest (and least expensive) research projects, get a written agreement detailing your expectations and goals before you authorize the researcher to proceed. Most professionals have a formal contract for you to sign. In addition, they may have a list of their normal methods, procedures, and policies that have been modified to fit your specific project.

Disputes do occasionally arise over the work done or not done—as when I questioned the work done in my second research unit on the ancestry of Martha Simmons. Make sure your agreement clearly spells out

- Your short- and long-range goals
- The time frame in which the project should be completed
- How often you will be updated on progress
- Any additional fees or expenses you are expected to pay (such as the costs of copies or travel expenses) and the limits you set on those extra expenses
- The schedule for payment
- The types of reports you will be receiving and their contents. Make certain you get a final report after the research is completed and evaluated.
- Contingencies for cost overruns or unexpected delays
- What will be done if either you or the researcher cannot fulfill the agreement
- Whether or not you give the researcher permission to publish or share this research. Even though you paid for the work to be done, it was the researcher's creative effort and he may want to publish it sooner or later.

If disputes arise that cannot be resolved through your communication with that individual (or if he fails to respond within a reasonable time), contact his credentialing organization—and notify your researcher that you are doing so.

Achieving Success

There are many ways to overcome brick walls on your family tree. Most of them involve four-letter words, such as *time* and *cash*. You can often achieve success on your own with enough time and work, but just as often the solution comes through a combination of the clues you gather, research done by distant cousins and shared with you, and the work of any professionals you hire. The important thing is to leave a legacy for future generations.

Chapter 15
Tracing Your Family Tree in the Twenty-first Century

TECHNOLOGICAL ADVANCES CAN BE A MIXED BLESSING FOR GENEALO-gists. It is easy to assume science has all the answers, when all too often those answers turn out to be incomplete. This chapter takes a look at some of the things technology can and can't do for genealogists. Three areas of technology that particularly impact family tree tracing are computers, the Internet, and DNA testing.

Computers: A Genealogist's Best Friend and Worst Enemy

Genealogists definitely have a love-hate relationship with their computers. They help us keep track of our research, share vast quantities of information and images, preserve what we have done, and access the Internet. They can also wipe out in seconds more work than ever before. They cost money, take time to learn to use, break down, and frustrate us nearly as much as our recalcitrant ancestors. Despite this, computing devices continue to proliferate among genealogists.

In August 2000, the U.S. Census Bureau reported that 51 percent of the households in America had computers. That percentage continues to grow. Even if you don't have one in your home, you'll end up using a computer in most libraries to browse their catalogs and search collections of genealogical records, either online or on compact discs.

Genealogists use their home computers, genealogy programs, and word processors constantly. Word processing has made the typewriter nearly obsolete. As mentioned in

Chapter 12, technology has made it much easier to publish histories, periodicals, and books of genealogical information. Consequently, these resources are being published in greater numbers.

On top of that, their quality has improved. Thirty years ago, only a small percentage of the genealogy books and periodicals published were indexed. Today, the vast majority are indexed. For example, in 1990 it took me only three days to thoroughly index my five-hundred-page family history book. Just five years earlier, it took a friend six weeks, using 3 x 5 cards, to index her book of a similar size. In just that short time, improvements in word processing had automated the indexing process.

Portable computers (also known as laptops or notebook computers) appeal to genealogists because they allow us to carry our computer files along on research trips. There is no other way I could take my fifteen feet of hanging files with me. It is also easy to take along other resources, such as the CD versions of the Family History Library Catalog and PERSI. If you know how to type, you can take notes much more rapidly with a laptop than by hand. This makes your notes more readable, easier to copy, and easier to share.

Another way laptops make it easier to share your research is through presentations. With no special training and just the software that came on his computer, my optometrist created a multimedia slide show for his parents' fiftieth wedding anniversary. He included images from photographs, newspaper clippings, and family documents with background music. He gave me a copy, which I used as an introduction to a class on creating multimedia presentations for family reunions. The class protested when I stopped his slide show to start my lecture—which was my whole point.

My laptop is a big hit at family gatherings. Not only do I use it for presentations, but I also use it (with a digital camera and scanner) to make copies of family portraits, old photos, important documents, cross-stitch samplers, quilts, and Great-grandpa's straight-edge razor. I then copy those images onto recordable CDs and share them with other family members.

Personal digital assistants, better known as PDAs, synchronize with your calendar and address book on your desktop computer. Some people even use them to access their e-mail. These devices are showing up more and more in the hands of genealogists in libraries and archives. By adding a folding keyboard, you can type notes into a PDA, just as you would on any computer, and easily transfer your notes to your desktop computer when you get home. Many genealogy programs have scaled-down versions of their software just for PDAs. This is one area where technology is advancing extremely rapidly.

Seven Reasons Genealogists Love the Internet

Advances in technology made the Internet possible. Genealogy is one of the most popular uses for the Internet. In less than a decade, it has radically changed the way genealogists trace their family trees. There are seven reasons genealogists love to use the Internet so much.

Resources

The Internet makes a world of resources available twenty-four hours a day, seven days a week right in your own home. No more waiting until the library opens to get a map showing where the town of LeRoy is located. I often contemplated the penalties for breaking and entering a public library in the days before the Internet was available.

Even if you don't have an Internet connection at home, free or low-cost access is probably available in many places in your community. Libraries, public schools, community centers, and cyber cafés are all places you can go to get online. Kiosks offering low-cost Internet access are springing up in such diverse places as airports, shopping centers, and business parks.

Research

What the Internet does for genealogical research is almost beyond belief. If the Internet did nothing other than let you access library catalogs online, it would be worth all the expense. No longer do genealogists plan expensive research trips to out-of-state locations without knowing if something is there for them to search. Research Guidance at the FamilySearch Internet site even tells you what to search next and where to look for it. It is like having a professional genealogist in your own home.

Reference

Genealogists use a great many different types of unique reference tools. I once purchased *Black's Law Dictionary* for a sizeable chunk of money. (It was a sizeable book.) I now simply go online to look up legal terms in specialty dictionaries. It is much faster than walking down the hall to my book room.

I frequently go online for help with the different calendaring systems used in the records I analyze. You can use the Internet to find out about the history of a geographic area, locate historical maps, gazetteers, specialty dictionaries, and free language-translation services. You can also download the latest versions of genealogy programs and other useful utility programs for your computer.

Reasonable

With an Internet connection, you save money by not having to purchase all the reference tools mentioned above. Plus, when you compare the number of trips I used to make to the local Family History Center and public libraries, I don't think my Internet connection costs very much at all. My husband certainly thinks it is money well spent to keep me at home. (Now, if he could just figure out some way to get his fair share of time on our computer . . .)

Retail

Everything from soup to nuts-and-bolts can be purchased online, including a wide variety of materials useful for genealogy. If you can't find what you need for free on the Internet, at least you can comparison shop. Letting your fingers do the walking on the Internet saves you shopping time, which can be better spent pursuing information about your family tree.

I don't, however, recommend buying anything online that is difficult to return or has to be tried on for size or comfort. For example, a computer keyboard needs to feel just right when you are typing on it. You can't tell that over the Internet. (I recently bought a wireless keyboard from an Internet site, but it was from a company I know has an excellent return policy.)

Reachable

The postman used to be my favorite person. I would hover like a vulture waiting for the arrival of the mail each day. When it came, I would immediately shuffle through the bills and advertisements looking for letters from other family tree tracers. I no longer hover by my mailbox—at least not the one outside the house. Most of my genealogy correspondence now takes place by e-mail. I still have to shuffle through the junk mail, but e-mail sure saves on postage and brings me nearly instant gratification.

A Zucknick cousin in Bavaria found me through a query I had posted on the Internet. He sent me an e-mail message asking what I knew about Zucknicks. It took me only a few minutes to go into my genealogy program and generate a report. I copied it into an e-mail message, which I sent to him. This took so little time that he was still online.

He e-mailed me right back, explaining that his English was not so good and it would take him about two weeks to translate my report. Knowing where to find a free, online translation service, I had it translated and sent back to him in two minutes. He immediately replied saying no one could have translated that twenty-page report so fast. I was glad to tell him how I did it, but I warned him it was a mechanical translation and might not always be correct.

Roaming

Just ask any genealogist who forgot to call ahead and arrived at the Arkansas State Library—only to find it was closed for Veterans Day. Yes, yours truly made this mistake. Thanks to the Internet, it is now much easier to plan effective research trips.

Using the Internet, I keep track of airfares and get discounts on hotels and rental cars. I check bus routes and train schedules before leaving home, and print maps and driving directions for the area I am visiting. I learned the hard way to print out not only the driving directions, but also a map of the area I am visiting. On one trip, I missed a turn and got lost. I spent the next hour trying to find my way back.

Most record repositories (libraries, archives, courthouses, etc.) have Web sites, which include such useful information as when they will be closed, parking availability, local places to eat, and the types of copy machines available.

Unfortunate Side Effects of Internet Use

The Internet brings us instant gratification, but its rapid growth may be making it harder for us to find what we are seeking. When you read a query in a local genealogy society's journal about the surname Jones, you have some hope it is about your Jones ancestor who lived in that area. But when you search a large, online database for the surname Jones, it is harder to recognize a possible link as you weed through the thousands of matches.

There are online directories and search engines, but currently it is hit-and-miss to find what's out there about your ancestral names, dates, and places. The growing trend is to cross-reference genealogical resources on the Internet. You can see this happening already at the Ancestry.com commercial site. There, you have an option to attach an online note to any of the records in their databases. These notes say such things as, "This census image lists my great-grandpa's name as J. W. Cannon. His full name was James Wallace Cannon. My Web site has more information about him at . . ."

Back when the Internet was young and the World Wide Web had not yet been born, I used a free service called the Roots Surname List. I listed the surnames I was hunting, plus their related places and time periods. For several years, one or two new cousins found me through this service each month.

Then the World Wide Web burgeoned. Genealogy Web sites proliferated to the point that it is a full-time job just to register my research interests online—even if I do so only at the high-traffic genealogy sites. Rarely do other researchers contact me these days through the Roots Surname list *(rsl.rootsweb.com),* which is a pity. It worked well for many years.

There are so many tools, and so much advice, and so many ways to contact and communicate with other family tree tracers through the Internet that there is another book in this NGS series about finding and using the Internet for genealogy. It is called *Online Roots: How to Discover Your Family's History and Heritage with the Power of the Internet* by Pamela Boyer Porter and Amy Johnson Crow.

The Evolution of Genealogy and Technology

The fact that the Internet keeps your research alive is both good and bad. Go to any of the big genealogy database sites and you will find my research. It is there under my name or the names of other researchers with whom I freely shared my work. But the information isn't up to date. I have since corrected many of my early mistakes—and those corrections aren't easily shown in most online databases. They are usually not corrected at all when my work was submitted by other people.

What is needed is a way to show the evolution of your research, one that will also help distant cousins stay in contact with each other and show where they agree or disagree about their family trees. Our genealogy programs need to show the progression of our information, not just the latest version of what we think is correct. When the Internet and our genealogy programs evolve to the point where they help us work in unison, rather than separately, then we will literally be able to build pyramids of pedigrees that last as long as the Egyptian pyramids. This is what I see in store for people tracing their family trees in the twenty-first century.

Testing Who's Who on Your Family Tree

DNA testing helps prove who done it—both on crime scenes and on some branches of your family tree. The operative word here is *some.* Currently, only your direct paternal ancestry (your father's father's father's . . .) or your direct maternal ancestry (your mother's mother's mother's . . .) can be analyzed—and the results give only a general range of generations back in time. For example, testing just one sample from one person cannot pinpoint which generation introduced the Native American genes on my pedigree.

Let me try to explain this as it was explained to me. Currently there are only three common types of DNA tests for genealogy:

- Y-chromosome tests (those that test the direct male line)
- Mitochondrial tests (those that test the direct female line)
- Native American marker tests (which can be done for either direct male or direct female lines)

See the FamilyTreeDNA Web site *(www.familytreedna.com)* for more information about DNA testing for genealogists.

But what about all those branches of ancestors who are not your direct male or female lines? In my family, we've always wondered if Grandpa Cannon was part Indian. Remember his picture with the Indian in Chapter 1? Currently, scientists can't test a sample of my cells to see if my maternal grandfather was part Indian because I am not his direct male descendant. Fortunately, my mother has one living brother who is, therefore, a direct male descendant of Grandpa (his son). At our next family reunion, I hope to convince my uncle to give a small sample of his cells to be tested for Native American markers.

If my uncle's cells come back with Native American genes, I'll move back another generation or two. Grandpa's father was supposedly John W. Cannon, whose only surviving male descendants, as far as I know, are my uncle and his two sons. But John had brothers. If I can find a direct male descendant of one of his brothers, if I can convince him to give cell samples, and if he also has Native American markers, I would know that the Native American ancestry came into my family farther back than Grandpa's father.

Science has continued to evolve to the point that the collection of genetic samples is easy and painless. Blood was once considered the purest form of DNA sampling. Now, you just swab your mouth for cheek cells or collect saliva using a special mouthwash.

Different types of genetic tests have different ranges. According to the salesperson who sold me the test for Native American markers, it has a range of four to eight generations during which the gene must have been introduced. This is one of the more expensive tests, and it isolates up to twenty-five different genetic markers.

Quite a few groups of genealogists with ancestors who had the same last name are banding together, finding a direct male descendant on their documented branch with that surname, and performing DNA tests. They want to see if they share ancestors in common or not. I have cousins I've persuaded to participate in the Hill DNA testing project. See E. Ray Hill's Web site *(www.livingston.net/hilldna)* for a much clearer explanation of DNA testing as it relates to surname studies.

Be a good consumer. Look for tests done by a reputable company. Usually such companies are affiliated with universities. Make sure the tests are regulated by a government

For more information about DNA projects, see the following Web sites:

- BYU Molecular Genealogy Project *(molecular-genealogy.byu.edu)*
- Sorensen Molecular Genealogy Foundation *(www.smgf.org/index.jsp)*
- Human Genome Project *(www.ornl.gov/hgmis)*
- Genetics, DNA & Family Health category at Cyndi's List *(www.cyndislist.com/dna.htm)*
- My Genetic Genealogy section at Ancestry.com (for subscribers only) *(www.ancestry.com/dna/mygg.asp)*

For more information about having your family DNA tested, see the following Web sites:

- Family Tree DNA *(www.familytreedna.com)*
- Genetica DNA Laboratories, Inc. *(www.genetica.com/services/index.htm)*

agency, thereby ensuring that your test results remain private. Not all companies doing genetic testing offer their services to genealogists.

At this time, only the clearly sex-linked and slow-mutating genes are understood well enough to calculate ancestry. The genetic markers currently checked for ancestral information represent only 1 percent of the information contained in a person's chromosomes. Studies are underway to unlock the secrets in the other 99 percent.

One such study is the Brigham Young University Molecular Genealogy Project. A sample of your cells is collected, along with your ancestor chart showing your direct (biological) ancestors for a minimum of four generations, including birth dates and places. You will not get information back from this study, but it does help scientists pinpoint various genetic markers by locality or ethnic group in which they are found—quite possibly down to a village level of geographic accuracy. Through such studies, genetic testing may become a more viable answer to our family tree questions in the future.

Genealogy in the Twenty-first Century

The twenty-first century holds great promise for genealogists. New technologies increasingly bring resources right into our homes and provide new ways to resolve old questions. While these technologies are a mixed blessing, they have undoubtedly increased the rate of success experienced by most family tree tracers who take advantage of them.

Am I worried about being left behind by such rapidly advancing technology? No way. Good technique still beats new technology—if for no other reason than the fact that genealogists are among the first to embrace new technologies. I hope you use the best of both worlds—the classic genealogy techniques explained throughout this book and the technological advances that are covered in the next book of this series, *Online Roots*—to fill the hunger that is in all of us to know our roots.

APPENDIX

National Genealogical Society Standards and Guidlines

THE NATIONAL GENEALOGICAL SOCIETY HAS WRITTEN A SERIES OF genealogical standards and guidelines, designed to help you in your family history research. NGS developed these as a concise way to evaluate resources and skills, and to serve as a reminder of the importance of reliable methods of gathering information and sharing it with others.

All of the NGS Standards and Guidelines appear in this book. They also appear online at *www.ngsgenealogy.org/comstandards.htm.*

Guidelines for Using Records, Repositories, and Libraries

Recommended by the National Genealogical Society

Recognizing that how they use unique original records and fragile publications will affect other users, both current and future, family history researchers habitually

- Are courteous to research facility personnel and other researchers, and respect the staff's other daily tasks, not expecting the records custodian to listen to their family histories nor provide constant or immediate attention
- Dress appropriately, converse with others in a low voice, and supervise children appropriately
- Do their homework in advance, know what is available and what they need, and avoid ever asking for "everything" on their ancestors
- Use only designated workspace areas and equipment, like readers and computers intended for patron use; respect off-limits areas; and ask for assistance if needed
- Treat original records at all times with great respect and work with only a few records at a time, recognizing that they are irreplaceable and that each user must help preserve them for future use
- Treat books with care, never forcing their spines, and handle photographs properly, preferably wearing archival gloves
- Never mark, mutilate, rearrange, relocate, or remove from the repository any original, printed, microform, or electronic document or artifact
- Use only procedures prescribed by the repository for noting corrections to any errors or omissions found in published works, never marking the work itself
- Keep note-taking paper or other objects from covering records or books, and avoid placing any pressure upon them, particularly with a pencil or pen
- Use only the method specifically designated for identifying records for duplication, avoiding use of paper clips, adhesive notes, or other means not approved by the facility
- Return volumes and files only to locations designated for that purpose
- Before departure, thank the records custodians for their courtesy in making the materials available
- Follow the rules of the records repository without protest, even if they have changed since a previous visit or differ from those of another facility

Standards for Use of Technology in Genealogical Research

Recommended by the National Genealogical Society

Mindful that computers are tools, genealogists take full responsibility for their work, and therefore they

- Learn the capabilities and limits of their equipment and software, and use them only when they are the most appropriate tools for a purpose
- Do not accept uncritically the ability of software to format, number, import, modify, check, chart or report their data, and therefore carefully evaluate any resulting product
- Treat compiled information from online sources or digital databases in the same way as other published sources—useful primarily as a guide to locating original records, but not as evidence for a conclusion or assertion
- Accept digital images or enhancements of an original record as a satisfactory substitute for the original only when there is reasonable assurance that the image accurately reproduces the unaltered original
- Cite sources for data obtained online or from digital media with the same care that is appropriate for sources on paper and other traditional media, and enter data into a digital database only when its source can remain associated with it
- Always cite the sources for information or data posted online or sent to others, naming the author of a digital file as its immediate source, while crediting original sources cited within the file
- Preserve the integrity of their own databases by evaluating the reliability of downloaded data before incorporating it into their own files
- Provide, whenever they alter data received in digital form, a description of the change that will accompany the altered data whenever it is shared with others
- Actively oppose the proliferation of error, rumor, and fraud by personally verifying or correcting information, or noting it as unverified, before passing it on to others
- Treat people online as courteously and civilly as they would treat them face-to-face, not separated by networks and anonymity
- Accept that technology has not changed the principles of genealogical research, only some of the procedures.

Guidelines for Genealogical Self-Improvement and Growth

Recommended by the National Genealogical Society

Faced with ever-growing expectations for genealogical accuracy and reliability, family historians concerned with improving their abilities will on a regular basis

- Study comprehensive texts and narrower-focus articles and recordings covering genealogical methods in general and the historical background and sources available for areas of particular research interest, or to which their research findings have led them
- Interact with other genealogists and historians in person or electronically, mentoring or learning as appropriate to their relative experience levels, and through the shared experience contributing to the genealogical growth of all concerned
- Subscribe to and read regularly at least two genealogical journals that list a number of contributing or consulting editors, or editorial board or committee members, and that require their authors to respond to a critical review of each article before it is published
- Participate in workshops, discussion groups, institutes, conferences and other structured learning opportunities whenever possible
- Recognize their limitations, undertaking research in new areas or using new technology only after they master any additional knowledge and skill needed and understand how to apply it to the new subject matter or technology
- Analyze critically at least quarterly the reported research findings of another family historian, for whatever lessons may be gleaned through the process
- Join and participate actively in genealogical societies covering countries, localities, and topics where they have research interests, as well as the localities where they reside, increasing the resources available both to themselves and to future researchers
- Review recently published basic texts to renew their understanding of genealogical fundamentals as currently expressed and applied
- Examine and revise their own earlier research in the light of what they have learned through self-improvement activities, as a means for applying their new-found knowledge and for improving the quality of their work-product

Glossary

Abstract: A summary of a genealogically significant record.

Accession number: A number assigned to a book or manuscript when it is placed within a collection housed in a library or archive.

Affidavit: A document written in the presence of an authorized person (notary public, court officer, etc.) while the author is under oath.

***Ahnentafel*:** A German word that means *ancestor table*. It is a name applied to a specific type of ancestor chart.

Alien: A person from a foreign country. See also **Immigrant**.

Ancestor: A person from whom you descend. This usually means you descend directly or biologically from that person, but it sometimes includes legal relationships, as well.

Ancestor chart: A graph or table showing your direct biological or legal (via adoption) lines of ancestry.

Approximated date: An educated guess based upon known facts. See example under "Date Dilemmas" in Chapter 5.

Archives: A government or institutional repository for records.

Biographical: Pertaining to a person's life.

Biography: An account of a person's life written by someone else during or after that person's lifetime.

Biological pedigree: The physical line of ancestry or descent based upon genetics inherited from birth parents.

Bond: A written agreement. It usually refers to the payment of a fixed sum of money by a specified date, if the conditions outlined are not met.

Calculated date: Determining when an event occurred based upon a person's known or stated age at a point in time (another event). See example under "Date Dilemmas" in Chapter 5.

Census: An official enumeration of the population of a country, region, or state.

Certified copy: A copy of an original document made and attested to by the officials who have charge of that original.

Certified Genealogical Instructor (CGI): An associate of the Board for Certification of Genealogists who presents an integrated series of classes that teach students to begin and continue their own genealogical studies. [Definition from Board for Certification of Genealogists, *The BCG Application Guide* (Washington, D.C.: Board for Certification of Genealogists, 2001), p. 15.]

Certified Genealogical Lecturer (CGL): An associate of the Board for Certification of Genealogists who delivers oral presentations that address genealogical sources, methods, and standards. [Definition from Board for Certification of Genealogists, *The BCG Application Guide* (Washington, D.C.: Board for Certification of Genealogists, 2001), p. 15.]

Certified Genealogical Records Specialist (CGRS): Associates of the Board for Certification of Genealogists who share common research and analytical expertise, demonstrating through their findings and written reports sound knowledge of the records within their specific geographic, ethnic, subject, or time-period areas of interest and experience. [Definition from Board for Certification of Genealogists, *The BCG Application Guide* (Washington, D.C.: Board for Certification of Genealogists, 2001), p. 2.]

Certified Genealogist (CG): Associates of the Board for Certification of Genealogists whose work extends to broadly based genealogical projects whose goal is finding the evidence, assembling the proof, and compiling a coherent historical account of the identities and relationships of *all the descendants* of a particular ancestor or ancestral couple. [Definition from Board for Certification of Genealogists, *The BCG Application Guide* (Washington, D.C.: Board for Certification of Genealogists, 2001), p. 2.]

CG: See **Certified Genealogist**.

CGI: See **Certified Genealogical Instructor**.

CGL: See **Certified Genealogical Lecturer**.

CGRS: See **Certified Genealogical Records Specialist**.

Chronology: The order in which events occurred, that is, birth, christening, marriage, children's births, death.

Circa: This means *about* or *near*. It is generally used in front of a date to signify that the date was approximated.

Civil records: Documentation of life events by a government agency, generally birth, marriage, divorce, and death.

Collateral lines: People with whom you share no immediate genetic connection, but who are of genealogical interest because they married into one of your ancestral families.

Compiled record: Information taken from several sources and combined to create a record. Examples are a family group sheet, biography, or family history.

Consanguinity: This means two individuals who are genetically related and share a common ancestor.

Degree of relationship: The distance between two relatives. See the "Family Relationships" section of Chapter 5.

Demography: The study of human population characteristics, such as size, growth, density, distribution, and vital statistics.

Descendant: The child, grandchild, etc., of an individual.

Descendant chart: A graph or table showing the descendants of a particular ancestor.

Emigrant: One who exits a country or region in order to live in another.

Enumeration: A listing or counting of people, such as a census.

Extract: A verbatim transcription of the genealogically significant portions of a record.

Family group sheet: A compiled record about a specific family that contains information about their major life events. See also **Compiled record**.

Family History Center: A genealogy library offering many services, as well as access to microforms loaned from the Family History Library in Salt Lake City, Utah. Family History Centers are found throughout the world, usually in a church building of the Church of Jesus Christ of Latter-day Saints, the sponsoring organization.

Family History Library: This library contains the world's largest collection of genealogical information. It is located in Salt Lake City, Utah, and operated by the Church of Jesus Christ of Latter-day Saints.

Family tree: Your immediate family, plus your ancestors and descendants as the roots and branches.

Forebear: See **Ancestor**.

Forefather: See **Ancestor**.

Gazetteer: A geographical dictionary listing place names and descriptions of those places.

GEDCOM: An acronym for GEnealogical Data COMmunication. It is a file format generated by most genealogical computer programs that enables family historians to share their work with others, no matter what genealogical program they are using. A way to create a generic copy of information stored in a genealogy program.

Genealogical society: A group of people who meet regularly to share an interest in genealogical research, education, and preservation. It is usually a nonprofit organization.

Generation: One step in a line of ancestry or descent. In terms of your ancestry, you are the first generation, your parents are the second, your grandparents are the third, etc. In terms of your descendancy, you are the first generation, your children are the second, your grandchildren are the third, etc.

Given name: This is a name given to an individual at birth, baptism, or shortly thereafter (up to a year or so in some cultures). This includes the first and middle names, except in cultures where the surname is listed first.

Grand-aunt or -uncle: Your grandparent's sibling. Many people (as do I) use the less-precise designation of *great-aunt* or *great-uncle.*

Great-grand-aunt or -uncle: Your great-grandparent's sibling.

Great-grand-parents: The parents of your grandmother or grandfather.

Gregorian calendar: Named for Pope Gregory XIII, who in 1582 ordered its creation to replace the Julian calendar. Most Protestant countries did not convert until 1752. Some countries, such as Russia, did not switch until the early twentieth century. See also **Julian calendar**.

Half-sibling: Person with whom you share just one parent; half-brothers and half-sisters.

Historical society: A group of people interested in the history of a certain locality, event, occupation, etc.

Immigrant: One who enters into a country or region with the intent to live there.

Instrument: A formal or legal document. Examples are deeds and wills.

Issue: The children of a person; lineal descendants of a common ancestor. See also **Descendant**.

Julian calendar: Named for Julius Caesar, it was used from 45 B.C. to A.D. 1582, or until a country converted to the Gregorian calendar. See also **Gregorian calendar**.

Kindred: A group of people who are related by blood.

Last name: See **Surname**.

LDS: Abbreviation for the Church of Jesus Christ of Latter-day Saints.

LDS Family History Center: See **Family History Center**.

Life events: A major event during a person's life, many of which are recorded in some manner. Examples are birth, christening, baptism, marriage, and death.

Lineage: Your direct descent from a particular ancestor.

Lineage society: A group of people who are descended from a qualifying ancestor, such as a patriot in the American Revolution, a Huguenot immigrant, or a soldier in the Civil War. Members must meet specific criteria.

Lineal descent: The direct line of descent from a particular ancestor. Also called lineal consanguinity.

Locality: The place in which an event occurred.

Maiden name: The surname a woman has at birth and is known by before she marries. In some cultures, this is her first name; in other cultures, her last name.

Manuscript: A book or other materials that have not been published.

Maternal: Related through your mother. My maternal grandfather is my mother's father.

Microfiche: Rectangular sheets of film on which microfilmed images are placed in rows and columns. This format is best for printed materials, such as books or computer files.

Microfilm: A photographic process that reduces images to a fraction of their normal size. Also, a roll of such microfilmed images. This format is best for handwritten materials but is used to record many printed materials, as well.

Microform: Refers to all the different types of media on which reduced photographic images are recorded. The most commonly used forms in genealogical research are microfilm and microfiche.

Naturalization: The process an immigrant goes through to become a citizen of a country.

Nephew: The son of your sibling.

Niece: The daughter of your sibling.

Offspring: See **Issue**.

Oral history: The history of a person, event, or place in the form of interviews taken from just one person or several. These interviews are generally recorded, then transcribed.

Original record: A document created by an eyewitness at or near the time of an event. Examples are a birth certificate, a marriage certificate, or a death certificate. This is less accurately called a *primary record* or *primary source*.

Paternal: Related through your father. My paternal grandmother is my father's mother.

Patronymic: A surname derived from a paternal ancestor, such as Lars Pedersen, son of Peder, and John MacDonald, son of Donald.

Pedigree: Your ancestry part of your family tree.

Pedigree chart: A type of ancestor chart. It is a line-graph showing your ancestors and their major life events (birth, marriage, death).

Periodical Source Index (PERSI): An index of genealogical and historical periodical articles created and updated regularly by the Allen County Public Library Foundation in Fort Wayne, Indiana.

Personal history: Your life story gathered together in the form of written accounts, diaries, scrapbooks, oral interviews, narratives, etc.

Postnomial: A title listed after a person's surname, usually in a shortened or abbreviated form. Examples are Jr., III, or Ph.D.

Posterity: See **Descendant**.

Primary record: See **Original record**.

Probate: The legal process for proving the validity of a person's will and distributing property to heirs after settling debts.

Progenitor: An ancestor, often the earliest identified, of a family line. The term is also used to refer to an immigrant ancestor.

Progeny: The descendants of a particular ancestor or person.

Propinquity: A sociological principle that states two individuals must be close in place and time in order to meet and marry.

Registrar: The official who records events and registers them with the civil government.

Research calendar: See **Research log**.

Research log: A form used to record the results of past searches, comments about the sources, and sometimes plans for future searches. Also known as a *research calendar*.

Secondary record: A document created some time after an event or copied from other sources.

Siblings: Your brothers and sisters.

Source: Any item or document relating to a person or event.

Source citation: A detailed list of information about a source (usually one you used to uniquely identify a particular event). This information is recorded on genealogical charts, forms, and reports.

Spouse: A husband or wife.

Step-parent: A person who marries one of your parents; step-mother or step-father.

Step-siblings: The children of your parent's spouse with whom you share no biological ancestors; step-brothers and step-sisters.

Surname: A person's family name. This usually means the person's last name, except in some cultures where the family name is listed first.

To-do list: Comments or reminders to yourself recorded in your research logs or database notes about other resources to check, possible new names to search, etc.

Tradition: Legends, customs, beliefs, etc., handed down from generation to generation, usually by word-of-mouth.

Transcription: Typed or handwritten verbatim copy; a copy of a record where an effort is made to represent the original as exactly as possible. No words or punctuation are changed.

Vital records: Civil records of birth, marriage, divorce, and death.

Vital statistics: The data about the birth, marriage, divorce, or death.

Index

National Genealogical Society

. . . . the national society for generations past, present, and future

What Is the National Genealogical Society?

FOUNDED IN 1903, THE NATIONAL GENEALOGICAL SOCIETY IS A dynamic and growing association of individuals and other groups from all over the country—and the world—that share a love of genealogy. Whether you're a beginner, a professional, or somewhere in between, NGS can assist you in your research into the past.

The United States is a rich melting pot of ethnic diversity that includes countless personal histories just waiting to be discovered. NGS can be your portal to this pursuit with its premier annual conference and its ever-growing selection of how-to materials, books and publications, educational offerings, and member services.

NGS has something for everyone—we invite you to join us. Your membership in NGS will help you gain more enjoyment from your hobby or professional pursuits, and will place you within a long-established group of genealogists that came together a hundred years ago to promote excellence in genealogy.

To learn more about the society, visit us online at *www.ngsgenealogy.org.*

Other Books in the NGS Series

Online Roots

Pamela Boyer Porter, CGRS, CGL
Amy Johnson Crow, CG

A practical guide to making your online search more effective and creative. Includes how to know if what you find is accurate and the best way to make full use of the Internet.

$19.99

ISBN 1-4016-0021-2

A Family Affair

Sandra MacLean Clunies, CG

Family reunions can create memories and celebrate a common heritage. Here's how to do it with a minimum of fuss and maximum of good times.

$19.99

ISBN 1-4016-0020-4

Planting Your Family Tree Online

Cyndi Howells, creator of Cyndi's List

How to create your own family history Web site, share information, and meet others who are part of your family's history and heritage.

$19.99

ISBN 1-4016-0022-0

Coming Soon

The Organized Family Historian

Ann Carter Fleming, CG, CGL

A guide to the best way to file, label, and catalog the wide variety of material and information related to a family history.

$19.99

ISBN 1-4016-0129-4

Coming Soon